JAMES F. MALCOLM 1962

THE COMPLETE

JAMES F. MALCOLM

A Collection of Writings by J. F. Malcolm

The Search for God

The Nature of Man

The After-life

Psychic Influences in World Religion

The Universe and Man

Published in 2009

by

SDU PUBLICATIONS
www.sdu3.com

for

The Spiritualists' National Union

ISBN 978-1-905961-13-9

Copyright © SNU 2009
www.snu.org.uk

Printed and bound in Great Britain by
CPI Antony Rowe, Chippenham and Eastbourne

INDEX

PUBLISHERS INTRODUCTION

SDU Publications is proud to be associated with the Spiritualists' National Union in the production of this book. This is our first joint venture and I hope it will be the first of many.

James F. Malcolm was a graduate of London and Glasgow Universities, he held degrees of D.Sc., Ph.D., and was an F.R.S.E., and for many years was head of the Bacteriological Department, West of Scotland Agricultural College, and for his distinguished work there, was awarded the O.B.E. He was also a Minister of the Spiritualist National Union and devoted much time and study to Spiritualist and Psychical Research.

He wrote five separate pamphlets which have been used by the S.N.U. Education Committee as part of their study courses for many years. This book brings into one volume all five pamphlets for the first time.

These pamphlets offer an in depth insight into Spiritualist philosophy, religious history and life in the spirit world. His insight and clear style of writing make what can be difficult subjects easy to understand.

I too am a S.N.U. Minister, yet reading these five pamphlets taught me so much, I hope they do the same for you.

MINISTER STEVEN UPTON
December 2008

i

THE SEARCH FOR GOD

AUTHORS FORWARD

I wish to acknowledge the help I have received in the preparation of this work from J. W. Herries, who contributed the Introduction, and advised me regarding, the sub-headings. My thanks are also due to the Rev. Thomas Jeffrey and Dr. John Winning for valuable criticisms and suggestions, and to Dr. Raynor C. Johnson whose books, "The Imprisoned Splendour" and "Nurslings of Immortality" (published by Hodder and Stoughton) have been freely used.

THE AUTHOR

INTRODUCTION

The problem of the Deity and the origin of life as we know it is still a mystery. Ordinary human beings are without any adequate guidance in their approach to an understanding or conception of the central focus and Controller of our vast and mysterious universe. The orthodox religions have little or nothing to offer towards a solution. Their testimony in some respects may be regarded as misleading. The personal God presented by the various books of the Old Testament is incompatible with modern knowledge and the teaching of Jesus, on which Christianity is based. Yet the tribal God of the Israelites has not been officially repudiated. Generations of children are puzzled by the inconsistencies of the Bible chronicles of a God who appears to be a cruel and vindictive tyrant, directing his avowed followers to exterminate their enemies, men, women and children, delighting in human and animal sacrifices, and threatening the world with incredible tortures and sufferings. No one, it may be said, attaches serious validity to the man-made God thus pictured; but these early representations of a Deity who has to be feared and propitiated still hold a place in conventional religion, recorded in what the rising generations are taught to believe is the embodiment of God's Word, the authoritative and directive voice of the Almighty.

One reason for the continuing reverence shown to this conception of early and savage peoples is that the Churches have nothing to put in its place. The emphasis is now, of course, placed on the more humane and spiritual ideas of the New Testament and the teachings of Jesus; but the old attitude implanted in the minds of generations of children still holds its place, casting shadows which often darken their later years. The doctrine of "fear," in its lower significance, still has its effect on the minds of a great portion of the human race.

Dr. J. F. Malcolm in this approach to a conception of the nature of the Deity in the light of modern knowledge has performed a notable and valuable service for all reflective men and women. He has brought to the exposition of his ideas an exceptional range of knowledge, historical, philosophic, classical and scientific, and also a keen and independent mind and a faculty of lucid expression which makes the results of his wide study and reflection readily available for ordinary readers. He has properly included in a modern treatise on this great central problem the investigations of eminent scientists in various fields who are convinced of the reality of human survival through psychic communications—which incidentally, are a continuation of the more valuable elements of the Biblical narratives and in full agreement with their witness. It is a work which the organised Churches should have attempted, but which the restrictions of their creeds have prevented, with the result that they have lost much of their influence on modern thought. The idea of an anthropomorphic Deity, a mere enlargement of human stature, is no longer tenable. Dr. Malcolm adopts the reasonable view that "God is so utterly transcendent in nature to man that the latter can never have any definite conception of the Divine Being, just as an insect can never have any definite conception of the nature of man, although both are forms of life. Man, however, can form some conception of His ways of working and therefore of His nature by studying the universe and the laws which operate in it." I am convinced that the S.N.U. in helping to make his conclusions available to a wide public has done an important service to the cause of true religion—a service which may have wide and vital consequences in a new and rational conception of the vitalising centre of the Universe.

God is Spirit, and cannot be restricted to any human embodiment. The suggestion of a central creative source of all things is in accordance with the Fatherhood of God, which is the first Principle of Spiritualism, and is a true interpretation of His relationship to humanity. This aspect of the Divinity, set out so convincingly by Dr. Malcolm, should bring a new hope and conviction, a sense of partnership and understanding, to many who have been walking in the partial darkness of conventionalised religion.

J. W. FERRIES.

25 Findhorn Place,
Edinburgh, 9.

1

DEVELOPMENT OF THE IDEA OF GOD

One of the most remarkable discoveries in anthropology, or the study of the human race, is that in all parts of the world there has been a common belief among primitive people that invisible beings, spirits or gods, were responsible for all the unexplainable phenomena of Nature. This belief, termed animism, has given rise to similar religious practices throughout the world in spite of differences in colour, race, language and environment.

There were many natural phenomena that primitive man could not understand but which appeared to him to be due to the activities of spirits or gods. For instance, there were terrifying earthquakes; volcanic eruptions in which flames and molten rock were ejected by an angry god from a mountain top; thunderstorms with destructive lightning discharges and in the thunder the awful voice of an angry god. Tornados, typhoons, floods, droughts, famines and disease were all attributed to the anger of gods. Even a twisted tree trunk or a prominent or queer-shaped rock was to be avoided at night as the possible lair of some malevolent spirit which could cause disease in the home or blight in the crops.

Fire was believed to be due to the activity of a benevolent god to whom worship and homage had to be paid, otherwise he might become angry and cause destruction in the home or in the vast forests. To evoke this fire-god into action, *i.e.*, to start a fire, two sticks had to be rubbed together. This may account for the fact that two crossed sticks, or a cross, formed a sacred symbol to many ancient nations even before the Christian era.

The sun was one of the first objects in nature to be worshipped. It gave light and heat, promoted the growth of vegetation and moved across the sky throughout the day. It was only natural that primitive man thought it was a god or the home of a god. Traces of sun-worship are found from the earliest times in all regions of the world—in India, Persia, Egypt, Greece, Australia, Greenland and America. The moon was also worshipped as a benevolent god owing to its light-giving properties. Eclipses of the sun and moon were dreaded in the belief that the gods were angry and had withdrawn their light.

ANCESTRAL SPIRITS AS GODS

Death was a particularly mysterious process. On the one hand, there was the *living* body with all its warmth and vital activity, and on the other, the *dead* body, cold and rigid, incapable of movement. Primitive man naturally concluded that at death *something* must have gone out from the living body; some invisible or shadowy form or spirit which had given it life. In the case of certain primitive people, the dead body was regarded with fear in the belief that it or its spirit or ghost might haunt the locality and trouble its surviving relatives. To prevent such hauntings, practices were adopted to restrict the activities of the corpse and spirit. For instance, the body was buried deeply or covered with a large stone or with a large heap of soil or stones. For the same reason the body might be badly mutilated or pinned down by driving a sharp stake through it, a practice carried out even in Britain with malefactors and suicides until a few centuries ago. However, with other primitive races, great respect was paid to the dead body; it was kept in a hut or cave and venerated in the belief that it or its spirit still survived. But where had this spirit gone? Was it still lingering near or had it gone to some common meeting place in an after-death world to live with its ancestors? These spirits had to be recognised as members of the tribe or family; they were interested still in their surviving

7

kinsmen and could be appealed to for advice and help. At the same time they had to be respected and even propitiated in some way to prevent ills befalling the tribe or family through their displeasure. Naturally, these spirits, especially those of the chiefs of the tribe, came to be regarded as gods.

BREAD AND WINE AS RELIGIOUS SYMBOLS

The growth and development of food crops from seed was also a mystery. It was commonly believed to be due to the influence of the god of the corn acting in association with the seed. For this reason it was considered necessary at time of sowing to make a sacrifice to propitiate the corn-god; a human (later an animal) victim in many cases was chosen for this purpose. The person sacrificed was supposed to represent, or be the incarnation of the corn-god, and his spirit, or the spirit of the god, was believed to enter the seed and animate the growing crop. The dead body of the victim—or if there were many fields, a part of it—was therefore buried with the seed at time of sowing and in some instances the blood was sprinkled on the seed. Thus the spirit of the god or of the person sacrificed, was believed to come to life again in the growing crop. To celebrate this resurrection, festivals were held at harvesting at which the first fruits or bread and wine were partaken of as symbolising the flesh and blood of the slain god or the sacrificial victim.

SPIRITUAL MANIFESTATIONS

Quite apart from these primitive beliefs and superstitions, primitive man would have actual experience of spirit manifestations, as the psychic faculty was apparently developed at an early stage in the evolution of man. (There is evidence of extra-sensory perception in animals). Thus certain people with clairvoyant or clairaudient powers would see or hear spirits. This would support the common belief in the existence of an after-death state. The psychic faculty would be more likely to develop and function freely in these early days as primitive man lived closer to nature than civilised people of the present age. Accounts of psychic experiences or spirit manifestations occur in the folk lore and historical tales of many ancient nations. According to the Old Testament, the ancient Hebrew patriarchs and prophets were gifted sensitives and so also, according to ancient Greek writings, were some of the ancient Greek scholars, *e.g.*, Pythagoras, Socrates, Sophocles and Empedocles. In the visitations from the other world which are recorded in the Old and New Testaments, the spirit responsible for the manifestation was frequently referred to as God or Lord, otherwise it was termed angel (Greek—*angelos*—messenger), messenger of the Lord, ghost or Holy Spirit. The expression used would depend largely on the beliefs and conceptions, not only of the person originally concerned with the spirit experience, but also of those handing it down by oral communication or in writing. The term used in the written tradition would also be subject to alterations in the various translations from one language to another.

Primitive man led a simple life and, unlike modern man, was not divided in his thoughts with regard to religion, work and home. He fully believed that spirits could intervene for good or ill in all that he did, whether he was hunting, making a canoe or offering a sacrifice to a tribal god. Their presence was an actual reality to him, and the only way to do things was that ordained by tribal custom to appease these spirits and ensure the welfare of himself, his family and the tribe. Thus primitive man was polytheistic in his beliefs; there were tribal and even family gods and spirits and in addition, gods of nature, and all had to be treated with respect and propitiated. But, at the same time, man in the savage state at all times believed that he himself had, like the gods, powers over nature ("supernatural" powers) which he could exercise by carrying out certain practices, which could be described as magical in character. Thus in many cases he did not regard the gods as being greatly superior beings to himself, and when they did not appear to answer his appeals for help, he might try to force or even frighten them with threats or other practices into carrying out his will. Later with advance in knowledge, he gradually realised how vast were the forces of nature and how feeble were his efforts to control them. This realisation, however, did not affect his belief in the potency of the gods or spirits to control these forces; indeed, it increased his belief in their powers. The fact that he himself was so feeble carried with it the conviction that the gods must be omnipotent.

MONOTHEISM

From these early and crude animistic and polytheistic beliefs there developed the elaborate pantheons or hierarchies of gods of the ancient Greeks, Romans, Teutons and other nations. However, with advance in culture there arose generally some vague conception of the One Supreme God, often symbolised by the sun, and this led ultimately to the monotheistic conception of the One Almighty God, the Creator and Sustainer of the Universe, who ruled over a large host of lower gods, spirits or angels of various orders, and who dealt with mankind through these spirits. But men have never been able to rise above anthropomorphic conceptions in their ideas of God; they have always thought of God in human form. In Genesis, it is stated that God created man in His own image, but it can certainly be said that man throughout the ages has conceived of God in man's own image.

HEBREW BELIEFS

The ancient Hebrews were at first polytheistic in their beliefs, but at an early stage in their history developed monotheistic ideas as a result of the teachings of their prophets. Their God, Jehovah or Jahveh, was Almighty and had created and continued to sustain the whole universe, but He ruled men in the manner of an earthly king, rewarding them for their good deeds and punishing them for their evil ones. Although their God had created all races of men, the Hebrews claimed that they alone were His chosen people. Thus He was to them a national god who, though loving and merciful to them, could hate the people of other nations with whom the Hebrews were at war. The Old Testament tells how Jahveh on various occasions commanded the Israelites to kill all men, women and children of other nations against whom they were at war.

THE CHRISTIAN CONCEPTION

The Christian conception of God is based not only on the teachings of Jesus but also on ancient Greek and Hebrew theology. (The Christian Church also believes that Jesus showed in His life and personality, qualities which throw light upon the nature of God). To the ancient Greek philosophers, Plato, Aristotle and Plotinus, God was the nameless, absolute and perfect spirit, infinite, omnipresent, omniscient, unchangeable and transcendent. On the other hand, the ancient Hebrews were taught by their prophets that God was perfect in holiness, wisdom and love, but He was also concerned with mankind and their morality. He was their Judge and His judgments could be seen in the history of their nation. Jesus, who had a thorough grounding in the high moral and monotheistic teachings of the Hebrew prophets, used these Hebrew conceptions of God as the basis of His teaching, but He developed the view that God was the Heavenly Father of infinite justice and mercy, who loved all mankind and sought their love and loyalty in return. He was an Almighty Spirit who could be appealed to by men in time of trouble and who could be thanked for all the blessings of earth life.

Accordingly, there are two very different conceptions in the Christian views of God: (a) the conception derived from the Greek philosophers that God is Transcendent, *i.e.*, above and independent of the universe and beyond relations with men and having no concern for moral values and pain and suffering and desire; (b) the Hebrew and early Christian conception that God is Immanent, *i.e.*, present throughout the universe as an indwelling and sustaining Spirit, for "in Him we live, and move, and have our being," and Personal in that He takes an active interest in mankind and all forms of life, even sparrows. Thus on the one hand, we have Transcendence and on the other, Immanence; also, the Infinite and Omnipresent as against the Personal.

PROBLEM OF PAIN

Philosophers and theologians since ancient times have been trying to harmonise without great success these different Greek and Hebrew conceptions of God. Dr. Matthews, Dean of St. Paul's Cathedral, suggests that they are "irreconcilable." Other questions also arise. For instance, there is the difficulty that an omnipotent and perfect God is yet the creator and sustainer of a world in which there is evil, pain and suffering, a world therefore which is far from perfect. It has been claimed that pain and suffering and evil are due to the fact that man has freedom of will and exercises this freedom in the wrong manner—for selfish ends. However, animals—which theologians claim have not free-will (although on rather doubtful grounds, as animals do appear to show an element of free-will, *e.g.*, in their play) also endure pain and suffering and must have done so long before man was evolved. Thus animal suffering cannot be attributed entirely to man's misuse of his free-will. Moreover, if God is unchanging and timeless in nature, how can He be the motivating factor and be immanent in a world which is always undergoing change, both in its animate and inanimate forms of matter, and which is also subject to the influence of time?

Aristotle was aware of such problems. He conceived of a Supreme God who was perfect and changeless, but he believed that such a God could not have been the creator of the world as it was imperfect; and He could not be concerned with such a world otherwise He would lose to some extent His own perfection. Aristotle thought that God's activity was entirely one of self contemplation. Nevertheless, He was the object of the world's desire and people yearned and strove for Him, and this was responsible for all the action, development and change in the world. God Himself, however, was unaware of such worldly activities and conditions and was not therefore responsible for the evil, pain and suffering in the world.

Against this view, it may be said that it is difficult to understand how such an aloof and disinterested God could be of significance as a principle of good in the universe and as a source of its moral order, or how He could be responsible for human ethical experience, *i.e.*, man's recognition of good and evil and his dislike for and striving against evil.

Certain eastern mystics have believed that God is merely an "impersonal, universal consciousness," not taking an active interest in the world and not motivating or willing anything to take place in it; but such a God could not be loved and held in awe and reverence by mankind. On the other hand, most nations have believed in a personal God, a God who could be revered and loved and worshipped and prayed to for help and guidance. Such a God, unlike an "impersonal universal consciousness," could be regarded as a loving Father, concerned with everything in the universe, even the fall of a sparrow, and continuously active in the universe.

DIVINITY OF JESUS

The Christian conception of God is based on the old Aristotelian and Ptolemaic belief that the earth is the centre of the universe, the sun, moon and stars revolving round it. This geocentric belief gave rise, as might be expected, to the religious doctrine that the whole universe was created primarily for the life of man on earth and that God's chief interest was in man, and that He sent His only begotten Son, Jesus, to the earth as a divine revelation to man. The early Church came ultimately to worship Jesus as God Himself.

The Doctrine of the Trinity was adopted by the Church at the Council of Nicaea, 325 A.D., to reconcile this worship of Jesus with the monotheistic theology of the Jews. This doctrine does not appear to be consistent with the general teaching of Jesus, St. Paul and the early Christian church. Although a Trinity is mentioned in St. Matthew's Gospel, chapter 28, verse 19, there are doubts whether these words are authentic words of Jesus. For instance, St. Peter and the other apostles appeared to be ignorant of Christ's commands given in that verse "to go and make disciples of all the nations baptizing them into the name of the Father and of the Son and the Holy Ghost," because according to the Acts of the Apostles, it was necessary for Peter to have a vision to convince him that he should go to Cornelius, a member of another nation, and he baptized Cornelius and his friends in the name of Jesus only. Moreover, he had later to justify his action to the other apostles and church leaders at Jerusalem. In interpreting the books of the New Testament, it must be remembered that they were first written a considerable time (30 to 70 years or more) after the death of Jesus, and in the succeeding three centuries the various scripts in use were altered and revised repeatedly in the determination to reconcile their statements on the doings and sayings of Jesus with the Church doctrines and practices prevailing in these later times.

Jesus never claimed for Himself that He was the only begotten Son of God or that He was the equal of God. This is clear from His sayings, "Why callest thou me good? There is none good but one, that is, God" (St. Matthew, chapter 19, verse 17); and "I ascend unto my Father, and your Father; and to my God, and your God" (St. John, chapter 20, verse 17). He also used to pray to God, and when troubled, ask Him for consolation and help, as at Gethsemane. (See St. Luke, chapter 22, verses 42 and 43.) Moreover, in the opinion of Dr. Matthews "even St. Paul nowhere definitely equates Jesus Christ with God." The conception of a Trinity of Gods, however, was not uncommon in ancient religions. The Egyptians as far back as the 18th century B.C. believed in the Trinity of Gods: Isis, Osiris and Horus. There were also Trinities of Gods in the ancient Persian, Indian and Greek religions. This may have had a profound influence in the adoption of a Trinity by the Christians. In this as in many other beliefs and practices, the new religion borrowed much from older religions, especially Mithraism. In "The Golden Bough," Sir James Frazer states, "In respect both of doctrines and of rites, the cult of Mithra appears to have presented many points of resemblance to Christianity. Taken all together, the coincidences of the Christian with the heathen festivals are too close and too numerous to be accidental. They mark the compromise which the Church, in its hour of triumph, was compelled to make with its vanquished and yet still dangerous rivals."

15

THE EXPANDING UNIVERSE

The Christian conception of God is on far too narrow a basis, when viewed in the light of modern knowledge of the universe. According to modern astronomical discoveries, our solar system belongs to a galactic system consisting of some 10,000 million suns or solar systems; our sun is only a comparatively small star far distant from the centre of the galaxy, in fact, near the edge, and having a brightness rather below the average. Many of these solar systems are believed to have planets. Moreover, far out in the depths of space, millions of light years away, there are millions upon millions of other huge starry systems, like our galaxy in course of evolution. Thus there may be millions and millions of planets in the universe as countless as are the grains of sand on a sea shore.

It has been accepted by religious thought everywhere in all ages that the most important aspect of the universe is the spiritual and not the physical, and that the primary purpose of our own planet is the provision of an environment for the evolution of living beings, especially man. However, this must not be taken as supporting the orthodox doctrine that the whole universe was created primarily for the life of man on this planet, because it is difficult to believe that the Divine Mind could be satisfied merely with the creation and distribution throughout space of countless solar systems with no associated forms of life except in the case of our own.

It is more reasonable to suppose that many other solar systems may also provide the environment for innumerable conscious beings to live and develop their spirit nature. These spirit beings may be like ourselves or in forms quite different from us, yet all will be of the Divine essence, *i.e.*, sons of God, and all of equal importance in His mind. Nevertheless, the Christian doctrine of the Trinity is difficult to reconcile with this probability that on countless planets there may be these conscious beings, who, like us, may have required and have had a divine revelation, in the form of a Christ. Dean Inge has said, "God's Word for this world was Christ but He may have had other words for other worlds." (See Dr. R. C. Johnson's "Nurslings of Immortality.")

THE VICARIOUS ATONEMENT

In considering this subject, it must also be borne in mind that modern science has thrown grave doubts on one of the principal doctrines of the Christian Church, namely the vicarious atonement of Christ. It is now generally accepted that man physically has been gradually evolved from the lowest forms of life and it is reasonable to infer that he has undergone a similar spiritual development. Thus there has been apparently no "fall of man" and therefore no need for an atoning sacrifice to reconcile man with God.

Moreover, even although man, owing to his misuse of free-will, had become sinful and, as a result, out of attunement with God, it is difficult to understand how a God who was righteous, just and merciful, and at the same time a Loving Father of mankind, would insist that a supremely upright and righteous person, namely Jesus, should be cruelly put to death as a sacrifice to effect a reconciliation between God and erring mankind. This would apply even although Jesus out of His love for man was perfectly willing to allow Himself to be sacrificed in this way. No earthly father would take pleasure in the murder of a son for this or any other purpose. Is God then less just and less merciful than His own creation? Moreover, there appears to be no reasonable purpose in such a sacrifice. How could a crime, such as the brutal torture and crucifixion of an innocent man, please God and reconcile mankind with Him? Would it not rather have had the opposite effect? Is it not more rational to believe that Jesus was prepared to stand up for the principles which He taught, even although by doing so, He incurred the hatred of the orthodoxy of the times and therefore the almost certain risk of a violent death? Not only were the priests and their followers jealous of His great success as a teacher and healer but they bitterly resented His outspoken criticism of their church and its leaders. The Jewish leaders may also have been afraid that His presence in Jerusalem might lead to insurrection and thus bring on them reprisals from the Roman army of occupation.

Belief in the vicarious atonement of a saviour-god slain as a sacrifice for the forgiveness of sins, occurred in many ancient religions long before the Christian era. The Egyptians worshipped a saviour-god Osiris; the Greeks, Dionysus and Prometheus; the Persians and Romans, Mithra; the Indians, Krishna; the Chaldeans, Bel. It is probable that the early Christians derived their belief in the vicarious atonement from these earlier religions. Even the ancient Hebrews in their Temple worship at Jerusalem sacrificed animals for the forgiveness of sins. In this connection, it must be remembered that St. Paul, who taught the doctrine of the Atonement, was brought up as a strict Jew of the sect of the Pharisees, and so was full of the "imagery of the ancient sacrifices—of an offering of a life in substitution for the wages of sin." Thus in the Epistle to the Hebrews, which in the English versions of the Bible is ascribed to St. Paul, it is said, "And according to the law, I may almost say, all things are cleansed with blood, and apart from shedding of blood there is no remission."

Modern spirit teachings do not uphold the doctrine of the vicarious atonement. They state that at death man can enter only that sphere in the spirit state to which his spirit has become attuned or fitted as a result of his earth life. There is no arbitrary judgment by God with recompenses for good and penalties or pardons for evil doing. It is simply a question of the relative spiritual progress made in earth life.

FALLIBILITY OF THE BIBLE

The Christian theology is based primarily on the Bible and the Church interpretation thereof, the Bible until the 18th or 19th century being regarded as the infallible word of God. But in the light of modern scientific knowledge, it has been found that inaccuracies are present in the Biblical records, *e.g.*, with regard to the Creation. The discoveries of Copernicus and others show that the earth is not, as implied in Genesis, the centre of the universe, but is merely one of the planets of a comparatively small solar system in a huge stellar galaxy, consisting of thousands of millions of suns, many possibly with, attendant planets. Also, the age of the earth would appear to be some 4,000 or 5,000 million years instead of only 6,000 or 7,000 years as indicated by the genealogical trees of the Old Testament. (Archbishop Ussher put the creation at 4,004 B.C., and this was widely accepted by the Church until comparatively recent times and even printed in the marginal notes of many editions of the Authorised English Version of the Bible.) Moreover, animal life has followed a course of evolution extending in all probability over the past 1,000 million years and man himself shows, for example, in the foetal stage of his life, evidence of evolution from the simplest unicellular forms of life, through the fishes and higher animals. Thus the creation of man did not take place, as stated in Genesis, in a single step from "dust of the ground."

Science itself as a result of its discoveries in various fields had become materialistic in outlook in the 19th century. The existence of spirit could not be demonstrated by any known scientific method and the so-called supernatural or miraculous happenings of the Bible could not be accounted for by the universal laws of causation established by science and thus did not fit in with other scientific data of the universe. Even the new science of psychology was largely materialistic in outlook. The personality and behaviour of an individual was shown to be profoundly affected by the condition of certain regions of the brain and the activity of the endocrine glands of the body. Hence it was claimed that mind, instead of being a thing apart from brain, was merely the activity of the brain and therefore there was no evidence of a spirit. Life in this world was believed to be the fortuitous result of various natural conditions and it did not persist after death of the body.

Auguste Comte, 1798 to 1857, the French philosopher who founded the "Positive" school of philosophy, claimed that there were three approaches to knowledge: (a) the primitive or religious, based on superstition, tradition and dogma, (b) the philosophical, based on logical analysis and (c) the positivistic or scientific, based on direct observation. According to him the last would prevail. He said "When science has done its complete work, it will conduct God to the boundary of the Universe and bow Him out with thanks for His provisional services." This summed up the attitude of the materialistic scientists and philosophers of the 19th century.

AUTHORITY OF THE BIBLE

Apart from the effect of the discoveries of science on the religious thought of these times, a critical examination of the Biblical text and narrative was being made by scholars and historians. This showed that much of the Bible, even the New Testament, was of doubtful origin and some of it was even self-contradictory in nature, hence it could no longer be regarded as an infallible authority. The lay people as a whole were also becoming better educated and many were now using their reasoning powers in regard to religion, especially in the light of these so-called "higher criticisms" of the Bible and the findings of science. Thus the creeds and doctrines of the Church were no longer blindly accepted, and as a result a wave of materialism swept over the world, which the Church could not hold back by the mere insistence on the necessity for and the virtue of faith in her teachings and dogmas. But while many people lacked this faith, they still remained members of the Church in which they had been reared, although there was a lack of reality and assurance in their religious life. For many, church attendance became a formality in which social respectability may have played to some extent a part.

MODERN SCIENTIFIC OUTLOOK

Since the beginning of the 20th century, the materialistic argument has lost much of its force; there has even been a tendency amongst scientists to put God back in the universe. There are various reasons for this. The mechanistic conceptions of the universe were formulated to a great extent on the classical dynamics based on Newton's laws of mass, force and acceleration; but Einstein's work has shown that these laws require to be revised as they do not take into account the relative speed of the observer, and they also require to be extended in order to make them applicable to atomic phenomena.

In addition, it has been found that the classical mechanistic conceptions do not explain entirely the behaviour of fundamental particles in the atom such as neutrons, electrons, etc., because, owing to the character of such rapidly moving particles, their position and speed cannot be simultaneously predicted with certainty. Atomic physics has also shown that the atom, instead of being a solid body as at first thought, in reality consists of infinitesimal electrically charged particles swirling around a central nucleus, and therefore what is apparently solid is not in fact so.

A Plan and a Planner

In the field of astronomy, the huge star systems scattered in space do not suggest a haphazard arrangement due to purely mechanistic forces arising as a result of chance or accident. There appears to be a design or plan and a purpose behind it all, and if this is the case there must have been a Planner. Many prominent astronomers have become convinced that there is a God behind the Universe. Johannes Kepler when observing the stars through a telescope said that "he was thinking the thoughts of God after Him."

Discoveries in the field of biology have shown that plants and animals can live only under favourable environmental conditions. These conditions have arisen on earth owing to the conjunction of many different factors. For instance, the earth is at a distance from the sun such that there is sufficient heat for organisms to live without danger of scorching. Also, the rotation of the earth in twenty-four hours prevents extremes of heat and cold which would make life difficult or impossible. Such extremes of temperature would arise if the rotation period were much longer, say, a week or ten days.

Moreover, the moon is sufficiently far from the earth to prevent the formation of huge tidal waves, which would inundate the land surfaces twice daily. In addition, the atmosphere of the earth is of such density that meteors, coming from interstellar space, burst into flames, and are dispersed before they reach the ground, otherwise they would be a constant source, of destruction and fire. The atmosphere also affords a certain amount of protection to animals from cosmic and ultra-violet radiation, which otherwise owing to its intensity might be harmful.

LIFE ON OTHER PLANETS

The argument that the many conditions, which enable organisms to live on earth, could hardly have arisen owing to chance alone, should not be pressed too far. For all our present knowledge, types of living organisms may exist elsewhere, *e.g.*, on other planets in our own or other solar systems, and these organisms may differ very greatly in form, structure and physiology from those on our own planet in order to deal with the vastly different environmental conditions on these other planets. For instance, the metabolism or body processes of the former may be based on quite different exothermic chemical processes from our forms of life. It is sometimes claimed that no living organisms can occur on certain planets owing to the absence of light or air, or owing to the presence of high temperatures or high concentrations of carbon dioxide or hydrogen gas. However, living matter has great powers of adaptation. Even on our own planet there are organisms which can exist in the dark or in absence of air or at high temperatures, *e.g.*, 75°C., or in presence of high concentrations of carbon dioxide or hydrogen. Indeed, the apparently infinite ways in which life can express itself may be taken as an indication of the limitless powers of a Divine Creator.

EVOLUTION AND PURPOSE

It is difficult to account for all the phenomena of life on a purely mechanistic basis. No biologist knows what constitutes the living principle in an organism, whether plant or animal, and the problem is no nearer solution although it is now known that the border line between inanimate matter and the lowest forms of living matter, *i.e.*, the viruses, is vague and difficult to define. The higher plants and animals have been shown to have evolved from unicellular forms of life, but it is unknown what started the process of evolution.

Although there is no scientific proof that evolution must have been directed, there is evidence of purposive and even experimental features, which could be taken as an indication of a Master Mind or Planner. Thus in the past hundreds of millions of years since the first forms of life appeared in the world, countless types of plants and animals have been evolved. Some of these could not maintain themselves indefinitely in the changing environmental conditions of the world and died out, as in the case of the giant reptiles of the Mesozoic Period, *e.g.*, the dinosaurs, and no further attempts were made to develop such types again. However, the types which were able to persist were frequently evolved further and new types formed from them.

Materialists may claim that those failure-lines of animals were not repeated owing to the elimination of unsatisfactory types by natural selection and that the ability to develop new types is due to some inherent property of the protoplasm, *e.g.*, that of mutation, but this does not account for the origin of such a protoplasmic property or the urge behind it to develop further the successful types.

EVIDENCE OF PLANNING

Further evidence of a Planner behind the process of evolution is shown by the development of complex structures, such as the eye and ear, in which difficult problems with regard to vision and hearing had to be overcome. Biologists may assert that it was possible for such highly specialised structures to arise owing to the production of many transient intermediate forms (many of which may have had selective advantages over their predecessors), and the immense stretch of time available for the final development of the perfect form. However, it is difficult to believe that such a complicated series of changes as was necessary, for example, in the production of the eye, could have been brought about fortuitously even from the numerous intermediate forms available, especially as, although in all cases the source of the organ is fundamentally the same, in various animals it may result from a different series of changes.

Moreover, at certain stages in evolution, for example, when aquatic animals first became amphibious or changed completely to a terrestrial mode of life, a complicated series of changes had to be made to enable the creatures to live in the new environment. For instance, they had to develop lungs and a new type of circulatory system, also legs for support and movement, and hair or some other protective device for the skin. Further, when creatures first attempted to fly and later when birds were evolved, many major changes had to be made in the body, *e.g.*, lighter bones, more powerful muscles for the fore limbs to convert them into wings, and feathers for air vanes and protection of the body. All these evolutionary changes had to take place before the creature could deal adequately with the new form of environment. Although there may have been many transient intermediate forms, for example, mud-fishes bridging the aquatic-amphibian gap, yet there must have been some definite mental conception of the ultimate form necessary; there must have been a Planner behind it all.

THE MECHANISTIC THEORY UNTENABLE

This is further borne out by the immense diversity in nature; the birds with bright plumage and remarkable singing powers; the brightly coloured flowers with their perfumes; the insects, some with marvellous colouring, *e.g.*, the butterflies. There is exquisite artistry and beauty in the design, colouring and structure of many of these forms of life for which mechanistic factors or powers of adaptation alone cannot account. There must have been a Master Mind, a Divine Artist.

The Planner is further shown by the marvellous transmission of a host of different characters from the parents to the offspring in the genes; by the wonderful instinctive behaviour of animals, for example, in the nesting and migration of birds, and the migration of eels and salmon; by the way in which nature maintains a balance, a pendulum-like dynamic equilibrium, so that one type or form of life does not outgrow or crowd out entirely other types. This balance is seen in the case of certain, wild animals, *e.g.*, lions and the creatures, such as antelopes, upon which they prey; also, in the case of insects and the plants and other insects upon which they feed.

THE LIFE FORCE

To sum up from the biological point of view, it may be said that in the "something" which is known as "life" there appears to be a tremendous force to survive, multiply, vary and in many cases to advance to more highly developed types. Although. the variation in itself, disciplined by the current environment, will automatically lead to evolutionary advance throughout the hundreds of millions of years at the disposal of the process, nevertheless, it is difficult to conceive how such a process with its tendencies for the development of higher forms of consciousness and greater states of awareness can be entirely accounted for by the chemical or physical properties of chemical substances, no matter how complex in nature they may be. Biologists may claim that it has never been proved scientifically that there is a "supernatural" force responsible for the urge behind the process of evolution and for its direction and control, but it must be borne in mind that nothing whatever is known as to what constitutes even life itself and what was responsible for the initiation of the process of evolution and the urge which is behind it and sustains it.

Alfred Noyes, the poet, has said of evolution:

"'Tis not the lack of links within the chain
From cause to cause, but that the chain exists;
That's the unfathomable mystery,
The one unquestioned miracle that we know,
Implying every attribute of God."

The science of psychology has also lost much of the materialistic outlook it had at the beginning of the present century. The work of Myers, McDougall, Freud, Jung and others, tended to show that the mind is not merely the brain in action, but is, in fact, distinct from brain and non-material in nature. For instance, in the mind there is a creativeness and a purposiveness and a power of reasoning which cannot be accounted for merely as activities of the brain cells. The mind can also criticise and formulate theories.

Further, the findings of the Society for Psychic Research and the work of Rhine, Soal, Gilbert Murray, Carrington, Hettinger and others, on extra-sensory perception showed that man has psychic powers which are not affected by space or time factors and are apparently not dependent on the action of the brain and nervous system; also, that the mind with all its memories and characteristic traits survives death of the body and so is distinct from the brain. It was found possible through sensitives or mediums, *i.e.*, individuals in whom the psychic faculty is well developed, to enter into communication with the "dead."

THE SPIRIT STATE

Such communications showed that there is a spirit state in which exist the spirits of all who have passed through earth life. The environment in which they live immediately after death depends on their spiritual development as a result of earth life; it is the environment to which they have become attuned in earth life. They have an active existence in the spirit state and can make progress by developing further their spiritual nature. These facts show that there is a meaning and purpose in earth life which it would not have if there is no survival of death, and they are also consistent with the belief that there is a God behind the universe.

Dr. J. B. Rhine, in discussing the implications of his psychic research work, has said, "The soul theory has now been confirmed." In a similar speculative way, we can now at least rationally conceive of the existence of a universal spirit equivalent to the modern conception of God."

PHILOSOPHIC BELIEF IN GOD

Philosophers have arrived at a belief in God for other reasons. Since ancient times they have recognised that in the universe there is a number of eternal principles or "values" or according to Plato, "forms": Truth, Goodness, Justice, Beauty and Happiness. They claim that these principles belong to an order or state of reality, which although non-material, is more real than the familiar world. These principles can be dimly apprehended by the human mind and recognised as the true materials of human knowledge and as the aims or ideals governing human behaviour, effort and aspiration. Thus, in realising what is good, in doing what is right and in appreciating beauty in any of its forms, a person is responding to the force of these principles. Philosophers claim that these principles are exemplars of a reality which exists independently of the human mind and this may be taken as implying the existence of a Divine Mind, an Infinite Personality, who knows and appreciates these principles and has been responsible for a moral order of which they are the expression in the universe which He has created.

2

THE NATURE OF GOD

According to spirit teachings received by prophets, seers and sensitives throughout the ages, God is Spirit; the motivating force in man is also spirit and this spirit is the same in essence as the Divine Spirit and comes in the first place from God. Thus there is a link between God and man, a link, which no matter how low the human spirit has fallen, can never be broken. Moreover, as the human spirit has emanated from the Divine Spirit, man can refer to God as the Heavenly Father, a fact recognised by Jesus in various sayings, for instance, "I ascend unto my Father, and your Father," and "Our Father, which art in Heaven." It is also recognised in the first Principle of Spiritualism, "The Fatherhood of God." And as all men can therefore be regarded as sons of God, the second Principle naturally follows, namely, "The Brotherhood of Man."

Spiritualists believe in the personal nature of God, a God Who is a Loving Father and who is concerned with all His creation and can be revered, loved, worshipped and communed with for fellowship and guidance. However, God should not be regarded merely as a Person, as this at most can be only one aspect of His whole nature.

God is so utterly transcendent in nature to man that the latter can never have any definite conception of the Divine Being, just as an insect can never have any definite conception of the nature of man, although both are forms of life. However, as the Divine Spirit has been responsible for the creation and sustenance of the universe, man can form some conception of His ways of working and therefore of His nature by studying the universe and the laws which operate in it.

Science has found that in the universe there is a conformity to natural law and order; there is also a creative productiveness showing evidence of design and purpose and frequently great artistry. Behind all and over all and sustaining all, animate and inanimate, material and non-material, in the universe must be an Almighty Force, a Creator of infinite wisdom, power and accessibility. In fact, Divine constructive thought associated with the power of creation must be a fundamental character of God.

THE HUMAN MIND

Moreover, as the mind of man is a manifestation of the spirit within him, and as this spirit is akin to the Divine Spirit, the human mind must have some relationship, however slight, to the mind of God. Thus the highest and best elements that can be found in the human mind should give some indication, although faint, as to the nature of the Divine Mind.

Man knows that there is a unity, a purposiveness and a creativeness in his own mind, which cannot be accounted for merely by the activity of the brain cells, but must be attributes of the spirit within him. There is also a love of Goodness, Truth, Justice, Beauty and Happiness, which is not material in origin but must be spiritual in nature, for these principles are expressions of another order of reality. The fact that the human spirit unhesitatingly accepts these ethical principles may be taken as an indication that it has *a priori* or intuitive knowledge of them due to their being expressions of the Divine Mind from which the spirit itself originates.

In other words, these principles may be modes under which the Divine Mind reveals itself to man, for if there is a God at the heart of the universe, these universal values may well be the means through which His nature is manifested.

Jesus fully recognised these ethical values and exemplified them in his life. However, all great religious teachers, leaders, and mystics throughout the ages, Buddha, Confucius, Lao Tse, Pythagoras, Socrates, St. Paul and St. Francis, realised them to a greater or less degree so that the divine spark glowed brightly in all their personalities.

These teachers all had the same traits. All were convinced of the reality of the spirit state and attached supreme importance to spiritual instead of worldly values. They led unselfish lives, in which all self-centred and worldly thoughts, passions, desires and ambitions were suppressed.

THE MESSAGE OF THE GREAT RELIGIOUS TEACHERS

Their teaching, no matter the age, country, civilisation or culture in which they lived, was essentially the same: "Do to others as you would they should do unto you"; be not proud, self-centred or selfish but think of others; control your passions and worldly desires; be spiritual in your outlook and actions. The code of ethics which they taught and practised in their lives can, as already mentioned, be regarded as the expression of the Divine Will, and an indication of a common inspiration throughout the ages, and this would also explain the essential similarity of the traits and teachings of these men in spite of their widely varied times and environments. This fact was recognised by St. Augustine, the great Christian theologian, for in one of his works he wrote, "For that which is now called the Christian religion really was known to the ancients nor was wanting at any time from the beginning of the human race, until the time Christ came in the flesh, at which time the true religion that had previously existed began to be called Christianity."

INSPIRATION

It is reasonable to suppose that the human mind in its most exalted moments of inspiration, *e.g.*, in states of ecstasy, should be able to have some slight consciousness or sense of awareness of the Divine Mind. Such moments are experienced not only by mystics, but also by musical composers, artists and poets, and provide clues as to the nature of the Divine Mind. Mystics tell us that at such moments they have the conviction that they are in contact with another state of existence, which is far more real than that of earth life; at the same time they have a sense of living more intensely and abundantly than in, earth life.

They also feel that they are in a state of at-one-ness (atonement) with a unifying universal Spiritual Presence. They have a sense of timelessness, selflessness and freedom from all narrow, self-centred and worldly thoughts and from all frustrating circumstances and inhibitions.

Over all there is a feeling of sheer joy and ecstasy in the goodness, truth and beauty of the things revealed. In such moments men sense, however dimly, the Divine Mind, for with an omnipotent God there can be no bounds, no limitations, no inhibitions; just complete harmony and joy in His work of creating and sustaining the universe.

God is Spirit, Eternal and Unchangeable, of Infinite Power, Wisdom, Justice and Goodness, and with a boundless Love for all His Creation.

THE NATURE OF MAN

"What is man, that thou art mindful of him? and the son of man, that thou visitest him? For thou hast made him but little lower than God, and crownest him with glory and honour."

Psalm VIII

I have to thank Miss M. C. Alston and Miss J. A. Hector for services rendered in the preparation of this work; also Dr. Winning who has contributed the Foreword.

THE AUTHOR

FOREWORD

Someone has said that, "Science has proof but no certainty; Religion has certainty but no proof." Nevertheless the inquiring mind of man will not be satisfied with religious affirmations alone. Tangible proof is demanded. This cannot always be forthcoming when we are dealing with imponderable substances that have neither weight nor shape. And so when Dr. Malcolm begins his treatise on "The Nature of Man" by saying, "Man is a Spirit" one is justified in asking, 'How does he know? What proof has he?' Perhaps a few words about the author of this booklet will help us to feel that Dr. Malcolm is not saying something without having first-hand information. He is a graduate of London and Glasgow Universities and holds the degrees of D.Sc., Ph.D., and is an F.R.S.E., and for many years was head of the Bacteriological Department, West of Scotland Agricultural College, and for his distinguished work there, was awarded the O.B.E. He is a Minister of the Spiritualist National Union and has devoted much time and study to Spiritualist and Psychical Research. On the S.N.U. Education Course he is a Tutor and Examiner in Psychology. Therefore when he makes a statement of any kind in this booklet on philosophy or science, it is backed up by a long term of University training in various branches of physical sciences and an equally long training in Spiritualist phenomena and Psychical Research.

The Nature of Man sets out to give a verbal picture of the physical structure of Man, followed by showing the link between Mind and Physical Brain, and finally dealing with the structure and functions of the Spirit Body as the citadel of the indwelling Spirit, or God immanent. This little booklet is a sequel to Dr. Malcolm's other book, "The Search for God," and as far as humanly possible proves that Man is an Immortal Being here and now, a God in the making, working and striving to reach perfection until he realises his at-one-ment with God—the Creative and Directive Power behind and beyond this Physical and Spiritual Universe.

Dr. JOHN WINNING,
Vice-President, S.N.U.

THE NATURE OF MAN

Man is a spirit. He is fundamentally of the same nature as God from whom he originates, and can therefore be said to be a Son of God.

Man comes forth from God and enters earth-life as an individual or separate entity. But he is not entirely independent because, in virtue of his spirit nature, he is linked with God for all eternity, no matter how undeveloped spiritually he may be.

Earth-life is but a short phase in the existence of his spirit. It is necessary to provide him with experiences in a physical environment, and in association with other men; experiences which will enable him to acquire a distinct personality, and to build up his moral character and develop his spiritual nature. As the spirit in earth-life has the power of freewill it can make wrong decisions, some of which may be of a low ethical or spiritual standard and therefore evil in nature, but it can learn to appreciate the harmful effects of evil behaviour and realise the merits of a good life. From the knowledge thus acquired of the effects of good and evil behaviour, it can develop a conscience with a sense of personal responsibility. Of its own freewill it can endeavour to live in a highly moral and spiritual manner, in attunement with the Divine Mind, and so fit itself for the next stage in its existence.

In earth-life a physical body is necessary to enable the spirit to function as an individual entity and acquire consciousness, or a sense, of awareness, of its physical environment. The spirit, however, cannot act directly on the physical body, but does so through the intermediary of a spirit body, which interpenetrates the physical. The spirit body appears to be a highly organised structure composed of substance of a higher order than that of the physical universe. It is subject to the influences of the spirit and is also affected by the condition of the physical body.

THE PHYSICAL BODY

The physical body is the one of which we are consciously aware. It consists of the same type of substance as the physical universe, being made up of the atoms and molecules of various chemical elements present in that universe. This body has been specially developed over a long course of evolutionary changes, extending over perhaps a thousand million years, to enable the spirit entity to function on the surface of the earth. In the process of evolution the different tissues of the body, *e.g.*, bones, muscles, blood vessels, nerves and glands, have been developed. Although these tissues may differ in function, their activities are co-ordinated, so that they work together in a harmonious manner to enable the whole body to maintain itself and carry out its various activities.

The body has the ability to grow, to renew worn-out tissue, to reproduce and to do work. The energy needed for carrying out such activities and for maintaining the body temperature, is obtained from the food by oxidising changes. The oxygen required for this purpose is derived from the air which is inspired into the lungs. The oxygen comes into intimate contact with the blood circulating through these organs. It is taken up by the red blood corpuscles and carried to all parts of the body, to be combined with the sugars and other substances present in the tissues.

THE MUSCLES

Muscles are necessary for the action of the organs of digestion, circulation and respiration. They are also required for carrying out the movements entailed in work and locomotion, and for this purpose are attached to the firm but flexible framework of bones, termed the skeleton. The bones are so jointed that the body can carry out a wide range of movements with great precision. The skeleton also gives support and protection to the internal organs.

THE NERVOUS SYSTEM

The nervous system controls and co-ordinates the activities of the various organs; it is responsible for the harmonious working of all parts of the body. It is made up of a central part, *i.e.*, the brain and spinal cord, and a peripheral part consisting of nerves connecting all parts of the body to the central part. The action of the nervous system may be automatic or involuntary, *i.e.*, carried out without the conscious working of the mind, as in the case of the action of the heart, lungs and digestive organs; or it may be voluntary, when it is due to the conscious working of the mind.

There are two types of nerves, namely sensory and motor. The sensory nerves form connecting links between the central nervous system and the sensory organs, *e.g.*, the eyes, nose and ears. These organs are influenced by external agents, such as light, smell and sound, and as a result, impulses are set up in the sensory nerves and are transmitted to the central nervous system. The motor nerves transmit impulses from the central nervous system to muscles, glands and other organs and thus affect their activities. They cause glands to secrete, and muscles to contract, relax or alter their rhythmical beat (as in the case of the heart). The central nervous system can carry out countless connections between the sensory and motor nerves, and thus act as a central control exchange.

THE BRAIN

In the brain there are not only *sensory areas* (receiving stimuli from sensory nerves) and *motor areas* (sending impulses through the motor nerves to the muscles or glands), but also *association areas* in which sensory experiences may be linked up with others of the same, or different nature. Hence the mind through the brain, instead of regarding each sensory experience by itself alone, can consider it in relation to others. As these association areas deal with mental images (visual, sound, etc.), memories and related ideas, the mind can remember its sensory experiences and link up the present with the past. At the same time it can make use of its sensory experiences, recognising and understanding happenings and conditions in the environment of the body. It is in virtue of these association areas that conscious memories, thoughts and emotions, may be stirred up by the recurrence of some past sensory experience. It has been claimed by materialists that all mental (even the higher) processes are based on the activities of these areas.

SIMPLE REFLEX ACTION

In some cases when an impulse is sent from a sensory organ through a sensory nerve to the central control, there is an immediate response in that an impulse is sent directly back through a motor nerve to a functioning muscle or gland. For instance, if a finger touches a hot object, an impulse from the sensory organs of the finger is sent at once through the sensory nerves to the central nervous system. There, the information is transmitted to motor nerves, which then convey an impulse to the appropriate muscles, causing them to contract so that the finger is withdrawn. This is an example of *simple reflex action*. These reflex actions are carried out automatically in response to certain stimuli; for instance, a speck of dust causes the blinking of an eye-lid, a bright light causes the contraction of the pupil of the eye, and an irritant in the nostril causes sneezing.

Simple reflex actions are occasionally due to the direct contact of sensory and motor nerves, but as a rule the linking is done through the central nervous system. In these cases the sensory impulse may also be transmitted to the brain, so that a sensation is experienced such as pain, heat, cold or smell.

The linking up of the central nervous system with the sensory and motor nerves enables the body to carry out a wide variety of reflex actions and in this respect to be highly adaptable. Thus changes of temperature, extreme exertion, emotional upsets, may affect the heart, the digestive or respiratory systems, or the lachrymal (or tear) glands. In many of these cases the individual is consciously aware of the reflex action, *e.g.*, shivering when cold, trembling when afraid, yawning when tired and laughing when amused; in others, the action is purely unconscious, *e.g.*, in the case of the action of the stomach and endocrine glands. In conscious reflex actions, the brain may to some extent control the process by activating muscles which have an opposing effect, as in checking a cough or a sneeze.

CONDITIONED REFLEX ACTION

The fact that one sensory experience may be linked or associated with one of a different nature, owing to their occurring together in the past, may cause the brain to react always to one of these stimuli as if the other were also present. This renders the reflex action more complicated and is known as a *conditioned reflex.* Thus a dog may salivate on hearing a dinner bell, even in absence of food, if it is the practice to ring a dinner bell each time he is fed.

The Behaviourist School of psychology claims that all human behaviour is due to conditioned reflexes and the thoughts, ideas and memories associated with these reflexes. But the purposive action and will-power of the human mind and its ability to reason cannot be accounted for on this basis.

THE SENSORY ORGANS

The sensory organs are responsible for all the so-called *sensory methods of perception.* These organs are the means by which the body can detect and keep in touch with conditions of its earthly environment. They enable the body to adapt itself to its surroundings, and thus survive. They were primarily evolved for finding food, for detecting other favourable environmental factors and for giving warning of harmful ones. In man and the higher animals, they have become highly specialised so that they can give precise and detailed information of environmental conditions—light, sound, smell, heat, cold, contact or pressure and balance.

Different sensory organs are responsible for the sensations of *pain, pressure (or touch), heat and cold.* They are located in most parts of the body, but especially in the skin. The numerous small sensory organs of pain in the skin give the brain warning of some harmful condition, *e.g.,* the presence of a sharp object, which if left unheeded, might lead to injury. The sensory organs of touch or contact are specially numerous on the palm-side of the fingers and on the tongue.

The sensory organs of *taste* are found in the mouth, particularly on the tongue. They can detect taste provided the substance is in the form of a liquid or is dissolved in the saliva. There are four fundamental tastes—sweet, sour, bitter and salt. The individual taste organs may not be capable of detecting all of these; some can detect only one, but others, two or more.

The sensation of taste may be combined in the brain with other sensations, such as smell, contact, heat or cold, and thus numerous flavours may be differentiated. Indeed, the flavour of certain foods is largely due to smell, as in the case of onions and coffee. Whether a taste is pleasant or not depends on various factors, *e.g.*, inherited traits, usage (as in acquired taste), ideas associated with particular tastes as a result of past experiences. In animals, inherited or innate likes or dislikes for various foods may be associated with their feeding habits, *i.e.*, whether they are herbivorous or carnivorous or, in the latter case, are carrion feeders.

The sensory organs of *smell* are located in the upper part of the nasal cavities. They are adapted to detect certain vapours or gases. The sense of smell was probably developed originally in our animal ancestors to detect not only food and harmful substances, but also other animals, friends or enemies. It is highly developed in many wild animals and enables them to search for prey and avoid their enemies, but it has become greatly diminished in man. Animals and humans differ widely as to whether particular smells are pleasing or not, for reasons somewhat similar to those in connection with differences in taste.

The sense of *sight* is of great importance to man, as it is responsible for most of his information about objects, other people, animals and plants in his environment. Even in his thought processes, he uses to a large extent mental visual images.

The eyes are sensitive to certain rays of light—those of wave length between 390 and 720 millionths of a millimetre. The ultra-violet, X-rays and gamma rays are below the range of visibility; the infra-red and wireless waves are above it. As gamma rays may be only three 1,000,000,000th parts of a millimetre and wireless waves may be five or ten miles long, the series of rays visible to the eye constitutes only an infinitesimal part of the wide range of electro-magnetic radiation in the universe.

Each eye has a mechanism, the iris, by means of which its opening, the pupil, is increased or diminished in size according to the intensity of light. Thus in bright light the opening is decreased, and in dim light or the dark, increased. This action is of a reflex nature. There is also a lens in the eye, which is automatically altered with great rapidity and precision to enable the eye to focus on objects at different distances. In addition, the eye can be moved to bring objects into the field of vision. The fact that there are two eyes, whose gaze can be directed simultaneously on the same object, provides for stereoscopic or three-dimensional vision. Thus man can gauge depth and distance.

The sense of *hearing* depends on the detection of the frequency of sound waves in the air by the ear drums. The human ear can detect frequencies of from 20 to 20,000 per second, and these are interpreted by the brain in the form of sound, of which the pitch varies with the frequency of the sound wave. Sound waves below or above this range of frequency are not heard by man. Man and animals vary in regard to the sounds which they can hear. For instance, dogs can hear sounds which are so high pitched that they are inaudible to man.

There is also a sensory organ of *balance*, which is of importance in connection with the maintenance of posture and balance.

SENSORY EXPERIENCES

Accordingly, in earth-life man has sensory experiences which enable him to be aware of, and respond to other people and creatures and conditions in his surroundings. Although there are a wide variety of these experiences, the various sensory organs are highly specialised, and in each case can deal only with a limited range of conditions. Much is therefore happening in the universe of which the individual is not consciously aware, as in the case of ultra-sonic sound waves and such electro-magnetic radiation as X-rays, infra-red rays and wireless waves. The sensory organs also are unable to detect "other-world" conditions of any kind.

THE MIND

MENTAL ASSOCIATIONS

During his waking hours man is continually receiving sensory stimuli from his environment, and these sensory experiences, together with the mental images, thoughts, ideas, memories and emotions associated with them, play an important part in his mental make-up. Indeed, the Behaviourist School of psychology claims that all behaviour in man and animals is due to simple and conditioned reflex actions and associated thoughts, and that the only way to understand their mental processes is by studying their behaviour. The behaviourists believe that these mental associations are responsible for all human thoughts, including the higher, and that the inference could be drawn that the brain and other parts of the nervous system are responsible for *all* man's mental activities.

OTHER MENTAL PROCESSES

Against this view, it may be said that much of human behaviour does not consist in mere automatic responses, simple or conditioned, to sensory stimuli, and the mental associations connected with them, but that there are other mental processes, such as those arising from inherited or instinctive urges and the sentiments associated with them. Those processes may be purposive in nature, the mind having a certain end in view and exerting will-power in striving to attain that end. In addition, man has the ability to reflect on his various sensory experiences, and he is swayed by emotions and desires. He is also capable of creative thought, can reason, form judgments and formulate theories. Moreover, there is some unifying, organising and controlling factor in relation to the mental activities, so that man can consider a situation as a whole and not as a number of separate sensory experiences and reflex motor actions.

MIND AND BRAIN

For these reasons, psychologists such as Myers, McDougall, Freud and Jung, have come to the conclusion that the purely mechanistic and materialistic theory of the behaviourists does not cover all the facts; there are mental activities, higher forms of consciousness, which cannot be accounted for as mere products of the brain and nerve cells, but which are due to a mind which is distinct from brain and is non-material in nature. This is also borne out by the fact that since ancient times man has been able to apprehend, although dimly, the ethical principles (the "forms" of Plato) of Goodness, Truth, Beauty and Justice. These are eternal values, which philosophers in all ages have recognised and unhesitatingly accepted as the true materials of human knowledge, and as the highest aims and ideals governing human behaviour, effort and aspiration. Love of these values cannot be of material origin, associated merely with brain and nerve cells, but must be spiritual in nature.

Further, the findings of the Society for Psychical Research, and the work of Rhine, Soal, Gilbert Murray and others, on extra-sensory perception show that man has psychic powers which are not affected by space or time factors, and are apparently not dependent on the action of the brain and nerves; also, that the mind, with all its memories and characteristic traits, learning and intellectual powers, survives death of the body and so must be distinct from brain and the physical body. It is therefore reasonable to assume that a non-material or spirit entity is responsible for our mental processes. In other words, the mind is a manifestation of the spirit of man, and the brain and nerves are merely the instruments by means of which the spirit governs and controls the activities of the physical body, and at the same time becomes aware of other creatures and of conditions in the earthly environment.

CONDITIONS AFFECTING THE MIND

Accordingly, there is evidence that the nervous system is merely the instrument which is used by the mind to keep in touch with its environment, and to control and coordinate the activities of the various organs of the body. But the activity of the mind itself can be affected by the nervous system. For instance, if the brain is injured or diseased, the mind may not be able to function properly through it and as a result the individual shows abnormal mental traits. In extreme cases the whole personality may appear to change. It has been found possible to cure certain neurotic conditions and even forms of insanity, by operating surgically on the brain or by subjecting it to electrical shock treatment. Thus patients who were in a state of utter depression or were violently insane, have been rendered care-free. The action of the mind may also be affected by drugs, especially those which act on the nervous system, such as sedatives, tranquillisers or stimulants.

The fact that the mental activities and apparently the personality of an individual may be affected by an abnormal condition of the brain, has been brought forward by materialists in support of their claim that there is no such thing as mind. They fail to appreciate that if the instrument (the brain) is faulty, the mind will not be able to function through it in a normal fashion.

The mind may also be affected by other physical conditions. For instance, a person who suffers from chronic indigestion is frequently irritable and readily upset. The *endocrine glands, e.g.,* the thyroid, adrenals, pituitary, etc., are of special importance. These produce secretions, termed *hormones*, which pass into the blood-stream and influence the action of other organs. For example, the adrenal glands, in moments of anxiety, fear or anger, produce a hormone, adrenalin, which increases the rate of respiration and of the circulation of the blood, while stimulating the activity of the muscles, so that the body is prepared for strenuous action, such as fighting or fleeing. The thyroid hormone stimulates the action of the heart and the digestive organs. It has a marked effect on temperament and on general intelligence. If this hormone is deficient, the health is impaired and the mind appears to be dull and sluggish. If it is in excess, the individual tends to become mentally unstable, tense and readily upset. Deficiency of the pituitary secretions during childhood causes growth to be stunted, but slight excess results in tall energetic individuals of high intelligence.

THE INFLUENCE OF INSTINCTS

In addition, the human mind is influenced by the innate drives or urges, termed *instincts*, to which it is subjected as a result of its being in association with a physical body which has been evolved through a long line of animal ancestors. From these earlier forms of life man has inherited three main types of instinct: self-preservation (*e.g.*, escape, combat, self-assertion, curiosity, acquisition and food-seeking); sex (*e.g.*, mating and parental); herd (*e.g.*, defence and social).

These instincts play an important part in enabling the individual to become adjusted to the conditions of earth-life. They are purposive in action and urge the mind to express itself in specific ways, and so have a profound effect on human behaviour. Under conditions which are suitable for their expression they may give great driving force to the individual, and thus be responsible for a life of striving after certain ends or ideals. If, however, an instinct has no opportunity of expressing itself freely in some natural outlet, or in the pursuit of some ideal in harmony with it, a state of mental tension may result. This may be prevented or reduced either by controlling the instinctive urge, or by redirecting it along other useful channels (*sublimation*), as in the case of an unmarried woman taking up nursing. In some cases, however, the mental tension arising from an unexpressed instinct is relieved by repressing it by forcing it below the level of consciousness into the unconscious mind. This may later have a harmful action on the mental health of the individual, giving rise to various forms of abnormal behaviour or perversions, *e.g.*, apathy, depression and hypochondria.

It must also be remembered that the state of the mind can affect the health of the body. Joy, hopeful expectancy and aesthetic emotion, have a stimulating influence, especially on the nervous system and the alimentary tract, whereas worry and other mental upsets, such as hatred, anger and jealousy, have the opposite effect. Thus good digestion is frequently associated with a happy disposition and a contented mind.

THE STRUCTURE OF THE MIND

There are three levels in the mind: the *conscious*, the *subconscious* and the *unconscious*. The conscious level is the part of the mind of which we are actually aware in our waking state. The subconscious and unconscious levels lie below the threshold of consciousness and we are therefore unaware of their activities.

The *conscious* mind is responsible for all those mental activities of feeling, remembering, purposing, willing and reasoning, of which we are actually aware when awake; also for all the voluntary actions of the body. It enables us to be aware of the impressions received through our sensory organs, and thus to know of, and respond to conditions in our physical environment. Owing to the fact that our sensory organs are highly specialised and therefore limited in their range of action, we are conscious of only a minute fraction of all that is going on around us at any time, and we are not directly aware of any activity in the spirit state.

In conscious activities, there is as a rule a *focal* and a *marginal* field of attention or awareness. Thus the mind is generally focused or concentrated on some particular object, thought, idea or activity (the focal field), but at the same time it deals casually with extraneous or marginal stimuli (the marginal field). For instance, in reading a book, the subject matter of the print occupies the focal consciousness, but the sound of a distant conversation or the noise of a passing car, takes up only the marginal. If, however, these marginal sounds become sufficiently loud to reach the focal area of attention, they distract the mind and interfere with its powers of concentration.

The *subconscious* part of the mind lies just below the level of the conscious and the latter is largely unaware of its activities. It stores memories of names and experiences, and of learning, which can be recalled at will. As a rule these are memories which have been recently acquired, but earlier experiences and knowledge may be recallable if they have made a strong impression on the mind.

The subconscious mind merges into the *unconscious*, there being apparently no definite line of demarcation. The unconscious mind appears to have great depths. It also is a storehouse of memories of past experiences and of learning, but these cannot be recalled at will. It is now generally accepted by psychologists that no experience or learning is ever completely forgotten, provided it made an impression on the conscious mind at the time of its occurrence. Even experiences of infancy can be recalled under certain conditions, *e.g.*, under hypnosis. There appears, however, to be some natural barrier to the free passage of thoughts from the unconscious, and even from the subconscious, to the conscious part of the mind, so that, although all parts are simultaneously active, the individual is as a rule unaware of what is happening below the threshold of consciousness. The workings of the subconscious and unconscious mind may become evident in moments of danger, of intense emotion or in dreams. But thoughts from the lower levels may not reach the conscious level in their original form; they may be altered in some peculiar or deliberate manner, or expressed in symbolic form.

As it is not possible to draw a hard and fast line between the activities of the subconscious and the unconscious parts of the mind, the term subconscious is used to cover both in the subsequent pages of this treatise. It is therefore employed in the same sense as Myers used the term subliminal.

ACTIVITIES OF THE SUBCONSCIOUS MIND

Although termed the subconscious level, it must not be thought that this part of the mind acts merely as a storehouse of memories, and that there is little or no mental activity. There is evidence that mental processes do occur in the subconscious, and that these are subject to the same laws as those of the conscious mind. Thus there is an element of striving and purposefulness in the subconscious activities. This may be due to the action of memories stored there, or to the inherited or instinctive urges which are active at this level of the mind.

The subconscious mind controls the action of the involuntary muscles, *e.g.*, those of the heart and stomach. It also influences the functioning of the endocrine and other glands of the body. It has therefore a profound effect not only on the mental but also the physical health. Conscious thoughts of worry, fear and hatred become impressed on the subconscious and thus lower the health of the body, just as confident, happy and unselfish thoughts raise it. The subconscious mind therefore plays an important part in the treatment of disease by suggestion and hypnosis, and also probably in spirit treatment, including absent healing.

The subconscious activities arising from stored memories or instinctive urges may have a profound effect on behaviour and personality. The spontaneous likes or dislikes, which an individual may experience for certain people or things, may be due to some instinctive action, or even to some innate power to judge at once a person's character; but it is most frequently due to the activity in the subconscious mind of memories of past experiences of a happy or unhappy nature. The person or object is linked up in some way by the mind with these memories, which although repressed by the conscious mind, are still active in the subconscious. Frightening or distressing experiences may be similarly repressed and although the subconscious mind does not allow them to be recalled, their memories may still play an active part and cause peculiarities in behaviour. Of course, experiences may be forgotten simply because they did not make sufficient impression on the conscious mind at the time of their occurrence.

DREAMS

Dreams are the products, often in dramatised form, of the subconscious mind. Everyone has dreams, but in many cases they cannot be recalled on awaking. According to Freud, dreaming is a necessary mental activity by which the unfulfilled desires and repressed thoughts, impulses and emotions, which are held in check by the subconscious mind, are released and find to some extent satisfactory expression in the conscious. But certain dreams, as will be discussed later, are due to the psychic activities of the subconscious mind.

Dreams may be affected by physical or physiological conditions, *e.g.*, noise, coldness, discomfort or indigestion, although these may not be given their true significance in the dream. Thus indigestion may cause palpitation of the heart of the sleeper, and as the subconscious mind may associate this condition with fright, the result may be a night-mare. In addition, these purely non-psychological stimuli may cause certain repressed memories or unfulfilled wishes to become active and find relief in their expression in the dream.

Accordingly, some dreams are of a simple nature, being merely the expression of some desire. Others are involved, arising perhaps from some repressed desire or complex, or from some psychic activity. They may also be variously disguised in their expression to prevent their unpleasant character awakening the dreamer. To disguise its nature, the dream may be put in symbolic form, as in the classic case of Pharaoh's dream of fat and lean kine. The same symbol may vary in meaning with different people. The symbolism may be highly dramatised, as, for example, when a person, studying hard for an examination, dreams he is trying to climb a precipitous rock. The disguise is said to be one of *displacement*, if some other object or person is substituted in the dream for the object or person in the repressed thought. *Condensation* is said to have occurred if the dream is concerned with the expression of several repressed desires; these have been combined in the dream owing to some common association or resemblance between them.

SUBCONSCIOUS MENTATION AND INTUITION

There is evidence that the subconscious mind has higher powers of comprehension and reasoning than the conscious. For instance, it appears to have the ability to estimate accurately the passage of time. This is shown by many people who can awaken at a predetermined hour. In fact, this sense of the passage of time is frequently more accurate in us when asleep than when awake. Also, a person under hypnotic suggestion, may carry out instructions at a time prescribed by the hypnotist, although this appointed time may be several days after the suggestion has been made.

Certain individuals possess an extraordinary power of making arithmetical calculations. This is due largely to subconscious mental activity and must be associated in some way with an insight into mathematical methods, yet it generally occurs in childhood and may disappear later in spite of mathematical education. Further, it is found not only in brilliant mathematicians, but also in individuals with apparently no knowledge of mathematics and even of low intelligence.

Subconscious activity may also be responsible for the migratory instincts of birds, the horning instincts of pigeons, the "sensing" of water from a distance by animals and the divining of water by man.

With people in general, if a problem or difficulty is dismissed completely from the conscious mind, the solution may later present itself spontaneously. As no conscious thought has been given to the matter in the interval, the problem must have been solved or the difficulty settled, by the activity of the subconscious mind, *i.e.,* by subconscious mentation. It is well known that questions have been settled in this way during sleep. Hence the soundness of the advice to a person who is confronted with a difficult situation, to "sleep over it." Mathematicians have solved problems in this way. They have become aware of the solution on awaking. So also have scientists been able to solve their problems and make original discoveries, sometimes in absence of any scientific data. In such cases as these, the subconscious activity involved has been termed *intuitive reasoning.* The person is said to have been guided by his *intuition* or to have had a "*hunch.*"

INSPIRATION

There are, however, more exalted forms of sub-conscious mentation, in which entirely original ideas, often of a constructive nature, come spontaneously from the subconscious mind into the conscious. This is known as *inspiration* and is characteristic of geniuses, although it is found to some extent in ordinary individuals. Tyrrell points out in his work, *The Personality of Man,* that "It is a highly significant fact that those creations of the human mind, which have borne pre-eminently the stamp of originality and greatness, have not come from within the region of consciousness. They have come from beyond consciousness, knocking at its door for admittance: they have flowed into it, sometimes slowly as if by seepage, but often with a burst of overwhelming power." Thus in true inspiration, the material frequently surges up spontaneously and unexpectedly into the conscious mind. It may have great, even dramatic, force and appear as in the nature of a *revelation* from some outside and unfamiliar or other-world source, giving the person concerned a feeling of elation or ecstasy—a common experience of great poets, writers, artists and musical composers.

Once the inspired material has entered the conscious mind, the true genius is able to interpret it and express it in words, musical notes or painting, so that it can be understood and appreciated by others. The material may be so transcendent or advanced in nature that the inspired individual has great difficulty in doing so. In the case of music and art, considerable knowledge and technical skill may be necessary. If the information is scientific in nature, it may be so advanced that it is not easy to find an explanation for it or prove its truth, when using the existing scientific methods and data available.

If inspired music or poetry enters the conscious mind gradually or over an extended period, there is time for the person concerned to absorb it and express it in suitable form, but if it breaks through in a sudden rush, altogether and complete, the individual may have difficulty in remembering it and expressing it in extended form with all the details in proper sequence. Chopin sometimes took weeks to write out a piece of music he had received in a moment of inspiration.

Many great musical composers, artists, writers and poets, have admitted that their works have come from beyond the threshold of consciousness, from sources which appeared to them to be at times outside their own minds, even other-worldly—in some cases, as if a greater being was supplying the inspired material. Shelley, Coleridge, Blake, R. L. Stevenson, Wordsworth, Mozart, Handel, Beethoven, Chopin, Schubert and many others, were inspired in this way. Socrates realised fully the subconscious nature of inspiration. He said, "I soon found that it is not by wisdom (*i.e.*, conscious thought) that the poets create their works, but by a certain natural power and by inspiration, like soothsayers and prophets, who say many fine things, but who understand nothing of what they say." (See *An Anatomy of Inspiration*, by R. E. M. Harding.)

Accordingly, intuition and inspiration are primarily due to the activity of the subconscious mind, and geniuses as a rule can tap the contents of their subconscious mind more readily than can ordinary individuals. But the conscious mind is required to interpret and express the inspired material in a form which can be appreciated and understood by other people. The question naturally arises as to how inspiration comes in the subconscious mind. Is it due to subconscious mentation or does it come from outside sources? In this connection it must be borne in mind that the subconscious mind has not only very high comprehensive and reasoning powers but, owing to its perfect memory, it has in addition a vast store of knowledge. These two factors alone could account for much of the information obtained by intuition and even by inspiration, but Myers claimed that to be the work of a genius, the inspired material must satisfy "two quite distinct requirements. It must involve something original, spontaneous, unteachable, unexpected; and it must also in some way win for itself the admiration of mankind." (See *Human Personality and its Survival of Bodily Death*, by F. W. H. Myers.)

Inspiration of this type can hardly be accounted for as merely the product of subconscious mentation, especially where there is something beyond the material world in the nature of the information obtained. Taking into account the fact that the subconscious mind has telepathic and clairvoyant powers (see later), it is reasonable to infer that the inspiration may have come partly or even wholly from outside sources, such as discarnate minds. This is borne out by information given in spirit communications through psychic sensitives. It is also supported to some extent by the fact that geniuses, in moments of inspiration, may show traits or mannerisms somewhat similar to sensitives under spirit control, as, for example, Handel in composing "The Messiah."

According to Myers, "the distinctive characteristic of genius is the large infusion of the subliminal (subconscious and unconscious) in its mental output; and one characteristic of the subliminal is that it is in closer relation than the supraliminal (conscious) to the spiritual world, and is thus nearer to the primitive source and extra-terrene initiation of life."

MYSTICISM

Mystical experiences also appear to come from beyond the range of the conscious mind. They are apparently associated with the exercise of the psychic faculty, and are essentially of the same nature as inspirational experiences, but are on a higher spiritual level.

In mysticism the individual approaches and has direct contact with the Divine Mind, and thus becomes aware of truths without the use of the intellect or the sensory organs. He thereby gains a clear and utterly convincing insight into spiritual and universal knowledge, especially with regard to the eternal values of Goodness, Truth, Justice and Beauty. The knowledge obtained is in all cases fundamentally the same, irrespective of the religion of the mystic; it is not restricted to any particular period, creed or nation—it is "cosmic, not denominational" in nature. It is free from the dogmas and doctrines which have arisen in all the world's religions as a result of the wrong interpretation or misrepresentation of historical facts. But it forms the basis of all the great religions. In fact, most of the founders and leaders of great religious movements in the past have had mystical experiences, *e.g.*, Christ, Gautama the Buddha, St. Paul, St. Francis of Assisi, Fox, Swedenborg and Wesley.

Mystical experiences in general are of the same basic nature. The mystic is frequently in trance and loses all sense of awareness of time and surroundings, but the experiences are vivid and overwhelming and give rise to a feeling of exaltation, joy and enlightenment. The knowledge obtained may be so ineffable or transcendent that the conscious mind finds it difficult or impossible to express it in words. It may, however, be transmitted in trance utterances or automatic writing.

The mystics were not merely individuals who spent their lives in meditation or in contemplation. In many cases they were energetic, forceful characters, whose mystical experiences appeared to spur them on to fresh activities, as with Joan of Arc, St. Francis and George Fox. Moreover, their experiences were not due to some abnormal condition of the mind, such as hysteria, but to the exercise of the psychic faculty. This is borne out by the fact that the information obtained could not as a rule be the result merely of subconscious mental activities, making use of the knowledge stored up in the subconscious mind. The mystical insight was generally of such an original nature that it must have come from some outside probably other-world, source, although it had to be put in earthly terms to enable it to be passed through to, and expressed by the conscious mind.

EXTRA-SENSORY PERCEPTION

The mind may obtain information by other means than by the ordinary sensory organs, *i.e.*, by *extra-sensory perception*. This may take the form of telepathy, clairvoyance, clairaudience, automatic writing or drawing, and trance speaking. In all these processes, the information is received in the first place below the threshold of consciousness, and therefore it would appear that the subconscious mind possesses the extra-sensory perceptive, or psychic, faculty.

TELEPATHY

The term *telepathy* denotes the extra-sensory communication of thoughts or impressions from one individual to another. The thoughts do not appear to be transmitted from the communicator or agent to the percipient by means of atmospheric waves or electro-magnetic radiation of any kind, as, unlike these physical phenomena, the process is not affected by distance, telepathy occurring perhaps just as readily when the two persons concerned are hundreds of miles apart as when they are in the same room. (Physical radiations decrease in intensity in proportion to the square of the distance they pass through.) Further, the process has never been detected by any instrument for recording waves or radiation of any kind, and no organ has been found in the human body which would be capable of generating or receiving such waves or radiation.

For these reasons it is now generally agreed that telepathy is not a physical process. This view is also borne out by the fact that, unlike the ordinary methods of transmitting information, no language or pre-arranged code, such as morse, is required; indeed, the persons concerned may not have a common language, only thoughts, impressions or visual images being involved. Further, there is generally only one percipient. This is as a rule someone who has a strong link with the communicator, such as family relationship, friendship or a common interest. The faculty is particularly marked in the case of identical twins.

There is a possibility that in telepathy no message is transmitted through space, but that the percipient becomes aware of the agent's thoughts, because their subconscious minds are in contact or attunement with each other, irrespective of spatial factors. The subconscious mind of an individual may not be confined to the particular locality occupied by the physical body; indeed, it may be free to function anywhere under suitable conditions, for example, when in harmony or rapport with another mind.

SPONTANEOUS TELEPATHY

In cases of spontaneous telepathy, the communicator is frequently in a highly emotional state owing to danger, illness, or some intense desire or longing; or he may be at the point of death. On the other hand, the percipient is generally in a relaxed condition, as in moments of abstraction or reverie, or when half-asleep. He may be asleep, and in that case the information received may take the form of a dream, which is usually characterised by its vivid and impressive nature, and perhaps by a mass of veridical details. These details and the "timing" may rule out the possibility of chance.

The telepathic communication may for some reason be retained in the subconscious mind of the percipient, so that he does not become consciously aware of it. But if it is passed in its original form from the subconscious to the conscious mind, its nature and meaning can be understood. In many cases, however, the communication, before it reaches the conscious mind, may have become so altered that its origin and purport are not clear; it may be put in symbolic form or changed in some peculiar and purposive fashion by the subconscious mind. In some instances the percipient, instead of becoming aware of having received a communication, has merely an unaccountable feeling of dread, depression or elation, depending on the nature of the communicator's thoughts.

TELEPATHIC COMMUNICATION BY SPIRITS

As the faculty of telepathy is possessed by the mind and not by the brain, it is retained by the spirit after death. In fact, telepathy appears to be one of the chief methods by which discarnate spirits communicate with one another, and with the incarnate.

The information given through mediums in automatic writing, trance speaking or drawing, comes in this way from discarnate spirits, and also perhaps from individuals still in earth-life, especially the sitters. This information is liable to be altered or coloured to some extent by thoughts in the medium's own mind (subconscious or conscious.) The extent to which such thoughts enter into what purports to be a spirit message will depend on a number of factors, *e.g.*, the degree of psychic development of the medium, the extent of the spirit control, and the presence of ingrained ideas in the subconscious. In some instances such automatic messages may come entirely from the medium's subconscious mind and not from spirit sources. The inspired work of geniuses, as already mentioned, may be the direct result of telepathic communications received from the spirit world.

TELEPATHY IN EVERY-DAY LIFE

In the case of the ordinary individual, telepathic communication from discarnate spirits, and individuals still in earth-life, is frequently, if not constantly, taking place. At the same time we can transmit to others, living and dead, our own thoughts. Our minds may be likened to wireless stations, which can both send out and receive messages. The information we receive in this way, however, is as a rule retained in the subconscious mind, and we have seldom any conscious knowledge of it. There may be some screening device in the mind or brain which prevents us from becoming readily aware of such information.

All things considered, life on earth would be rendered more difficult and more complicated if our conscious minds were fully accessible at all times to those of others. Further, we would have difficulty in focusing our attention on, and adjusting ourselves to, our material environment if we were simultaneously aware of thoughts from individuals in earth-life and from those in the spirit state. But even although the conscious mind is not aware of such thoughts, they may influence the individual for good or ill.

By right thinking and by aspiration we bring our minds into attunement with those of higher spirits, *e.g.*, our guides or "guardian angels," and become subject to the influence of their thoughts. On the other hand, by leading vicious or depraved lives we attract vicious or spiritually undeveloped individuals, incarnate as well as discarnate, and become subject to their evil influences. Similarly, we can influence others, incarnate and discarnate, for good or ill by our thoughts. Kindly and sympathetic thoughts are helpful to others, whereas spiteful or critical thoughts have the reverse effect, besides being harmful to our own mind. Hence by expecting the best from a person, we are more likely to get it. For the same reason, the united thoughts of a group of earnest people may influence national leaders or start reform movements. It is possible that a feeling of sympathy or antipathy between persons may have in itself been due to a telepathic contact.

TELEPATHY AND PRAYER

Discarnate spirits become aware of our thoughts as a result of such telepathic contacts. In fact, prayer is based on this method of communication with the spirit world. Hence, in praying, it is essential that we attune our minds to God or to our spirit helpers. It has been said that our whole life should be a prayer, *i.e.*, one of spiritual attunement to God, and that when we pray, instead of constantly making pleas to Him for this and that, we should rather thank Him for His boundless love and His countless blessings. We should have complete trust in Him and His spirit messengers to help us in our spiritual endeavours.

Socrates believed that our guardian spirits are perfectly aware of our requirements. They know them better than we do, therefore it is unnecessary to specify them in our prayers. He approved of the old Greek prayer, "Give us, O God, what is good, whether we pray for it or not; and avert from us the evil, even if we pray for it." Nevertheless, by focusing our attention on our particular needs, and by making specific requests in our prayers, our minds are more likely to become adjusted to enable the prayer to be answered. However, what we regard as our needs may be considered by our spirit helpers to be actual hindrances to our spiritual development.

EXPERIMENTAL WORK ON TELEPATHY

Spontaneous cases of telepathy, especially where the information is of a detailed nature and there is exact timing in the transfer of the information, can be highly evidential to the persons concerned, but may not be so to others, who may claim that the results could be due to coincidence or chance or to leakage of information through the sensory channels. To meet these objections, experiments have been carried out under carefully controlled conditions by a number of investigators, such as Rhine, Soal, Tyrrell and Carington. In these experiments, card detection or other tests were used, which could be carried out repeatedly.

Such experimental work, unlike cases of spontaneous telepathy, is at a disadvantage owing to the lack of emotional or dramatic content, and to the two persons concerned in the experiment being in a normal state of mind. The percipient may even be concentrating on the experiment instead of being in a state of relaxation. Under such conditions the process is much less effective than in spontaneous cases. But such experimental tests have the advantage that they can be repeated again and again, perhaps thousands of times, and this enables results to be examined statistically so that the effects of chance can be ruled out. The result of such work provides clear evidence of the existence of the faculty of telepathy.

TELEPATHY IN ANIMALS

Animals appear to have extra-sensory faculties. For instance, dogs have been known to see human spirit forms; also, to act either as the agent or the percipient in telepathic communications with man. The howling of a dog just prior to, or at the time of its master's death (although they may be miles apart) is a well-attested phenomenon. It is possible that the special gifts, naturally possessed by certain animals and birds, of direction finding, homing, migration and water finding, may be at least partly due to extra-sensory powers; as well as their ability to foretell dangerous situations arising from avalanches, earthquakes and volcanic eruptions. The concerted wheeling in regular formation in the air of large flocks of birds, *e.g.*, crows and starlings, can hardly be accounted for on a purely sensory basis. There may be some form of telepathic communication to control their movement and constitute what might be termed a group mind of the birds.

CLAIRVOYANCE AND CLAIRAUDIENCE

In *clairvoyance* the percipient has an extra-sensory vision of some other individual or some scene or event, either in the physical world or in the spirit state. The clairvoyant impression is first received in the subconscious mind and then presented to the conscious mind as a visual image. This may be externalised by the conscious mind, so that it is apparently seen by the eyes. This, however, is a false impression, as the vision would still be observed if the percipient was blind-folded or in darkness. The clairvoyant image is occasionally altered, perhaps in some peculiar manner, as in the case of Pharaoh's dreams of the fat and lean kine, and the full and blasted ears of corn, where it is put in symbolic form.

As with telepathy, the process does not appear to be affected by space or time factors. The vision may be of some event at any distance in time or space. Where the vision is of a distant friend it is almost impossible to determine whether the process involved is telepathy or clairvoyance, as both occur under practically the same conditions.

Clairaudience is the extra-sensory perception of sounds, *e.g.*, speech. It may occur alone but is frequently associated with clairvoyance. For instance, spirits seen clairvoyantly are frequently heard to speak. In clairaudience the impressions are received in the first place in the subconscious mind, but the percipient may be under the false impression that he has actually heard the sounds, as in the case of the child Samuel in the Temple, and Jeanne D'Arc. Socrates was also guided throughout his life by a spirit voice, in which he placed implicit trust.

SPONTANEOUS CLAIRVOYANCE

Spontaneous cases of clairvoyance and clairaudience, like telepathy, occur most frequently when the percipient is asleep or in a relaxed condition, half asleep or in reverie. The information contained in the vision or speech may be of so detailed a nature as to render it highly evidential. The percipient may see the event, not as the individual concerned in it would see it, but as a spectator. Thus he may witness the death of a friend and subsequent happenings to the body. This would show that the vision was due to clairvoyance and not telepathy.

Persons at the point of death occasionally become clairvoyant, and have visions of relatives and friends. Almost invariably the people seen are in the spirit state, although their deaths may have been unknown to the percipient. It could be claimed that these visions show that a dying person is met by his spirit friends as he enters into the spirit state.

MEDIUMISTIC CLAIRVOYANCE

Sensitives as a rule are clairvoyant, but the information given by them in mediumistic communications may have been received not only by clairvoyance, but also by telepathy from the dead, or even from the living. At the same time, it may be coloured by their own conscious or subconscious thoughts. To promote the exercise of the psychic faculty, the activity of the conscious mind of the sensitive may be subdued by auto-suggestive or hypnotic methods, *e.g.*, crystal gazing.

In spirit healing, the medium, in attunement with the spirit healer, becomes the channel through which the latter works. The illness is diagnosed by the spirit and appropriate treatment given, healer and medium working together. But it is possible that healing mediums may diagnose disease by clairvoyance; or by telepathy if the subconscious mind of the patient is aware of the abnormal condition. (As the subconscious mind controls the action of the involuntary muscles and the various glands of the body, it seems reasonable to suppose that it may become aware of any abnormality in their condition.) The handling of an article, *e.g.*, a handkerchief, belonging to an absent patient serves to direct or canalise the medium's psychic faculty on the particular individual, so that a diagnosis can be made.

Absent treatment of disease is based on the linking up of the healer or his spirit control with the patient and, being entirely dependent on psychic, and not on physical forces, is not affected by space factors. It can therefore be carried out irrespective of distance. Sometimes the sensitive may have a clairvoyant vision of the patient and his surroundings.

EXPERIMENTAL WORK ON CLAIRVOYANCE

Much experimental work has been carried out to obtain evidence of clairvoyance. Such investigations have been conducted under conditions somewhat similar to those for telepathy, but precautions were taken to exclude the possibility of telepathy by ensuring that no living person had any knowledge of the matter being used in the test. For instance, in the card detection tests, the cards were shuffled by purely mechanical means and not handled by any person before or during the experiment. Thousands of these card detection tests have been made and the results examined statistically to rule out the effects of chance. These tests provide clear evidence of the faculty of clairvoyance.

In certain experiments where sensitives were asked to determine messages in sealed envelopes, or objects in sealed containers, telepathy between the sensitive and those who had prepared the material for the tests could not be ruled out. The reading of a posthumous message may be due to telepathy between the sensitive and the dead writer of the message, but this can hardly be accepted as complete proof of survival, as the medium may have read the message clairvoyantly. Book and newspaper tests of clairvoyance have been made, in which the sensitives determined words or phrases in certain specified parts of books in libraries; also, words in particular columns of next day's newspapers (in some cases at a time before the type had been finally set up).

PSYCHOMETRY

In the case of certain sensitives, telepathy or clairvoyance can be induced by their handling, or perhaps seeing, an article which was at one time in the possession of the person to be contacted, whether dead or alive. This is termed *psychometry*. The article itself is not the source of the extra-sensory information; it merely makes an impression on the subconscious mind of the sensitive, and focuses or canalises his psychic faculty on the possessor of the article. Thus the extra-sensory matter may contain information of events which happened to the person before he possessed the article, or after it left his possession. Also, after the article has been handled by the sensitive, it can be destroyed without affecting the extra-sensory process.

Psychometry may be of importance in the reading of posthumous letters in sealed envelopes. It may also to some extent be responsible for individuals being impressed by the "atmosphere" of old houses, castles, dungeons, monasteries and abbeys. It may play a part in certain forms of haunting.

WATER DIVINATION

Water divination or *dowsing* appears to be a form of extra-sensory perception in which the presence of underground water can be detected. A small forked twig, usually hazel, is frequently used, the main stem of the twig being pointed upwards by holding one branch of the fork in each hand. In presence of water the twig turns round in the hands until the stem points downwards. The process may be due to some latent extra-sensory faculty of the subconscious mind, perhaps of the same nature as that enabling animals to detect water from a far distance. The twig may serve the purpose of quietening the conscious mind and stimulating the psychic faculty of the subconscious. The actual turning of the twig appears to be due to subconscious muscular action.

EXTRA-SENSORY PERCEPTION AND EARTH-LIFE

The fact that all these forms of extra-sensory perception are purely mental processes in which the brain plays no part, shows that mind can act independently of brain and is therefore distinct from it. The brain is merely the instrument by means of which the mind controls the physical body and thus enables the incarnate spirit to function in an earthly environment. The brain, however, by exercising a restrictive action on the mind, prevents the individual from becoming consciously aware of extra-sensory (including other-worldly) matter. This enables the attention of the individual to be focused on the findings of the sensory organs, and on the muscular activities of the body. Thus he can concentrate better on worldly affairs and so gain a fuller experience of earth life.

It has been suggested that extra-sensory perception may have been the original method by which primitive forms of life kept in touch with their surroundings, and that the sensory organs were developed later when, in the course of evolution, organisms became more highly specialised in their relationships with other organisms and with their earthly environment. With the development of the sensory organs, the extra-sensory faculty has fallen largely into disuse with regard to the physical conditions of the environment. Nevertheless, in earth-life we are subject to countless extra-sensory influences from purely mental or other-world sources and may be affected thereby although largely unaware of the fact.

Earth-life is a highly specialised form of existence, in which a physical body has been evolved to enable the spirit to function in the material environment. The facts of extra-sensory perception show that there is another state of existence—the spirit state. As our sensory organs are not affected by, and therefore cannot detect, any form of radiation from that state, our conscious mind is unaware of the conditions and happenings there. On the other hand, our subconscious mind, owing to its psychic faculty, may be cognisant of such other-world information and under suitable conditions, *e.g.*, a relaxed state of mind, may be able to pass some of this knowledge through to the conscious mind, although in the process it may be altered so much that its true significance is not recognised.

PRECOGNITION

The mind may obtain information of future events by telepathy from the living or dead, or by clairvoyance. This is termed *precognition*. As these extra-sensory processes are due to the action of the subconscious mind, the individual concerned is unaware of how the prediction is formed. Precognitions are therefore quite distinct from the ordinary *inferential predictions* of our daily lives, in which events are foreseen from a knowledge of human arrangements or intentions (*e.g.,* the running of railway trains) or from a knowledge of scientific data and natural laws (*e.g.,* the rising and setting of the sun, eclipses of the moon, tidal movements, etc.). In such cases the foreknowledge is acquired by the conscious mind from existing information or by the use of its reasoning powers.

Cases of spontaneous precognition occur in waking impressions or in dreams, *e.g.,* the dreams of Joseph and Pharaoh. The prophetic death-bed blessings by the ancient patriarchs of the Bible were probably of the same nature. But evidence of this psychic process has been obtained experimentally using card detection and other methods. In the card detection tests, certain percipients were able to detect cards prior to their selection from the pack. In newspaper tests, certain sensitives foretold the precise position of certain words in the following day's newspaper, even though at the time of the prediction the setting and arrangement of the type had not been completed.

ACCOUNTABLE PRECOGNITIONS

In some cases it is possible to explain how the precognition could have been made. For instance, if a person had made up his mind to visit an old ruin, he might sometime before his visit have a clairvoyant vision or dream of the building. The conscious thoughts of the oncoming visit may have promoted the action of the clairvoyant powers in his subconscious mind. Thus when he actually went to the ruin, he would think he had seen it before.

In many precognitions, the factors which will cause the event foreseen may be already in existence at the time the prediction is made. Our conscious mind is unaware of

71

these factors and therefore unable to foresee the event, but our subconscious mind or that of another individual, dead or living, may have more complete information and be able to make the prediction. For example, the precognition of a death in the near future might be possible owing to the sensitive (by clairvoyance) or a communicating spirit having knowledge of an illness, which will possibly cause the death of the particular person at the time foreseen. Similarly, an aeroplane disaster might be precognised, if some mind, incarnate or discarnate, had become aware of a defect in the machine and gave the sensitive the warning.

Although an event is foretold, it does not necessarily mean that it is bound to occur. It may take place only if the factors at the time of the prediction are allowed to persist. Hence once a prediction is known, steps may be taken to prevent the occurrence of the event foretold. If, however, the precognition is vague, its true significance may not be recognised and the warning may be ignored. The fact that the precognition is frequently in the form of a warning of danger or illness serves to indicate that there is a purpose behind it. Some individual, dead or alive, is trying to give guidance and help.

UNACCOUNTABLE PRECOGNITIONS

In precognitive communications from spirits, the reasons for the precognition may be stated. But in many cases no explanation is given. In fact, it would appear to be impossible to explain how an event such as an accident can be foretold months previously, where the happening is due to a factor which is not in operation until a few seconds before the event, as in the case of a car smash due to a dog crossing the road.

There is also the difficulty that in precognitive clairvoyance the extra-sensory process does not appear to conform to the universal law of cause and effect, for how can the mind apprehend a predicted event, *i.e.*, an effect, as it were "out of the blue." The process also appears to be independent of the time factor and therefore outwith all ordinary human experience, time being a mental concept to account for the fact that our minds experience, in earth-life, a sequence of states of awareness.

As the subconscious mind, in clairvoyance, can become aware of events, irrespective of their occurrence in the past, present or future, it would appear that, unlike the conscious mind, the subconscious is not affected in its action by time. From this it may be inferred that there is a state of existence outside our space-time universe of which our conscious mind has no direct knowledge. In this other-world state, time, as we know it on earth, does not exist, there being no beginning and no end. As our subconscious mind can function in that state it may be assumed also that it can persist for ever, and that therefore the spirit must survive bodily death.

FREEWILL AND DETERMINISM

At first sight the facts of precognition apparently give support to the belief that all our future acts are predetermined and that there is no freedom of will in earth-life. Since ancient times the problem of *freewill* and *determinism* has occupied the minds of philosophers and religious scholars. Those who believe in man's freedom of will claim that in earth-life we have complete freedom of choice in making decisions; we are not compelled to do so in any way by external or internal influences. Our decisions are therefore free from the principle of causation and are to some extent spontaneous in nature, so that they cannot be definitely or infallibly predicted. According to this belief, we are entirely responsible for our own actions; we have real moral freedom and in most cases a sense of duty and responsibility, and so experience a feeling of guilt when we do wrong. This is in agreement with fundamental Christian teaching, although it is difficult to reconcile complete freedom of will with the Omnipotence of God.

On the other hand, the determinists believe that there is no such thing as freewill, but that all our decisions are determined by external and internal factors over which we have no control, *e.g.*, inherited instincts and traits, upbringing, education, environmental influences, past experiences and conditions of health. These factors do undoubtedly have a considerable effect on our thoughts and desires and are therefore bound to influence us in making decisions, so that they are not made spontaneously. We all recognise this fact in our daily lives, and in our educational, social, public health, penal and other systems. The determinists, however, go so far as to assert that *all* future events are predetermined or "fixed" beforehand, that there is no freedom of will, and that precognition provides proof of this.

In the past, certain theologians have claimed that God has predetermined every event in the world, and has also decreed that certain people, the "chosen" or "elect," are fore-ordained to be saved, while the others are doomed to perdition. This doctrine is termed *predestination*. It is based on the belief that God rules the world according to a fixed plan, and that man, being utterly sinful, has no chance of being saved without the intervention of God.

Against this belief, it could be argued that, if God is Omniscient, He must have foreseen all things from eternity, and so must have foreseen the occurrence of evil and must have fore-ordained that it be allowed to occur. If that is the case, all man's actions are predetermined and any efforts he may make to change his destiny are useless. Under such conditions he can hardly be held responsible for his actions; and morality and duty, and responsibility and repentance for evil-doing can have no meaning. Such a doctrine tends to promote fatalism.

In spite of all the arguments in favour of determinism, the fact remains that we are all quite certain in our consciousness that, whatever the circumstances, in making decisions we have freedom of will, *i.e.*, the power to choose what we think to be the right course of action. Further, when we realise later that we have made a wrong decision, we are fully convinced that if we had so willed at the time, we could have made the right one.

It is not possible to reconcile the theories of determinism and freewill. The truth of the matter appears to be that in neither case is determinism or freewill ever absolute. It would seem that in earth-life we have freewill, but at the same time are influenced to a greater or less extent by many deterministic factors, such as inherited traits, environment and upbringing. In effect, we have freewill within limits. It can be said that only within these limits are we morally responsible for our actions. However, even in our free-will decisions we may be influenced, although unknown to us, by spirits interested in our welfare, but we cannot be forced to act against our will. The final decision always rests with ourselves; in this way only can we become morally responsible beings.

PRECOGNITION AND FREEWILL

The fact that we have freewill does not preclude the possibility of precognition, because discarnate spirits may have such a wide knowledge of our character and the effects on us of various deterministic factors that they are able to foretell future events in our lives. It is possible that only certain events can be foretold in this way, and even these cannot be predicted infallibly and in full detail. At the same time, as we have freewill, we may be able to take avoiding action if fore-warned about coming events.

The Divine Plan of our lives has been roughly sketched out for us beforehand, but we are responsible for filling in the details in our daily lives. Although we have a certain amount of freedom in filling in the details, we are influenced and guided, and if we accept this, we cannot go too far from the original design. Thus the future is only "fixed" in broad outline; the details are "plastic" and only become fixed by us in the actual present.

It is of vital importance to us that we should have freedom of will to choose between right and wrong. If our behaviour was controlled entirely by deterministic forces we could make no spiritual progress.

The degree of freewill increases with our spiritual development. A man of low spirituality, unlike a really good man, may be governed almost entirely by deterministic factors, such as his animal instincts and physical desires. As a rule he fails to realise that this is so, being under the impression that the compelling urge of these factors is but the expression of his own freedom of choice. Such a person, however, can widen the scope of his freedom and at the same time can become more spiritual in nature, by striving to control his natural desires and emotions, and by endeavouring to lead a less self-centred life. On the other hand, a really good man (one in whom, according to Aristotle, virtue is "a settled habit") by the exercise of his freewill can resist or control deterministic factors, and in this way can develop still further his spiritual nature.

Spirit Communications through Mediums

Most sensitives can tap their subconscious minds for material, while still retaining their normal waking consciousness, *i.e.*, without becoming entranced. Such material may contain information from (a) the subconscious mentation of the medium, (b) her clairvoyant activities, (c) the minds of sitters and others on earth with whom the medium is in telepathic rapport and (d) discarnate spirits. The information passed on by the medium to the sitters may contain material from all these sources, besides being coloured by her own conscious thoughts, and it may be difficult to determine how much of the "message" is from one source and how much is from another.

Certain investigators go so far as to assert that much of the material given in mediumistic communications does not come from discarnate spirits at all, but from these other sources. They also claim that even though the information is quite unknown to the sitter or to his friends, a sensitive can search out the particular individual with the appropriate knowledge and sift his mind for it from a mass of other thoughts. Further, that a sensitive can carry out a clairvoyant search of books in libraries and elsewhere for the required information, and that she is able to arrange all the facts thus acquired and dramatise them to give a satisfactory simulation of the particular spirit personality. However, it is extremely doubtful whether the mind of a sensitive has such wide selective powers of extrasensory perception, and at the same time is capable of arranging and dramatising the material. Such claims are based on an assumption which is far more fantastic than that the information has come from spirit sources. Nevertheless, it must be admitted that many Spiritualists are far too ready to accept statements in mediumistic communications as coming from discarnate spirits, especially where such information is already known to the sitters.

THE TRANCE STATE

All mediums are "overshadowed" when en rapport with spirit helpers. Some retain consciousness. With others, consciousness is diminished, in which case the term used is *trance*. In the latter case, the medium ceases to a greater or less extent to be aware of the conscious level of her mind but is in touch with some level of the subconscious. At the same time she can give expression to material from that deeper level in the form of trance speaking, writing or drawing. Such "messages" may contain subconscious thoughts as well as material from telepathic and clairvoyant sources and from discarnate spirits, but conscious thoughts are largely eliminated.

In the trance state another personality from that of the medium is manifest and is apparently in control of the proceedings. This control describes other spirits and passes on messages from them or gives instructive addresses. Although these controls may show characters and traits quite different from that of the medium's normal personality, some investigators claim that they are merely subconscious creations or psychological build-ups of the medium, which simulate spirit controls. On the other hand, most Spiritualists believe that, although this may hold good in certain cases, the majority of these controls are what they claim to be, *i.e.*, discarnate spirits which have become associated with the sensitives, and act as links between the latter and discarnate spirits wishing to communicate. They safeguard and protect the sensitives, when in trance, against intrusion by undeveloped spirits.

The degree of trance varies from light to deep. The former may be regarded as inspirational in nature rather than as actual spirit control. It may be analogous to what occurs with geniuses in moments of inspiration. Under such conditions much of the inspired matter may come from subconscious mentation. But in deep trance there is a very close association between the mind of the sensitive and of the spirit, and the latter may actually control the medium's brain and perhaps her mind. Under such conditions the subconscious thoughts of the medium are largely, if not, completely, excluded. At the same time the controlling spirit usually provides evidence of a definite personality, quite distinct from that of the medium. Moreover, the medium may speak in a language foreign to her, but which was that of the spirit control in earth-life. This is the explanation of the "gift of tongues" of the Apostles at Pentecost, and it is a phenomenon with sensitives at the present day. For instance, messages from an ancient Egyptian spirit were obtained through the English medium, Rosemary. These were in the ancient Egyptian dialect and gave the hitherto unknown vowel sounds, thus enabling a vocabulary of the language to be built up.

PROOF OF SURVIVAL

The problem of proving survival after death has been rendered much more difficult since psychic research work has revealed the wide scope of extra-sensory perception. Many investigators even go so far as to assert that telepathy between the medium and other living persons, or clairvoyance, is largely, if not entirely, responsible for communications purporting to come from spirit sources.

There is no doubt that a sensitive may obtain information in these ways, and this must be borne in mind in determining the evidential value of mediumistic communications. But it is highly probable that the messages are from spirit sources if the information given is quite unknown to the sitter or to any of his friends. Moreover, it has never been proved that a sensitive has the wide powers of telepathy and clairvoyance claimed by these investigators.

Spirit communications have certain characteristics, which provide evidence of their other-world origin. Thus they may show evidence of personal traits and mannerisms, different from those of the medium. They may also show peculiarities in speech or dialect, specialised knowledge and "shared" memories. There may be evidence of independent planning and purpose. While the information given in the communications should have been known to the spirit purporting to give the messages, it will be all the more evidential if it is unknown to any living person and not obtainable from books or records. Of course, it must be veridical, *i.e.*, capable of proof, as with the Glastonbury Abbey communications, in which plans and dimensions of the ancient abbey were received through a medium, and these, on excavation of the site, were found to be correct. The information may be precognitive in nature. In this case, time will prove or disprove its validity.

PSYCHO-KINESIS

Just as the mind can receive information by extra-sensory in addition to sensory methods of perception, it can bring about physical or motor effects by extra-muscular as well as by the normal muscular action of the body. Such extra-muscular action is known as *psycho-kinesis* or *tele-kinesis.*

Evidence of psycho-kinesis has been obtained by Rhine and others in experiments designed to determine whether it is possible by the power of thought to influence results in the throwing of dice. Thousands of these experiments have been carried out, and the results have been examined statistically to rule out the effects of chance. These investigations show clearly that the mind has this extra-muscular motor faculty. The psycho-kinetic power is not affected by variations in the method of throwing the dice, but appears to be influenced by more or less the same factors as extra-sensory perception, *e.g.*, the effects on the experimenter or agent of boredom, fatigue, distractions and drugs.

ECTOPLASM

Certain mediums are capable of producing psycho-kinetic effects, *e.g.*, raps, bangs and other sounds, the levitation of their own body or of objects (even heavy tables), the movement of articles at a distance, the altering of the weight of bodies and the playing of musical instruments with which they are not in actual contact. These phenomena are brought about by rods and other structures made of a material substance, termed ectoplasm, which exudes from the body of the medium and sometimes from the sitters. The medium is usually in a state of trance.

Ectoplasm varies greatly in character. (1) It is frequently invisible and intangible, especially in the production of raps. (2) It may be sufficiently condensed to form a vapour or a solid, in these cases being visible and frequently tangible. (3) It may be soft, like muslin, or hard and solid. (4) It may be luminous and may show bright "spirit lights." (5) It is sensitive to daylight but not to dull red light or infra-red rays. (It is worthy of note that Christ's appearances after death were as a rule in the morning, "while it was yet dark," or in the evening.) The character and structure of the ectoplasm are varied to meet particular requirements, *e.g.*, rigid rods with hard smooth ends for the production of raps, and rigid rods terminating in suction pads for grasping smooth flat surfaces, as in table levitations.

MATERIALISATIONS

With certain mediums the ectoplasm may be built up into complete human forms or into parts of the body, *e.g.*, hands and feet. At the same time lights, cool breezes and perfumes may be produced. These *materialised* human forms may be solid and tangible, and may be capable of movement and of carrying objects from place to place. Crookes, and Richet and Geley, carried out comprehensive investigations of such *materialisations*. Richet and Geley were able to obtain moulds of wax made from materialised hands and feet. To do this, they carried out experiments in which the materialised forms were dipped in melted paraffin wax, then withdrawn and dematerialised, leaving behind thin moulds of wax. Plaster casts were then made from the moulds. These casts showed impressions from the veins of the hand or foot, and the lines on the skin. Further, the wrists of the gloves of wax were so small that no normal human hands could possibly have been withdrawn through them.

Nothing is known as to how ectoplasm is formed, exuded from the body of the medium, and energised. In paranormal physical phenomena it forms the instrument by which the psychic force acts. Crawford showed that such phenomena as rappings, table tiltings and levitations are produced by ectoplasmic rods acting in accordance with common mechanical laws. At the same time, some directing intelligence is needed to control the formation of the ectoplasm, to vary its structure and govern its movements, so that the particular phenomenon can be produced. This directing intelligence may be the sub-conscious mind of the medium or of one of the sitters, or it may be the mind of a discarnate spirit. In the last case, if the materialised form can speak (*direct voice*), or write messages with a pencil on paper, it may give sufficient information to establish its identity. On the other hand, the spirit may provide evidence of its identity by materialising with the characteristic features, scars or blemishes of its one-time earthly body, as Christ did in the Upper Room; or it may give thumb prints, as in the case of the dead brother of Mrs. Crandon of Boston.

APPORTS

Associated with materialisation is the process whereby one form of matter is passed through another. Thus complete rings of wood may be interlocked; also, objects, commonly termed *apports*, may be brought into sealed rooms. Apports frequently consist of small articles, *e.g.*, ornaments and books, but occasionally of flowers and even living animals and birds. To enable their passing through the walls of a sealed room, the apports (or a part of the wall) would require to be dematerialiscd first and then, after their entrance into the room, rematerialised.

POLTERGEISM

Poltergeist phenomena are psycho-kinetic in nature and apparently involve the use of ectoplasmic structures. These phenomena vary widely in character. They may consist of noises, such as raps or bangs, or the sound of the movement of furniture, even in its absence. There may also be the actual movement of books, furniture and kitchen utensils; the "controlled" flight of objects, and a lowering of the temperature of the atmosphere.

There are records of *poltergeism* since ancient times. The phenomena are as a rule associated with an adolescent person, most frequently a girl. This individual apparently provides the ectoplasm and the psychic force required for the process, and so acts as the medium, although perhaps quite unaware of the fact. There is, however, in each case a directing intelligence controlling the process. In general, this is believed to be an undeveloped or earthbound spirit— hence the use of the German term, "poltergeist," meaning a boisterous or noisy spirit. Frequently there is a malicious element in poltergeism. In other instances it is purposive in nature and when the reason is discovered and the spirit satisfied the disturbances stop.

APPARITIONS

Apparitions are supernormal appearances of persons (frequently in a moment of crisis or dying), or of discarnate spirits. They may be purely subjective, *i.e.*, thought forms or mental images, as a rule telepathic in nature, or they may be objective and therefore capable of being seen and in some instances touched by the various persons present.

These objective forms may be to a greater or less extent ectoplasmic in nature, one of the persons present acting as a materialising medium. Practically nothing is known as to the nature of apparitions in general, but there is probably a gradation of types between the purely subjective form and the completely materialised.

Apparitions are occasionally associated with, or haunt, a particular locality, house or room, and in such cases they may always act in the same manner and then disappear. Such forms are commonly termed *ghosts*, and the place is said to be *haunted*. In some cases the haunting appears to be quite meaningless. In other instances it is purposive in nature. Thus the Hydesville haunting appeared to be due to the spirit of a pedlar, who wished to call attention to the fact that he had been murdered in the house and his body buried in the cellar.

To sum up, the spirit in earth-life has a physical body to enable it to function on the earth. By means of the organs of that body, it can be aware of, and keep in touch with, its material environment. In addition, the spirit has extra-sensory experiences in earth-life due to its possession of psychic powers. These enable it to keep in touch with other beings, discarnate as well as incarnate. Thus the spirit has at one and the same time contacts with the spirit world as well as the material. It has also the power to bring about the movement of earthly matter without the use of the muscles of the body, and it may be reasonably inferred that this extra-muscular or telekinetic power is retained by the spirit after death and is used by it in the after-life.

THE SPIRIT BODY

The spirit cannot act directly on the physical body, but does so through the intermediary of the spirit body—sometimes termed etheric or spiritual body, or eidolon

(Ancient Greeks). Thus the spirit body is the link between spirit and the physical body, being affected, on the one hand, by the activity of the spirit and, on the other, by that of the physical body.

NATURE OF THE SPIRIT BODY

Practically nothing is known about the nature of the spirit body. It is frequently claimed to be etheric in character, but the existence of an ether has not been generally accepted by scientists. The spirit body appears to be of much finer material than the physical, being undetectable by the ordinary sensory organs and therefore intangible and invisible. It can, however, be seen by clairvoyants, and according to their descriptions it is the exact counterpart of the physical body. It is more permanent in nature than the physical body, and is not subject to the continual breaking down and building up processes, which the latter undergoes during life on earth. It also persists after the death of the physical body, and enables the spirit to function in the spirit world as the physical body does on earth.

FUNCTIONS OF THE SPIRIT BODY

The spirit body appears to be so constituted and organised that energy or other interactions can occur, on the one hand, between it and the spirit, and on the other, between it and the physical body. As a result they can influence one another. Thus material from the spirit can be transmitted to the brain and other parts of the nervous system of the physical body. Since the spirit manifests itself in the mind or mental activities, the matter transmitted in this way will include thoughts, desires, purposes, and also extra-sensory and psycho-kinetic matter. At the same time, sensory and other material are transmitted by the spirit body in the reverse direction, *i.e.*, from the physical body to the spirit.

The spirit body probably plays an important part in the spirit treatment of disease, the healing forces from the spirit control or the sensitive being applied through the intermediary of the spirit body. Further, a spirit control may be able to diagnose disease from the condition of the spirit body, as the latter may reflect the, state of health of the physical body.

In Theosophy, it is claimed that, in addition to the spirit body, there is an astral body, but in Spiritualism such a distinction is seldom made. The spirit body is frequently termed the soul, but this term is also sometimes used for the spirit itself, as in the Principles of Spiritualism.

THE SPIRIT

THE DIVINE ORIGIN OF THE SPIRIT

There is in all living organisms a life-giving, vital or motivating principle, termed *spirit*. It is essentially of the same nature as the Divine Spirit and comes in the first place from, and is sustained by, God. This has been recognised by philosophers and theologians in all ages. For instance, Herbert Spencer believed that man is "ever in the presence of an infinite and eternal energy from which all things proceed," and St. Paul, quoting from an ancient Greek poet, stated "For in Him (God) we live, and move, and have our being."

The spirit in man constitutes the real Self or Ego, and is linked with its primal source, God, for all eternity. Thus man can refer to God as the Heavenly Father and at the same time consider himself to be a son of God. This is recognised in the first two Principles of Spiritualism, "The Fatherhood of God" and "The Brotherhood of Man."

CHARACTERS OF THE SPIRIT

The human spirit, being akin to the Divine, is transcendental in nature and therefore beyond the power of human understanding. In fact, to know spirit would be to comprehend God.

Spirit has apparently no form or substance, and cannot act directly on physical matter, but does so, in the case of living organisms, through the agency of the spirit body. It is the activating factor behind the mind; the latter may be regarded simply as the activity or expression of the spirit. There is no proof that this is so, as the nature of spirit is unknown, but as Descartes said, "cogito ergo sum" (I think therefore I am).

The association with a physical body in the material environment of earth-life restricts the activities of the spirit and isolates it to some extent from other spirit entities. This probably enables it to develop as a separate individual without undue interaction with or interference from other spirits. At the same time it gains a definite and fixed personality which is capable of adjusting itself to different environments. Further, the experiences of earth-life enable it to develop its spiritual nature.

THE DISCARNATE SPIRIT

Being immortal, the spirit persists after the death of the physical body, and still retains all the knowledge, experiences and other memories of earth-life. It will also now be able to recall the memories of the other-world contacts which it had during earth-life. (These psychic contacts, being subconscious, seldom reach the conscious mind of the incarnate spirit, but are stored up in the sub-conscious.)

The spirit after death may be aware of space and time factors, but is not conditioned by them as it is in earth-life.

Thus space and time have not the same meaning in spirit-life as they have on earth.

A discarnate spirit cannot manifest itself in the material world except through the use of a medium's body. Owing to its telepathic powers, it is to some extent aware of the feelings, desires, aspirations and thoughts of an incarnate spirit, especially when directed to it, as by prayer. The discarnate spirit may also be able to influence the thoughts and actions of an incarnate spirit, and in this way may have a profound effect in helping the latter to develop its spiritual nature.

While it is not possible for man to understand the true nature of spirit, some indication as to its character may be obtained from the highest and best elements in the human mind. Thus, there is a purposiveness and creativeness in the mind, and a love of the ethical principles of wisdom, courage, temperance, truth, justice and beauty. These mental qualities must arise from the spirit of man—not from his physical body. In fact, they are fundamental attributes of the Divine Spirit from whom he originated.

CONCLUSION

Man is a spirit, and earth-life is but a brief phase in the endless ages of his existence. It is a phase in which he has, for the time being, a physical body to enable him to function as an individual in a material environment.

THE PURPOSE OF EARTH-LIFE

Although the fundamental principle of his existence is spiritual and not material, the life on earth is of profound importance as it enables him to build up a definite and stable personality and to develop his spiritual nature, and so become fitted for the next stage of existence. As he has a physical body he is affected by its weaknesses and inherited traits and by the conditions of the material environment.

He is also influenced by his interactions, good or bad, with his fellowmen. Thus difficulties and hardships arise. In many cases these are due to the fact that he has freedom of will and is making mistakes. He must be free, however, to make his own decisions; otherwise he would merely react to other people and to surrounding conditions according to deterministic factors, such as his animal instincts, and thus would be unable to develop a sense of responsibility. Having freewill he can fight against such factors and strive to lead a life of high ethical standard. In this way he can become a responsible moral being, showing evidence of his kinship with the Divine Spirit.

Nothing in the universe can be achieved without exertion. This applies not only to material but also to spiritual things. A continuous effort is required to carry out the duties and overcome the obstacles of earth-life, but all the striving and the hardship involved in achieving worthwhile things has a training and disciplinary effect upon the individual. Such activities, if carried out with a glad and willing heart, and not to the exclusion of spiritual things, enable a man to make spiritual progress. A life which is easy and free from difficulties, leads to indolence and apathy; while one devoted to pleasure and self-indulgence results in selfishness and satiety. These are qualities which are not conducive to spiritual achievement.

Man has developed a social instinct from the herd instinct of his animal ancestors. But communal life, if it is to be successful, depends upon the unselfish conduct of the members of the community. Thus from the social instinct in man there has arisen a code of ethical behaviour, which a good man observes and derives happiness in doing so. The keynote of his life is love, which finds its expression in service to others.

THE DIFFICULTIES OF EARTH-LIFE

Man, being a spirit, has infinite possibilities for spiritual progression, and if he can but trust in God and try to realise the spiritual significance of his existence on earth, his difficulties will not appear so formidable. Many of his troubles may be due to wrong thinking and can be avoided by changing his mental outlook. But he may have no moral courage or stability of character, and so be leading a purposeless life, without desire to make spiritual progress. Instead of striving against adverse conditions he may prefer to drift along on a sea of daily circumstances.

Man is responsible for his own spiritual welfare and cannot be compelled to lead the good life. However, by living in attunement with the spirit world, he can obtain help and guidance to meet his troubles. Instead of availing himself of this limitless source of power, he may be content with a debased life and, owing to selfishness, jealousy or conceit, may be frequently at variance with his fellowmen. As a result, there is disharmony and ill-will. In this connection it must be remembered that peace and good fellowship within a community, and even a nation, depend upon the interactions or personal relationships of the individual members. Thus by living in harmony with his fellow-men, man is playing his part in the realisation of the true Brotherhood of Man on earth.

Man has made great material progress in the last few hundred years. He has acquired a vast amount of knowledge and can control to a great extent the forces of nature, but he has made comparatively little spiritual progress, and in most cases his life is not of high ethical standard. In fact his scientific discoveries have far outstripped his spiritual achievement. As a result, there is a grave risk of these discoveries being put to ill-use, *i.e.*, for destructive purposes instead of for good. There is therefore an urgent need for a profound spiritual upsurge throughout the nations of the world.

THE HUMAN AND THE DIVINE MIND

As man develops spiritually he comes to appreciate the spiritual value of ethical qualities, such as goodness, truth, justice and beauty. These are "eternal values" or "principles" recognised by all spiritually minded individuals throughout the ages, no matter their religion or nation. Man realises that these values are the essential basis of human wisdom, and are the ideals governing human behaviour, effort and aspiration. The love of these principles is not material in origin, but spiritual, for they are the expressions of an order of reality, a moral order, which is Divine in nature. The fact that the human mind at its highest level unhesitatingly accepts them, shows that it has, in virtue of its spiritual nature, intuitive knowledge that they are expressions of the Creator's Mind.

As man becomes aware of his true spirituality he realises that he is not an isolated individual, but a member of a vast community of spirits, incarnate and discarnate, all linked together in a Brotherhood, having a common origin in God. He can form no clear conception of God, although he knows that he, personally, is essentially of the same nature as the Divine Spirit from which he came.

He has learned from the discoveries of science that throughout the vast universe in which he lives, things do not happen in a haphazard manner, but that there is a unity, a design and a purpose behind it all; also a conformity to law and order. Thus he realises that there is a Mind at the heart of things, a Mind which shows Infinite Wisdom, Power and Creativeness; is purposive in nature and systematic in all its activities. Although Omnipotent and Omniscient, it is the Mind of a Heavenly Father, who is concerned with all His

Creation, who can be revered, loved, and communed with for fellowship, help and guidance by all his earthly children.

In the words of Isaiah:

"They that wait upon the Lord shall renew their strength; they shall mount up with wings as eagles; they shall run, and not be weary; they shalt walk, and not faint."

THE AFTERLIFE

I have to thank Miss M. C. Alston, Mr. C. Hodgkinson and Dr. J. Winning for services rendered in the preparation of this work.

THE AUTHOR

FOREWORD

With regard to this subject, the question arises naturally of how much reliance can be placed on any accounts of the after-life which must be based of necessity on information obtained through psychic sensitives or mediums. Can such information be relied upon, or is it largely a figment of their imagination? This question has been dealt with fully in the text, but a few words here may not be out of place.

It may be said at the outset that to those who do not believe in survival after bodily death, this work is of no value, and there is no need for them to read further. On the other hand, most people of all religions believe in survival, and it is for them the following remarks are made.

If individuals survive death, there must be an environment in which they can exist and function. As the sensory organs of the physical body have been developed to detect conditions only in our material world, we have to rely for our knowledge of the after-life on the descriptive accounts received through psychic sensitives. Such information may consist of clairvoyant impressions or "out of the body" experiences, in which glimpses are caught of the spirit regions and the inhabitants. Mystics throughout the ages have told us also of such other-world experiences. But by far the most important and comprehensive accounts of spirit-life are those given by discarnate spirits themselves in mediumistic communications.

All such information has to be accepted with a degree of caution, as it is liable to be "coloured" by the mind of the sensitive, especially if she has fixed ideas on the subject. There is also the difficulty that the information may be of such a nature that it cannot be passed through in its original form so that it may be understood by earth-conditioned minds. But one is justified in placing some reliance on such accounts, if the medium has shown herself accurate in other communications which were verifiable; and if the information is more or less in agreement with that of other mediums in other parts of the world, or in other ages. At the same time the accounts should appear to be reasonable and satisfactory to common sense. After all, there is a system and a continuity running throughout the physical universe, and one would expect this to extend also into the spiritual, especially as they appear to have a close inter-relationship. Hence there must be some similarity or connection, however slight, between earth and other-world conditions.

Other than these psychic methods, there is no way of acquiring knowledge of the after-life. By refusing to accept such mediumistic information one automatically closes the door against proving survival after death and of gaining any knowledge whatsoever of the spirit state.

It might be claimed by orthodox Christians that the New Testament records of survival and the spirit-life should be sufficient for all mankind. While Jesus undoubtedly gave convincing proof of survival to his followers, it is said in St. Matthew's Gospel that "some doubted"; and the Jewish Church in general refused to believe in his after-death appearances. There are many doubters of these Biblical records even among Christians at the present day. Moreover, the accounts of the after-life given in the New Testament are meagre and scanty. In St. John's "Revelation" the description is so coloured by the Eastern imagination as to appear too fantastic for the modern Western mind to accept. In any case, it must be remembered that the New Testament accounts of Jesus' after-death appearances and of the spirit-world are based on psychic experiences similar, if not identical, with those of the present time, and therefore if the modern ones are ruled out, it is only logical to reject those of the Bible.

J.F.M.

THE AFTER-LIFE

ANCIENT AND MODERN BELIEFS

From a remote age there has been a widespread belief in the survival of the human spirit after death, and consequently in a spirit state of existence. But the ideas of what happens after death and of the nature of the after-life have varied greatly with different peoples. In some cases, the conceptions were vague; the spirits after death were thought to be of a highly attenuated or shadowy nature, existing in some dim underworld—the hades of the Ancient Greeks. In other cases there was a definite idea that the spirit world was very similar to the material; that it was a continuation of it on a higher plane, and that the spirits there had as real and substantial an existence as in earth-life.

With advance in civilisation and the recognition of certain moral values, there arose the belief that those who had led a good life on earth by observing accepted moral standards, religious rites, or tribal customs and taboos, were rewarded after death. They were allowed to enter an ideal state of existence, the classic or Hellenic elysium or the Jewish or Christian heaven, whereas those who had led an evil life were punished for their misdeeds by being forced to go into a place of endless torment, termed hell, from which there was no escape.

At first, it was generally held by the Jews that there was no resurrection of the dead, but that a person survived merely in the lives and minds of his children and their descendants. Later, there arose a vague belief in an after-life, but it was a shadowy kind of existence in an underworld. At the time of Jesus, the sect of the Pharisees believed in survival after death, the good spirits being rewarded and the evil ones punished. On the other hand the sect of the Sadducees claimed that there was no such thing as spirit, no life after death and no spirit state.

It is worthy of note that certain Christian theologians have believed that immortality is not an inherent quality of the spirit, but is a reward by God for a life of faith and good works. According to this view unworthy spirits, instead of being condemned to a life of endless torment in hell, are completely obliterated.

"THE TRANSMIGRATION OF SOULS"

Apart from these conceptions of what happens at death, there has been since ancient times the belief in the "transmigration of souls." This was held by the Ancient Egyptians, the Ancient Greeks and the Druids, and is still an important doctrine in Hinduism and Buddhism, two of the most ancient and most important religions in the world.

According to the Orphic teachings of the Ancient Greeks, the spirit at death passed to the underworld or hades, where it was either rewarded for its good deeds or punished for its evil ones. In the former case it was reborn as a human being and in the latter as an animal. This transmigration of the spirit was not eternal, as a spirit which had passed through three good lives, and therefore had been found guiltless three times, was allowed to enter elysium, the "land of the blest."

The Druids (see "The Faiths of the World" by Rev. James Gardner, M.D.) believed that if a man led a brave and virtuous life, his spirit went at once to Flath-Innis, the elysian island or heaven. However, if he led a bad life, his spirit returned to earth as an animal; then at death, he reincarnated again as a man. This procedure was repeated until his spirit was fit to go to the elysian island. In earlier Druidic teaching, an evil person was not reincarnated but went to Ifurin, "the isle of the cold land" and fierce animals.

According to the Hindu and Buddhist religions, man passes through a series of earth lives, in which he ascends or descends on the spiritual scale depending on whether these lives are good or evil. This progression of the spirit, up or down, obeys what is termed the Law of the Deed or Karma, which states that "From Good must come Good, and from Evil must come Evil." By leading a succession of good lives, man ultimately reaches the ideal state of bliss (nirvana in Buddhism), but a series of evil lives causes him to fall lower and lower spiritually until he may reincarnate as an animal or insect, and even, in the Jain religion, as a plant.

HEAVEN, THE IDEAL STATE

With different religions, there has been great variation in the beliefs of what constituted the ideal after-death state or heaven. The ancient Egyptians had various ideas of this state. To some, it was a western place of light and rest; to others, it was a land where they would be united with their saviour-god, Osiris, and would cultivate corn crops and fruit trees. There was also an Egyptian belief that the spirit after death had a cycle of disembodied existence of thousands of years, and then returned again to inhabit the original physical body, hence the necessity for preserving the body by mummification.

The ancient Greeks hoped at death to go to an elysium of meadows, on which grew a profusion of the eternal asphodel and other flowers. Homer described elysium as a beautiful meadow at the western extremity of the earth, on the banks of the river Oceanus, where the spirits led a life of perfect happiness—"no snow, nor storm, nor rain, but the cool west wind breathes there forever." Hesiod thought of heaven as an elysian island by the ocean, where heroes exist without pain, and earth produces her fruits three times each year. In later times, elysium with its bliss for those whom the judges considered worthy, was thought of as occurring in the underworld.

The Red Indians of North America conceived of heaven as "the happy hunting grounds of the west," a land of forests, streams and lakes, teeming with all kinds of animals, and with an ideal climate.

The Hindus, since ancient times, have held that the ideal or perfect state, reached after a series of virtuous earth lives, is one in which man loses all sense of conscious existence as an individual, as he becomes merged with the Supreme God, Brahma. The Buddhists believe that after a series of incarnations in which man frees himself from all earthly desires and passions, he reaches nirvana, an ideal state of complete attunement to the Divine Existence. It has been described as a "deep passionless calm, all desire hushed, because sense of being is hushed." While it is a state of supreme consciousness, it is believed by some to be the end of all existence as a conscious individual.

EARTH CONDITIONS AND IDEAS OF THE AFTER-LIFE

It is evident that with many races, the idea of what constituted heaven was determined largely by the conditions under which the people lived on earth, especially by the hardships from which they suffered and from which they longed to be free when they entered the spirit state. Thus the Semitic tribes, which inhabited the arid, sun-scorched sandy Arabian deserts, thought of heaven as a fertile, shady, well-watered oasis, a Garden of Eden, in which they dwelt in tents with beautiful women, or houris, in attendance. In contrast with this, the wandering or nomadic northmen of the cold far north of Europe, who were often in a half-starved, half-frozen condition, conceived of heaven as a valhalla, where the spirits of the dead, after a day of manly sport, could sit at night before huge fires, feasting and drinking. Consistent with these ideas, the races of Arabia believed that hell was an ever-lasting fiery furnace, whereas the northern races thought it was a dark bitterly cold region.

CHRISTIAN BELIEFS AND SPIRITUALISM

Christians have commonly held throughout the ages that the earth-life determines irrevocably for all eternity man's after-death state, *i.e.*, whether it is to be in heaven or hell. This is the old doctrine of the "saved" and the "damned," or the "sheep" and the "goats," which was preached to strike fear into the hearts of all would-be evildoers.

Until comparatively recently, Christians adhered to the ancient belief of the Jews and other Semitic races that hell was a fiery furnace, where the spirits of those who had led an evil life on earth, were condemned to suffer endless agonies from heat and thirst. They had no definite conceptions of heaven, except that it was a place of endless worship and adoration of God—ideas derived largely from the accounts of heaven given in the Revelation of St. John. But the impoverished and downtrodden peasants of early Christian and later times thought of heaven as a celestial city, gleaming with precious stones, pearly gates and golden streets, where all their longings for plenty, human fellowship, comfort and happiness would be fully satisfied.

At the present time many Christians prefer not to think of the after-life because it calls up repressed fears of death and the unknown. This may explain why they have as a rule only vague and even crude ideas of the spirit-life. But the same may be said of the followers of most of the other great world religions, *e.g.*, Judaism, Hinduism and Buddhism. On the other hand, Spiritualists have a definite and realistic conception of the life after death. This is based on the information obtained in communications from spirits living there, and not, as with other religions, on ancient records and mythology. These spirits tell us of a state of existence after death which is quite as real as that on earth, and which, at least at first, bears some resemblance to the latter. To the orthodox Christian, this may appear to be too materialistic a conception of the after-life. Against this, it may be said that the orthodox beliefs appear vague, unnatural, and even fantastic to the modern mind, and will become more so with increase in scientific knowledge and education.

THE NATURE OF THE SPIRIT STATE

THE REALITY OF THE AFTER-LIFE

As spirits survive bodily death, there must be a state or environment in which they can exist and function. As our sensory organs are quite unable to detect the matter or conditions present in that state, we have to depend for information on the communications from discarnate spirits, or from the clairvoyant or "out of the body" experiences of sensitives.

Materialists will claim that such information is quite unreliable, as they hold the view that man does not survive death and there is no such thing as extra-sensory perception and mediumship. But we know that survival and extra-sensory perception have been amply proved by investigations carried out in the past hundred years, so we need not be unduly concerned with the views of materialists. Surely, we can attach some credence to the accounts which a medium gives of the after-life, if she has proved to be trustworthy with regard to communications on other matters, and all the more so, if her descriptions of the spirit state are in agreement with those of other mediums.

According to such mediumistic information, the environment in the after-life is just as real as in earth-life, but the conditions in the former vary with the spiritual development of the spirit passing over from earth-life. The spirits who have led a good life pass into higher regions, where the conditions are somewhat similar to those on earth, but on a far finer and grander scale. However, those who have led an evil life, go to lower regions which are gloomy and miserable.

Apart from mediumistic communications, it is possible from our knowledge and experience of our earthly environment to postulate to some extent what the conditions in the spirit state are likely to be. We are justified in doing so, as we know that in the Divine Scheme of Creation, there is a fundamental unity and a continuity running throughout all things, animate and inanimate, in the material part of the universe, and we can reasonably assume that this unity and continuity extend into the spiritual. Hence the conditions of spirit-life must bear some relationship and even resemblance to those of earth- life. In fact, the newly arrived spirit may be impressed with the familiar nature and naturalness of the new surroundings. It may even think that it is still living under earth conditions and not "dead"; it has simply fallen asleep and awakened in a strange part of the world. This conception of the after-life may appear too materialistic to those who think of it as some kind of formless state, in which spirits live in a highly tenuous or "ethereal" condition. But such an existence would not meet the needs of an individual who had just passed over from earth-life.

THE ETERNAL NATURE OF EXISTENCE

While proof of survival after death does not necessarily prove that spirits live for all eternity, spirits tell us they believe that life is eternal. They also claim that there is no end to the progress they can make, contrary to the view held by many Christians that heaven and hell are states of perfect bliss or complete damnation, determined by a good or evil earth-life for all eternity. In addition, spirits believe that, no matter in which region they are living, there is always a higher one beyond. In all these cases there is this further step, and that may be taken as an indication that there is no end to progression in all its aspects and therefore no end to individual existence. Is it reasonable that in God's scheme of creation a definite personality of high spirituality, wisdom and experience, should be built up over the ages in an individual only for the latter to become merged with God with loss of identity in the end?

However, we should not give too much thought to such speculations, but rather devote our energies to preparing ourselves for the next step in our spiritual progress, thus fulfilling the Will of our Creator. There is an old Chinese saying, "A journey of a thousand miles begins with a single step." Let us make sure that we are preparing ourselves for that step.

MEDIUMISTIC DESCRIPTIONS

Much information of the spirit state has been obtained in spirit communications through many mediums in all parts of the world. The descriptions of conditions in the spirit-life are rational and largely in agreement. The differences which occur are as a rule of a minor nature, no greater than would be found in accounts of earth-life from people of different races and habits: Eskimos, Arabs, Australian Aborigines, Chinese and Europeans; or from people living under equatorial or polar conditions.

Such mediumistic descriptions are liable to be distorted or coloured to some extent by the mind of the sensitive. If she has firmly held beliefs on the subject (due perhaps to training and education), there will be a combination of her ideas and those of the spirit communicator. Thus the communications received through the mediumship of Swedenborg, were affected by his orthodox religious views;

his hell was one of endless torment from which there was no hope of escape.

In addition, the information received is bound to be limited in scope by the difficulties of passing other-world material through the mind of the medium. Much of it may be beyond the powers of comprehension of the incarnate mind and be therefore intransmissable. For instance, the discarnate spirit, being free from the restrictions of the physical body with its brain and sensory organs, which are very limited in their range of action (see "The Nature of Man,"), may have greatly enhanced powers of perception, especially as the psychic faculties will now be more freely exercised. Thus it may be able to apprehend and appreciate more clearly the true nature of things around it, and may have experiences which are beyond the scope of our understanding. Moreover, the significance of time and space must be quite different in the spirit state from that on earth. The human mind, like the physical body, has been developed through ages of evolution to deal with an earthly environment. It may therefore have become so highly specialised that it is unable to comprehend readily things of another order of existence, which are not consistent with its preconceived ideas and beliefs.

The Matter of the Spirit Regions

The matter of the spirit world is of a different order from that of earth-life. It is of a much finer quality or a more subtle nature than that of the material universe and as a result the one cannot react with or affect the other directly; indeed, the one could interpenetrate the other without interference. Further, as the sensory organs of our physical body have been developed to detect conditions only of the earth state, we cannot become aware of the presence of matter in the spirit state or of the spirit entities there, except by extra-sensory modes of perception, such as clairvoyance.

INTERPENETRATION OF PHYSICAL AND SPIRIT MATTER

That the material and the spirit state can interpenetrate without interference with each other, is not so difficult to understand, when we remember that what appears solid to us in the physical world, *e.g.*, a wall, consists in reality of empty space in which extremely minute electrically charged particles are in rapid motion. These particles are so minute that the distances between them are as great in relation to their size as the distances between the planets in our solar system. If all the protons and electrons and other elementary particles of the human body could be pressed together so that there was no space between them, the amount of matter thus produced would be so small as to be invisible. We feel a table to be solid because our bodies are of the same basic nature, and their swirling electrical particles cannot interpenetrate those of the table, or, in other words, there is a repulsive action between their electro-magnetic fields.

While interpenetration may thus take place freely between the material and the spirit state, it is possible that it may also occur between the different regions (see later) in the spirit world. If this is so, it provides the answer to the question, how can there be room in the spirit state, for all the millions and millions of spirits who have passed through earth-life. It must also be borne in mind that even in the material universe alone, there is no beginning nor end to space; it is infinite And the same must apply to the spirit regions—in fact, it is doubtful whether the term, space, should be applied to the spirit state, as it is merely an indefinable conception of the mind in regard to the material universe.

PHYSICAL BODY OF NO USE IN THE AFTER-LIFE

From what has been said, it follows that the physical body would be of no use to the spirit in the non-material environment of the after-death state. It is merely an instrument which has been evolved to enable the spirit to function in the material universe. Those who believe in the resurrection of the physical body, fail to realise that such a body can function only in a world of the same order of matter, atoms and molecules, as its own substance. Thus a belief in a physical resurrection also entails a belief in a physical or material heaven. If heaven is of this nature it should be detectable by our sensory organs in earth-life, provided it is not situated beyond the range of optical visibility—and such remoteness has never been claimed, even by those who hold this belief. In this connection, it is worthy of note that St. Paul said, "Flesh and blood cannot inherit the Kingdom of God." (1 Corinthians 15, 50.)

Christians base their belief in the resurrection of the physical body on the after-death manifestations of Jesus, but it is quite clear from the Gospels that he did not appear in his physical body but in one of ectoplasm, a psychic substance derived from his psychic apostles and women followers. Thus he could become visible and tangible suddenly in a closed room and then could vanish or fade away. He could appear only under certain conditions, *e.g.*, in dim light—in the morning "while it was yet dark," or in the dusk of the evening or in the upper room; or in presence of mediumistic people, such as his apostles. He could not appear in absence of these conditions, for instance before the High Priest or Sanhedrin. Also, at times he could not be recognised or touched, as would be the case with an incomplete materialisation, but not with a physical body. Moreover, if he had a physical body after death, where did he get his clothes, for they also would be in this case material in nature? The presence of the nail and

107

spear wounds does not prove that it was his physical body, because in materialisations the ectoplasmic body may have the scars and other blemishes of earth-life for purposes of identification. The empty tomb also does not show that Jesus had a physical resurrection, as the body in the tomb may have undergone dematerialisation, a process which has been shown to be possible by modern psychic investigation. The psychic power for such a process may have been available, as some of the persons preparing the body for entombment were probably sensitives, as in the case of the apostles and some of the women.

CHRISTIAN BELIEFS

Christians believe that the resurrection of Jesus from the dead was unique, but St. Paul recognised that this was not the case, as shown by his words in 1 Corinthians 15, 13, "But if there is no resurrection of the dead, neither hath Christ been raised," and verse 16, "For if the dead are not raised, neither hath Christ been raised." The remarkable feature of Jesus' death was his later appearances (objective and subjective) to his followers. He thus proved to them that he had survived death. He was able to do so because the apostles and some of the women were sensitives.

There was also the Christian belief, still held by certain churches, that after death the spirit slept until a day of general resurrection. On that day it rejoined the physical body and then was judged to determine whether it was fit to enter heaven, or was so debased that it had to go into hell. This belief, however, entails, as previously mentioned, belief in a physical heaven. It is also not consistent with the teaching of Jesus, because in the parable of Dives and Lazarus, the spirits of these men after death passed *directly* into the spirit world, Dives going to a low region and Lazarus to a higher one. Also, their physical bodies had been discarded; indeed, Jesus states that the body of Dives had been buried. That there had been no prolonged period of rest is shown by the fact that Dives wished to have warning of their oncoming fate sent to his brethren still at his father's house on earth.

Moreover, it is worthy of note that the remains of human bodies have been found, which were buried thousands of years ago, in the case of Neanderthal man, perhaps 50,000 years or more. If these bodies are awaiting a general resurrection when they will be reunited with their spirits, where are the spirits meantime? It does not appear to be reasonable to assume that they are existing in a purely dormant or inactive condition throughout these long ages. There is also the question of what happens at a general resurrection of the physical body in the case of a person, *e.g.*, a missionary, who has been eaten by cannibals.

Who has prior claim to the molecules of the original body, the missionary or the cannibals? Further, if a man in earth-life had a leg amputated in Africa and later died in Britain, at a general resurrection of the physical body does his leg travel through space to rejoin the rest of the body? These questions show the absurdity of the belief in the resurrection of the physical body.

ENTRY INTO SPIRIT-LIFE

THE PASSING TO THE SPIRIT STATE

At death, the spirit discards the physical body completely, never to make use of it again, and clothed in the spirit body which it had in earth-life and which persists after death, it passes directly into the spirit world. At first there may be a short period of sleep to enable the spirit to rest and relax, and get rid of all ties with the physical body. At the same time it gains in strength and becomes adjusted to the new conditions of life. This short rest is all the more needful, if the passing has been abrupt or violent, or if there has been a prolonged illness with much suffering. However, a person who has endured much with patience and fortitude may thereby have made spiritual progress, becoming thus better fitted to enter higher regions after an initial rest.

As it is only the physical body that grows old, an aged person at death enters the spirit state in full vigour of life. A child, on passing over, has to be specially cared for and reared and educated, to enable the mind to become fully developed.

On waking, the individual is met as a rule by spirits specially trained for this work, and these help him to become adjusted to the new environment. Relatives and friends, who have passed on previously, will also be present if there are strong bonds of friendship. But these helpers and friends may have great difficulty in making contact with, and in convincing a person that he has passed over, if he is undeveloped spiritually, or has fixed ideas that the spirit does not survive death or lies asleep until a day of general resurrection. He may refuse to believe that he is dead, especially if he has died suddenly or unexpectedly, or he may be too proud to accept help. He may be so concerned about his earthly affairs and possessions as to be "earth-bound" and unapproachable. Sometimes a spirit is so confused and bewildered that he can be contacted only by someone still on earth, presumably because the earth state is the only one with which he is familiar. Hence the value of "rescue circles" conducted by groups of individuals in earth-life under the leadership of a reliable medium, with the object of getting into touch with and helping such spirits.

Accordingly, when a person dies, there is a need for helpful and kindly thoughts and prayers for the departed spirit, so that assistance will be given by spirit helpers and friends to enable him to become quickly adjusted to the new conditions of existence. Excessive grief on the part of the bereaved may cause distress to a spirit who has just entered the spirit-life.

As a rule the period required for rest and adjustment to the new environment is short, only a few days, but it may be extended for a long time, if the spirit through prejudice or ignorance cannot realise that he is "dead," or is too proud or obstinate to accept help from spirit friends.

ENTRY INTO THE SPIRIT REGIONS

There are many regions in the spirit world, or as Jesus said, "In my Father's house are many mansions." They differ from each other in spiritual level; the higher the region the more spiritually developed are those who can live in it, and the greater the radiance of the environment.

According to many spirit communications, there are seven main "planes" of spirit existence, and these are believed to form concentric zones round the physical world. They are also frequently referred to as "spheres," but this term is also sometimes used to indicate the various regions on a plane. For all we know, there may be far more than seven main divisions or planes in the spirit state. It is also doubtful whether they form concentric zones or spheres round the earth. For these reasons and to avoid confusion, the terms, plane and sphere, have not been used in this treatise, and instead, the various parts of the spirit state have been referred to simply as regions or realms.

The spirit, after the initial period of rest, passes directly into the region to which it has become spiritually fitted or attuned as a result of earth-life. Those who have led good earth lives, pass into the higher realms, *i.e.*, heaven, or the Spiritualist summerland, but evil spirits enter the lower or "dark regions." (The terms "higher" and "lower" are used not to indicate the relative position in space of these regions, but to signify the relative spiritual development of the spirit inhabitants.) There is no arbitrary judgment by

God with recompenses for good and pardons or penalties for evil-doing. It is simply a question of the relative spiritual progress made on earth. "God is not mocked; for whatsoever a man soweth, that shall he also reap." And no special privileges are attached to the following of any particular religion or to the belief in any creed. As St. Peter said, "I now see how true it is that God has no favourites but that in every nation the man who is god-fearing and does what is right is acceptable to him" (Acts 10, 34). All are God's children, whether baptised or initiated into a particular faith or not, and spiritual progression is open to all. But a debased spirit must go into a lower spirit region; it could not function in a higher one.

As spirits can exist only in realms to which they have become spiritually fitted, the inhabitants of each region will be more or less of the same spiritual development. Thus it may be said that in the after-life the spirits become arranged according to spiritual level. There is, however, no division according to race, colour, religion, earthly possessions or social standing; these are of no importance in the spirit state. But in each region or at each spiritual level, certain spirits will be drawn together into harmonious communities by some common interest or purpose in their life, or by similar religious beliefs which they may retain for a time after death.

THE INFLUENCE OF RELIGION

Although entry into the higher spirit realms is not dependent on any belief in a creed or religious dogma, nor on baptism, there is no doubt that certain religions provide a better atmosphere or training ground for spiritual development in earth-life than others. While there is a measure of truth in all the great religions of the world, not one by itself has the full truth, nor does it point the only way to God. This is fully recognised in the Hindu religion, in which it is claimed that "the number of ways to an Infinite God must be infinite," or as the mystic and poet, Rajjab, said 400 years ago, "The forms of worship of different sects are like so many small streams which move together to meet God, who is like the Ocean."

In nearly all religions there is a definite emotional appeal to the individual, great importance being attached to devotional services to the Divine Being, as in Christianity, Mohammedanism and the Bhakti School of Hinduism. In a few cases, the approach to God is of a more intellectual nature, stress being laid on meditative practices, as in the Jnana School of Hinduism. Another path to God in Hinduism is by works, *i.e.*, Karma. In this matter much depends on the stage of civilisation and on the upbringing, education and even the temperament of the individuals concerned. Certain religious practices, rituals or beliefs may have a spiritually uplifting effect on one race and not on another, *e.g.*, the cross and altar are of profound significance to Christians, the totem pole to North American Indians and various other totems to primitive tribes in Africa and Australia. The use of these religious symbols, beliefs and practices, may be justified in certain stages of spiritual development in that they may help to train the individuals to follow a higher ethical standard of life and to focus their thoughts on spiritual rather than on worldly values. But they are only a means to an end and not the end itself—and that is the development of a person's higher spiritual nature.

THE DOCTRINE OF THE VICARIOUS ATONEMENT

The question of the vicarious atonement of Jesus as a sacrifice to God for the forgiveness of the sins of mankind, has already been discussed in "The Search for God." It was held in this religious doctrine that man was originally in a state of perfection, but as a result of the sin of one individual, Adam, mankind became essentially evil, or in a state of total depravity, and therefore could not possibly pass at death into the higher spirit realms, except for the atoning sacrifice of a saviour-god. Beliefs in saviour-gods occurred in many ancient religions long before the Christian era, and it is probable that the early Christians derived their belief in the atoning sacrifice of Jesus from these earlier religions. It must be remembered that St. Paul, who preached the vicarious atonement of Jesus, had been brought up in the traditions and teachings of the Pharisees, who believed in the shedding of blood for the remission of sins. It is now, however, generally accepted that physically man has been gradually evolved from the lowest forms of life. Also, that the earliest human beings were not in a state of primitive innocence or perfection, but were savages governed entirely by their bodily desires and instincts, and thus little higher than wild animals in their mode of life. In the course of thousands of years they have become gradually civilised and have advanced to higher ethical standards of living. Although during this period setbacks have occurred there has been no general "fall" throughout the world. Instead, there has been on the whole a gradual spiritual advancement. Hence there has been no need for an atoning sacrifice by a saviour-god to bring about a reconciliation of God with mankind.

According to most Christian teachings in the past, entry into heaven depended largely on *faith*, since no matter how greatly a person had sinned, if he repented at the time of death for his misdeeds and believed in the saving grace of the atoning sacrifice of Jesus, he would be saved from hell and allowed to enter heaven—"washed in the blood of the lamb."

Modern spirit teachings do not uphold this doctrine. They state that death-bed repentance is of no value, unless accompanied by a sincere desire to make good or atone in the spirit-life for the evil done; further, at death man can enter only that region to which he has become spiritually fitted as a result of his earth-life. Man therefore merely reaps what he has sown.

PERSONAL RESPONSIBILITY

Certain theologians in the past, *e.g.*, St. Augustine, have claimed that God has not only predetermined every event in the world but also has decreed that certain people, the "chosen" or "elect," are fore-ordained to go to heaven, while the others are doomed to go to hell. This doctrine, termed predestination (see "The Nature of Man"), is based on the belief that man is utterly sinful and has therefore no chance of being "saved" without the intervention of God; also, that all his actions are predetermined and any efforts he may make to change his destiny are useless. Under such conditions man can hardly be held to be responsible for his actions; and morality, duty and responsibility for evil-doing can have no meaning. Such a doctrine leads to fatalism and is utterly refuted by spirit communications, as these insist on each person being responsible for his own thoughts and actions in earth-life and thereafter.

Sooner or later in the after-life, the individual will recall with regret all his past faults, misdeeds and lost opportunities for doing good. He will also realise that to make spiritual progress he will require to get rid of these faults, and to make amends, if possible, for all the evil and suffering he may have caused to others.

THE HIGHER SPIRIT REGIONS

RESEMBLANCE BETWEEN THE HIGHER SPIRIT REGIONS AND THE EARTH-LIFE

The conditions of the part of the spirit world to which a spirit passes after a good earth-life, will resemble to some extent those of earth. Thus the new environment will appear somewhat familiar or natural to the newly arrived spirit. It may even think it is still living under earth conditions and not "dead." In fact, it may not realise it has entered the spirit state, but may think it is in some strange part of the world, until it is greeted by relatives and friends, who it knows have already passed on.

Owing to the fact that there is this similarity in earth and spirit conditions, the newly arrived spirit is enabled to make use of the knowledge it has gained and the experiences it has had in the material environment of earth-life, and as a result it can adjust itself more readily to the new conditions. Even any technical or manipulative skill acquired on earth, *e.g.,* in craftsmanship, in playing musical, instruments, or in drawing, painting, dancing or sport, will still be of use to the spirit, otherwise such skill would be merely an earthly accomplishment or discipline,

THE MIND UNCHANGED AT DEATH

The human mind being essentially the working of the spirit and not of the brain, is unchanged at death. Even after a good earth-life, the individual on entering the spirit state does not all at once become omniscient. His mental powers and moral outlook are the same as on earth, but keener as they are not now restricted in their expression by the physical brain. All the earth memories, conscious and subconscious, are retained, including those of the other-world or psychic contacts with discarnate friends made during the sleeping or waking state on earth. The latter, being largely subconscious in nature, are not as a rule consciously remembered until the spirit enters the next life. A mother in earth-life may have such contacts with a dead child, and be subconsciously aware of its progress in spirit-life. She will therefore have no difficulty in recognising the child, when she herself passes over.

Thus at death, an individual may recognise spirits and scenes in the new environment of which he was not consciously aware on earth. These memories of past contacts will tend to reduce the strangeness of the new surroundings and so lessen any shock of the passing to spirit-life.

THE FUNCTION OF THE SPIRIT BODY

In earth-life, the physical body required food, water, air and warmth, to keep it in health; and the mind had to have sensory experiences to enable it to acquire a sense of awareness of its surroundings and to develop its intelligence. The spirit after death does not require the various necessities of a physical body, such as food, water and oxygen; and clothing is created by the power of thought. However, for the continued existence of the spirit as an individual entity in the after-life, the new conditions must be such that the spirit is fully aware that it does exist, and at the same time can express itself and function in the new environment in as real a fashion as it did on earth. In other words, the discarnate spirit should be able to act on, and be aware of, the things, events and conditions around it. It does this by means of the spirit body, which it has retained after death. This body is of so refined a nature compared with physical matter that it cannot be detected by the sensory organs of our physical body. But it is as real and substantial in relation to the spirit environment as the physical body is to the earthly.

According to the spirit communications received through Anthony Borgia (see "Life in the World Unseen"), the spirit body is the spirit counterpart of the physical body and by its means the spirit can detect (see, hear, taste, smell and feel) and react to things and conditions, and carry out work in the after-life in much the same way as it did through the physical body on earth. However, the spirit body does not require food, being apparently sustained, according to Borgia, by spiritual or radiant energy from its environment. While it does not suffer from the diseases of earth-life, it is affected by the state of the mind and the spiritual development of the spirit. Thus the spirit bodies of the inhabitants of the higher spirit realms are always more radiant and of a higher order of matter than those of the spirits in the lower regions. According to Borgia, the spirit body at death will be sound if the earth-life has been spiritually sound, but ugly and warped if the earth-life has been evil.

THE REALITY OF THE SPIRIT STATE

Accordingly, the spirit can function in the spirit state in much the same way as it did in the material environment prior to death. And the new environment will be quite as real and tangible to the spirit body as the earth was to the physical. However, the earth environment will not now appear or feel real and tangible to the discarnate spirit. The terms "thought state" and "illusory state" have sometimes been applied to the spirit existence, but these terms should not be used as they give rise to the false impression that the spirit state is unreal. We are no more justified in using them for the spirit state than discarnate spirits would be when referring to earth conditions.

The reality of the environment in which a spirit exists, depends upon whether it is functioning at the time in its physical body or only in its spirit body. The incarnate spirit finds the earthly environment real and tangible, but the spirit realms unreal and intangible. With the discarnate spirit, the converse is the case. It follows from this, that the spirit state and its inhabitants could be in our midst, and could even interpenetrate our earthly environment without our being consciously aware of the fact.

THE MENTAL POWERS OF SPIRITS

The human mind undoubtedly remains unaltered at death. It does not change in character, but has the same traits, desires and memories, and even the same false beliefs, that it had in earth-life. It is no longer associated with a physical body with its brain and nervous system and so will not be affected by *bodily* needs, desires and instincts, except where these have become ingrained habits of thought. As it does not now have to provide for these bodily requirements, it should have plenty of time for acquiring knowledge, for exploring the new world around it, for service to others and for recreation. It does not immediately acquire infinite knowledge, *i.e.*, become omniscient, but acting through the wider scope of the brain and sensory organs of the spirit body, it will now have far greater ability to appreciate the conditions around it, to express itself and acquire fresh knowledge. There will be ample opportunities for doing useful creative work. Thus life will become more real and more deeply enriched than on earth.

In addition, the faculty of extra-sensory perception, *e.g.*, telepathy, can be exercised much more freely. Hence, discarnate spirits can be aware to a great extent of each other's thoughts, although their minds need never be wholly disclosed. It is possible that this telepathic awareness is largely prevented in earth-life by the association of mind with the physical brain, or by the fact that the conscious mind cannot readily obtain the telepathic information from the subconscious mind, the latter alone having telepathic powers. With people in earth-life, it may be necessary that the mind is not exposed to this wide telepathic awareness, otherwise the spirit might have difficulty in developing individual traits and character and in establishing its personality. There might be so much telepathic interference from the thoughts of other individuals that its own spiritual development would be hindered. Moreover, in earth-life, unlike in spirit, people of different degrees of spiritual development, *e.g.*, good and bad individuals, are living together in the same community, and under these conditions such telepathic powers might be a source of much embarrassment and trouble. At the same time emotional experiences are felt more keenly and feelings are expressed more openly in the spirit-life, as the mind is now free from the limiting or blunting action of the physical brain.

Owing to the wide scope of the telepathic faculty in the after-life, spirits can readily affect each other by their thoughts. Thus there can be no dishonesty, nor dissimulation of thoughts and feelings—spirits know each other as they really are and not as they may pretend to be. If a spirit has decided ideas, beliefs or interests, which differ from those of the rest of the community, it cannot hide the fact, and will be obviously out of harmony with the others. Hence it must either modify or discard these ideas or beliefs, or go to a community with which it is more in harmony.

In this telepathic exchange of thoughts, no language difficulties arise, and friends can readily contact each other, although in different regions.

THE CREATIVE POWER OF THOUGHT

In the spirit environment, there will be the spirit counterpart of ground, grass, flowers, fruit and other trees, rivers, lakes, houses and gardens, very similar to those on earth but of far greater beauty and grandeur, so that spirits will live there in great happiness. It may be contended that, as in the case of the beliefs of races in the past, this description is merely a representation of our ideas of the ideal conditions under which we should like to live on earth—a cottage in the country, fields, trees, lakes and hills.

There is an element of truth in this, for after all, we do in the end actually create our own heaven.

The power of thought is a great creative force even on earth, *e.g.*, buildings have to be planned in the mind before they can be constructed. But in the after-life, as the mind has much greater freedom of expression, its creative powers, are greatly enhanced. Moreover, the substance of the spirit state being more refined than that of earth, may be more readily acted upon by, or more responsive to, the creative forces of the mind Thus one can readily understand that the combined thoughts or desires of a community of spirits of the same degree of development, reinforced strongly by the creative and directive powers of more advanced spirits, must have a profound effect in creating the environmental conditions, natural features or scenery, and buildings, etc.

Accounts of such creative work have been given in spirit communications. For instance, in the Rev. G. Vale Owen's automatic script, "The Life Beyond the Veil," Vol. 3, there are details of the construction of a large temple by a group of spirits, working together in close harmony under the control of a highly advanced spirit. There was in the first place a general conception in the mind of each spirit of the design of the temple. A site was chosen, and then the building was constructed in stages by the creative will power of the group. The master spirit directed and controlled the creative forces and added the final touches to the structure. The spirits had to rest after each stage in the construction work to renew their creative powers. According to this account, the temple was real and substantial, and not merely a mental image or a figment of the imagination.

Such accounts show how misleading are those conceptions, which claim that the after-life is a purely mental state, dependent on the "inner minds" of those present in it, so that a "good" spirit may see the grandeur and beauty of heaven around it, and an "evil" spirit, in the same surroundings, only the desolation of hell. Such a state of affairs would lead to utter chaos in spiritual relationships and the spirit-life would have no meaning. To enable the spirits in each region to lead a rational purposeful life, and thus make spiritual progress, the environment must be not only real and substantial, but stable, so that the various natural features, buildings and other things, have the same appearance to all the inhabitants there. Of course, one region may appear shadowy or unreal to the spirits of another, just as all parts of the spirit world are to us on earth.

SPACE AND TIME IN THE AFTER-LIFE

Space may not have the same meaning in the after-life as on earth. For instance, there may be interpenetration of the different spirit realms; and of these regions and the material world. The possibility of this is shown by the fact that spirits may be present in our midst without our being aware of it.

Moreover, there must be some profound difference between the spirit state and earth conditions, because, according to spirit communications, spirits not only travel from place to place by the ordinary methods of locomotion, *e.g.,* walking, but they can also travel instantaneously by concentrating their thoughts on where they wish to go. It is possible that the spirit would have this power in earth-life, but for the fact that its powers of locomotion are restricted by the physical body. In the sleep state on earth, the spirit may leave the physical body and visit other parts of the world or the spirit realms. Under certain conditions psychic sensitives may also have these out-of-the-body experiences, but care must be taken to distinguish them from what is merely "travelling clairvoyance."

At the same, time, the conception of space in the spirit-life cannot be discarded. For, if the environment is real and substantial to the spirit inhabitants of a region, it must have all the features, such as fields, woods, lakes, houses and gardens, spread out in some form of space.

The conception of time in the spirit-life appears to be different from that on earth. Spirits tell us that in the spirit state there is no sun, but that in the higher realms everything is brightly illuminated, with no shadows. Thus there are no alternating periods of day and night, and no succession of seasons or years, so that solar and sidereal time do not exist. But there must be some form of time, otherwise there would be no sequence of events and therefore no progression. Thus it may be said that time is reckoned by work done, services rendered and spiritual progress made. But the fact that discarnate spirits can attend regularly spiritualist circles and séances held at definite times, shows that they must direct their activities in accordance with some form of time—unless they come merely when they know, by telepathy, that their presence is expected or desired by the mediums or the people gathered for the meetings. Indeed, it could be said that spirits can determine the passage of earth time by telepathic contact with people still in earth-life.

FAMILY AND FRIENDLY TIES

Spirits will tend to form harmonious communities in a spirit region, being drawn together because of similar spiritual development, similarity in character, ties of friendship and by some common interest. Like attracts like, and spiritual affinity and character are of more importance in this connection than blood relationships, in which there may be wide differences in personality. Owing to the close affinity which exists within such a community, there will be close co-operation between members in their work and other activities. At the same time, there will be no disharmony, such as arises in earth-life, from petty jealousies and clashing of interests.

Husband and wife, if there is a strong bond of love between them, will continue to live together when both pass over, but if one is more advanced spiritually than the other and is therefore in a higher realm, then he or she will endeavour to help the other until both can be together again. If there is not this strong bond of love between them, they may separate in the after-life or may work together as friends. Parents still retain their affection for their children, and will recognise them, as already mentioned, even though the latter passed over at an early age and have grown up in the spirit state. This also applies to still-born babies.

ABSENCE OF EARTHLY TROUBLES

In earth-life, suffering and hardship arise from fatigue and illness of the physical body, malnutrition or lack of warmth and shelter. As the physical body is discarded at death, there are no such physical troubles in the after-life. But a spirit may require to rest or relax after strenuous mental efforts of any kind. Although food and drink are no longer necessary, spirits may retain for some time after death the desire for eating and drinking, and they are able to satisfy such cravings by the creative power of thought. It is said that there are orchards with fruit which spirits may eat. Smoking may be practised at first by addicts, but not by advanced spirits.

Trouble is also caused in earth-life by the striving for material advantages, such as wealth, power and social position. These are of no importance in the spirit state.

Money is no longer required as spirits can meet the needs of themselves or others by creative thought. Further, there is no need for spirits to live huddled together in overcrowded areas, a source of much hardship and unhappiness on earth, as there is no end to the space available and their homes can be spread out over a wide area. No matter how far their homes are from their centre of occupation, they can travel instantaneously by the power of thought.

The conditions in any region depend largely on the spirit inhabitants. When individuals pass to spirit-life, they still adhere largely to the ideas and practices and religious beliefs of earth-life, and as a result there is at first a great diversity of thought and in mode of life. But as they increase in knowledge and wisdom, they outgrow these beliefs and superstitions and can live happily in communities with other individuals, who may have been originally of a different colour, race or faith.

Of course, suffering and pain may arise in spirit-life from mental and emotional states. However, as spirits progress and advance to higher spirit regions, they observe higher and higher ethical standards, and there should not be any disharmony such as arises in lower regions and on earth from selfishness, greed, conceit and jealousy.

LEADERSHIP IN THE SPIRIT-LIFE

Each of the regions in spirit-life will be under the guidance and control of leaders, who, owing to their advanced spiritual nature and greater wisdom and experience, are well qualified for this purpose. Many of these leaders may actually belong to higher realms. On earth, a person may be in a position of authority or leadership because of social position, wealth or other influence. In spirit-life, leadership is not acquired in these ways, but by spiritual qualifications, wisdom and experience. Thus the higher realms are soundly and wisely governed, and good order, prevails, as although the spirits at all times have freedom of will, they must be guided by their leaders, if they are to remain in harmony with the rest of the community and make spiritual progress. These leaders, however, act not only, as rulers, but also as helpers and friends to all under their control.

Many people expect to be in the direct presence of, and even to see God or Jesus immediately they pass into the after-life. They overlook the fact that only the most advanced spirits are fit to enter the highest realms where there may be a full manifestation of Jesus. Of course, Jesus may manifest himself to some extent at lower levels for special purposes. It is very difficult to conceive of a direct manifestation of God in personal form at even the highest level, but for all we know a limited one might be possible.

Spirit-life Not Entirely Devotional in Character

The life after death is not an idle, dreamy, purposeless existence, but one of activity and responsibility. Many Christians still believe that it is of a purely religious character; a life of fervent religious emotion in which angels with wings and perhaps harps play an important part, and the spirits of those who have led a good earth-life devote all or most of their time to praising and worshipping God. But as the spirit communicator of Swedenborg pointed out in his description of heaven, God does not require to have this endless praise, worship and glorification. In any case a continual service of this kind would quickly lead to the utter boredom and indifference of those taking part in it, provided death has not completely altered their character and interests. Does it appear to be consistent with the nature of a Heavenly Father, who is concerned with the spiritual welfare and happiness of all his children, that He should be content with this endless worship and praise, when so much could be done by the spirits concerned in the helping of other spirits, incarnate or discarnate? Swedenborg also shows, in his communications, how a life in heaven spent wholly in feasting or in wandering about a beautiful garden, would lead to satiation or utter boredom, and at the same time would be quite purposeless.

DUTIES IN THE AFTER-LIFE

There is plenty of work for spirits in the after-life. There are duties to be carried out in connection with the general life and activities of the community or region to which they belong. Houses, institutes, gardens and other sources of interest and occupation, have to be constructed and attended to. Buildings, already in existence, may have to be enlarged or adapted to new requirements.

SERVICE TO OTHER DISCARNATE SPIRITS

Service to others forms an important part of the spirit's activities, help being given to those in need of it in the same or in a lower part of the spirit world. For instance, individuals who have just passed to spirit-life require assistance to enable them to become adjusted to the new conditions of existence. They may require to be nursed in a rest home so that they can recuperate after a long or painful illness. There may be a difficulty in convincing some newly arrived spirits that they are no longer under earth conditions, but are actually in the spirit state. Such spirits may have ingrained ideas about death and may not be convinced of their true condition until brought into contact with relatives or friends who have passed on previously; or until reminded of details of their last days on earth and their passing to the spirit-life. They may also have to be taken to some familiar place, *e.g.*, their old home, and shown the difference between their new state and that of their friends still on earth.

In addition, missionary and rescue work has to be carried out for spirits in the lower regions, to enable them to realise their undeveloped or debased condition and encourage them to strive to develop their higher spiritual nature. No sincere plea for help is ever ignored, no matter how low the spirit may have fallen.

There are also duties to be carried out in the care and nursing and rearing of the children in the spirit world. All the children have to be trained and educated to enable them to develop in spiritual nature and in intelligence and wisdom. Those who have died in infancy or have been still-born or feeble-minded, require special treatment to compensate for the earthly experiences which they have missed.

MINISTRY OF SPIRITS TO MAN ON EARTH

Guidance and help and healing have also to be given to those still in earth-life. This can be a potent source of good provided the individuals on earth are in attunement with their spirit helpers. The latter can become aware of incarnate thoughts and desires, especially if expressed to them in prayer, the process involved being that of telepathy between minds en rapport or in attunement with each other.

This work of service to people in earth-life is commonly referred to as the "Ministry of Angels," the term angel being used in the Bible for a spirit messenger or messenger of God. (The word "angel" comes from the Greek "angelos" which means messenger.) Some believe that angels are of a different order of creation from the spirits of the "dead," but the seers, Andrew Jackson Davis and Swedenborg, claimed that angels are in all cases the spirits of human beings, who have lived on earth. This is also supported by the fact that in the Bible the terms angel and spirit are occasionally used interchangeably, as in Acts 8, 26 and 29. Further, in Judges 13, an angel is also referred to as "man" and "man of God."

The Jews came ultimately to believe that there was a guardian angel for each individual in earth-life. Indeed, it has been said that they put "a layer of angels between God and man." This belief is against the Christian doctrine that there is no need for any other intermediary between God and man than Jesus, as in the latter, Christians have "direct, unhindered and first hand access to God." However, this Christian teaching does not appear to be consistent with a common sense and realistic outlook. Why should God not have agents everywhere in the afterlife as on earth? In earth-life our friends and others are willing to help us, when we are in difficulty, and this must apply also to those in the spirit world, for there is a system and a continuity running throughout the universe, spiritual as well as physical. Thus discarnate spirits will try to help each other, and if possible mankind still on earth. These spirit helpers, like our earthly ones, do not come between those they help and God; they simply act as His intermediaries or agents.

If a person in earth-life wishes to appeal to God directly, there is no reason why he should not do so, but the answer to his prayer may come through his spirit guide or guardian angel, or some other spirit friend, or even through some person still in earth-life who has been prompted from the spirit world. For all should be God's agents and any help that anyone can give is in accordance with God's will, even although the inspiration or prompting may have come through a number of intermediaries.

WORK AND SPIRITUAL PROGRESS

Thus work in the service of others has to be done in the spirit state, but an individual does not require to do work for which he is not fitted or which is of an uncongenial nature. He cannot be forced to carry out duties in the after-life, but if he fails to do so, he will not make spiritual progress and will not be in harmony with the other spirits in the community. He will therefore either have to readjust his mode of life and accept his responsibilities or go to another region.

Failure to carry out the duties in the after-life leads to spiritual stagnation. A person on earth may be able to lead an indolent, selfish life, and have all kinds of privileges owing to his worldly wealth or social position, but such a life does not make for spiritual progress. Also, at death all these material advantages have to be left behind, as in the case of the rich man, Dives, in the parable. His body was being buried with great pomp and ceremony, while he was alone in the spirit state, stripped of all his possessions, and in utter misery owing to his lack of spiritual progress.

EDUCATION IN THE SPIRIT-LIFE

In the spirit world, learning is encouraged, especially that leading to increase in spiritual wisdom. There are places of instruction, institutes or colleges, and libraries with books and other records, for those desiring to have more knowledge of the sciences, arts and music. Individuals who have been interested in any of these subjects on earth, may continue their studies in the after-life. Others who have been unable to do such work in earth-life, can now do so if they desire. There are no limits to the resources and facilities available for such purposes.

Under suitable conditions the results of such studies may be passed to those on earth, as in moments of inspiration. Tyrrell in his work, "The Personality of Man," claims that "those creations of the mind, which have borne pre-eminently the stamp of originality and greatness" have come from beyond the range of the conscious mind, and they have done so "not only with power, but often with something exotic and other-worldly about them." Many authors, poets and artists, *e.g.*, Shelley, Wordsworth, Keats, Bunyan and Stevenson, were inspired in their work in this way; so also, no doubt, were certain scientists. Moreover, advanced scientific information may be given in communications through mediums with little or no scientific training. For instance, Andrew Jackson Davis, in his psychic communications, "The Principles of Nature, Her Divine Revelations, and a Voice to Mankind," asserted that there were nine planets in our solar system. At that time only seven had been discovered, but another two were found later. He also gave the density of the eighth planet, which was later found to be correct. Also, Hudson Tuttle, a youth with little or no education, produced automatic writings showing scientific knowledge of so profound a nature as to be quoted by the philosopher Ludwig Buchner, and the biologist, Charles Darwin, in their works.

There is music in the spirit world, especially in the higher regions, and it is claimed in spirit communications that in the higher realms there is a relationship between music and light, which shows itself in glowing changes of colour. Music plays an important part in spirit-life in bringing about harmonious conditions and spiritual upliftment; also, for soothing and revitalising spirits, who have just come from the lower regions or from earth-life. Spirits may study music in all its aspects, there being special halls for musical and dramatic instruction, as well as for entertainment. The great musicians of the world can continue their work after death, and under favourable conditions the results of their labours may be passed on to individuals still on earth. Much of the inspiration in earth-life of great musical composers, *e.g.*, Beethoven, Mozart, Chopin, Schubert, Handel and Wagner, has come from spirit sources.

Increase in knowledge and wisdom makes for spiritual advancement. However, spirits with fixed or ingrained ideas and religious beliefs may be quite unreceptive of other information, and as a result their spiritual progress is hindered. Thus those belonging to certain religious denominations may retain for a long time particular beliefs and dogmas. They may even form separate communities, where they can live in harmony with others of the same faith. Later, as they acquire more wisdom, they will gradually discard their peculiar beliefs and intermingle with other spirits.

THE LOWER SPIRIT REGIONS

Individuals who have led an evil earth-life are so undeveloped spiritually that they are not fit at death to enter the higher spirit realms, and so must go to the lower regions, commonly referred to by Christians as hell. There, they live along with other evil spirits.

The lower regions are cold, dank and desolate, with little or no light and no vegetation. The life there is one of misery, suffering and spiritual darkness. These conditions are not imposed on the spirit inhabitants by a vengeful God, but are created by their own evil thoughts and actions. Nevertheless, the environment is real and cannot be regarded as a mere mental state.

THE MENTAL CONDITION OF LOWER SPIRITS

Many of the spirits in the lower realms are in a dazed condition, having perhaps little or no recollection of earth-life. They may not know where they are nor even realise that they are dead, and they may be unapproachable by higher spirit helpers.

Certain individuals live in solitary misery, brooding in despair over their seemingly hopeless state. They may have a feeling of remorse for their past misdeeds, but may be so despondent that they cannot make an effort to improve their condition. Others may be too self-willed and proud to admit that they are in a debased state and are alone to blame.

Those who in earth-life set great store by their wealth or possessions, will now realise that, like Dives in the parable, death has stripped them of all these material advantages. They may even be tortured by the thought that others are now making use of their former possessions. Suicides will realise that they have not escaped from their responsibilities and difficulties by ending their earth-life. In fact, their difficulties may be greatly increased owing to their having entered spirit-life before their work on earth has been completed. Many lower spirits have some good in them, but owing to an evil twist or trait in their nature, have failed to live a good life. Selfishness and jealousy have frequently been the root of all their trouble.

Lower spirits in many instances prefer to live in communities of those of like nature to themselves. As these spirits are frequently utterly wicked and sadistic in nature, much suffering arises among them from their own vicious and cruel habits. Certain ones by sheer strength of personality become leaders, venting their evil passions and hatred on all those in their power, until they themselves become the victims of even more powerful spirits.

Accordingly, in the lower realms there is suffering, fear and misery, and little or no striving for spiritual progress. For a time, perhaps lasting ages, the debased inhabitants refuse to recognise spiritual values in their mode of life and cannot be influenced by higher spirits. They continue their evil ways and sink lower and lower, until they become sated with their own wickedness. At last they begin to realise that they alone are responsible for their condition. They yearn for relief and appeal for help. They have at last reached the turning point in their life in these lower realms. A higher spirit may have been able to influence them, for God's power extends even to the lowest depths of hell.

No matter how low a spirit has fallen, no matter how debased it is, no sincere plea for help is ever left unanswered. But the spirits in these regions, like all other spirits, incarnate and discarnate, having free will, cannot be forced to abandon their evil mode of life. Guidance and assistance can be given to them only provided they are prepared to accept such help.

THE REMEDIAL NATURE OF THE LOWER REGIONS

The old belief that hell was a place of everlasting damnation and torment from which there was no escape, was a figment of medieval minds. Such a hell would serve no useful purpose and would not be consistent with a merciful, all-loving Father. If there was no possibility of escape from the lower regions, it would be far better that evil spirits should suffer complete annihilation at death, a belief that has been held by certain Christian theologians.

The lower regions are undoubtedly places of suffering, but they are remedial in nature. The conditions there are such that sooner or later the wanderers from the paths of righteousness, no matter how far afield they have strayed, will, like the Prodigal Son, find their way home to their Heavenly Father. God never fails and therefore not one of His children can be irretrievably lost.

The process of spiritual regeneration is slow; it is easier to undo wrongs and get rid of vicious habits on earth than to do so in the lower regions. To repent of an evil action does not mean that the spirit is freed from the responsibility of having committed the deed, for it may, still have to make amends for any hindrance or harm it has done thereby to the spiritual development of others.

SPIRITUAL ADVANCEMENT

SPIRITUAL PROGRESSION

There are many realms in the spirit world, and advancement is open to all spirits, even to those in the lowest regions. When an individual has made sufficient spiritual progress and acquired enough spiritual wisdom, he becomes fitted to go into a higher region. Spiritual wisdom must not be confused with intellectual power; a spirit may have much spiritual wisdom without being highly intelligent and vice versa. Advancement also does not depend upon the holding of certain religious beliefs or the carrying out of various religious practices. *The keynote of religious life in the spirit realms is love and service to all.*

No spirit can enter a higher region until ready for it; nor can it live in a community to which it is not spiritually attuned. The rate of progress made and therefore the time spent in any part, will vary with different individuals, but even after a good earth-life, advance may be slow at first, spirits being happy and well content to remain for a time in those parts of the higher regions already described.

When an individual passes to a higher realm, he may be leaving friends behind, but there is no regret or sorrow as he can still keep in touch with them by the power of thought. Also, he can readily visit them whenever he desires, and they will become ultimately reunited when those left behind make sufficient progress to advance to the higher region.

ENVIRONMENT AND SPIRITUAL PROGRESS

The matter of any one region is always more refined than that of lower ones, so that the former is not normally visible to the inhabitants of the latter. Moreover, spirits in becoming attuned to a higher realm, have spirit bodies of a more "ethereal" nature, so that they also are not normally visible to lower spirits. But they can condition themselves so that they can be seen and spoken to by lower spirits. The fact that the matter of a higher region may not be visible to the spirits of a lower, does not mean that the higher region is not as real as the other. No matter where the spirit is, the environment seems as real as the earth does to incarnate beings.

With advancement to higher and higher realms, spirits find that the environmental conditions become less like those on earth. There is for one thing far more light, so that everything is much brighter. Indeed, lower spirits would be dazzled by the intense brilliance and suffer great distress.

The scenery becomes marvellous in beauty and grandeur, far beyond our earthly powers of imagination. Spirit communicators tell us of ranges of high mountains, their peaks in the bright light glowing in colours—white, gold and red; also, rivers and streams flowing through meadows and woods, their waters clear and sparkling. The meadows are carpeted with flowers redolent with perfume; the woods contain a great variety of fine trees, rich in colour.

There are cities with magnificent buildings, halls, temples, institutes and residences. The various edifices are surrounded by green lawns and fountains, and gardens with a profusion of flowers and fruit and other trees. Unlike those of lower parts of the spirit world, the buildings are made of highly translucent material, like glass or crystal. This may be of different colours and glistens in the light, like precious stones. As the colour of material used may vary with different buildings, a city may give forth a blaze of many-coloured light.

HIGHLY ADVANCED SPIRITS

The spirits themselves, as they advance to the higher realms, become more radiant and beautiful in form, and their clothes, which correspond in nature with the wearer's spirituality, also become much finer in character.

In these regions, differences due to colour, race and religion, have disappeared, and there is an all-pervading peace and harmony. This is also fostered by the fact that the individuals become more self-less in their outlook, and realise more clearly that they are linked together in a common brotherhood, which may include, for all we know, not only the spirits from earth-life, but also perhaps those from life in other planets of the universe.

The spirits in these high realms, with their much greater knowledge and wisdom, have much higher powers to understand and appreciate the nature and unutterable beauty of everything around. They can also express themselves more freely in the environment. Thus they have a very real existence, and the joys of living are greatly enhanced. According to the Borgia communications (see "Life in the World Unseen"), "they are not shadowy unreal people, but, on the contrary, they are like ourselves, capable of feeling and exhibiting the emotions of their fine natures, capable of human understanding, of human thought, and as easily susceptible to laughter and free-hearted merriment as were we ourselves."

THE MORE ADVANCED REALMS

The conditions in the more advanced realms are utterly beyond our conception. Myers (see "The Road to Immortality" by Geraldine Cummins) states that the individual spirit comes to realise that it is not completely independent, but that it is in close communion with a number of other spirits, the association being referred to by Myers as a "group-soul." This enables the spirits to share their knowledge and experiences, past and present, without loss of their individuality. He also tells us of a state of timelessness, and says that form or shape is no longer essential for the functioning of the spirit.

We can, however, rest assured that in each of these realms the spirits will find ample scope for further spiritual advancement and increase of knowledge. There will also be no end to the opportunities for service to other spirits (no matter from which part of the universe they come), and to

God in His work of creating and sustaining the vast universe with its millions of galaxies and countless solar systems, and the myriad forms of life, incarnate and discarnate.

It is possible for every spirit, even those in the lowest spirit regions, to advance to these high realms. The individual may take ages, even aeons, to do so, but life is eternal and there is thus no end to the time that is available, and there is also no limit to the help that can be received. To make this progress, the spirit need not adhere to any particular faith. No religious body has the right to assume that it alone can ensure "salvation." The paths to the summit are open to all, for as the Lord Krishna says, "By whatsoever path you come to Me I shall welcome you, for the paths men take from every side are Mine."

AT ONE WITH GOD

There appears to be no end to the progress that a spirit can make, and as it rises to greater and greater heights, it will find even more highly advanced spirits and hierarchies of spirits. It will also acquire a more profound understanding and appreciation of the nature and purpose of all things in the universe from the beginning of time, and will thus be able to apprehend more clearly the original conception of the Universe in the Mind of God, and the Love and Creative Force which brought it into being and sustains it.

At the same time the spirit will acquire a deeper sense of contact with the Divine Mind, and will realise more and more fully that it is essentially of the same nature. Thus it will draw closer and closer to God, until it is in a state of complete at-one-ment with Him without losing its individuality or identity. Then it will know that it is in truth a Son of God.

PSYCHIC INFLUENCES
IN WORLD RELIGION

I wish to thank Miss M. C. Alston for her advice, guidance and helpful criticism in the preparation of this work; also Miss J. A. Hector, Professor K. W. Braid, O.B.E., and Dr. J. Winning, for their services in the revision of the script.

THE AUTHOR

FOREWORD

Man lives in a vast, apparently boundless universe, his physical existence being but a mere moment of time in the limitless ages of eternity. During his earth-life he is consciously aware only of his physical environment, his sensory organs having been developed to detect merely physical conditions. Thus he is not directly conscious of the non-physical or psychic.

Early man knew that by doing certain things he could get definite results, and he reasoned from this that there must be a cause behind everything. Hence he came to believe that there must be some unseen power to account for the universe, a power which brought it into being and was responsible for all that happened therein—an Almighty Being or God, who could think, reason and do things. This God was invisible, and reigned supreme over a large number of minor gods or spirits. Such ideas were held by most ancient peoples.

In all ages, however, there have been individuals with psychic gifts, who were aware of "other-world" conditions and of discarnate spirits. These seers or prophets have had a profound influence on human thought, and have even initiated great religious movements. In fact, all the great religions of the world owe their beginnings to the work of such sensitives.

Their teaching, being spirit-inspired, was the same in essence, no matter the age or stage of civilisation in which they lived. With the passage of time, however, the original message was unfortunately overlaid with materialistic accretions. This has been responsible for the wide diversity of creeds in the different religions.

In the following work, an attempt has been made to show the influence which such psychic individuals, under spirit guidance and inspiration, have had in the development of the great world religions.

J. F. M.

PSYCHIC INFLUENCES IN WORLD RELIGION

THE BELIEF IN SPIRITS AND GODS

At an early stage in the history of man, he developed a belief in spirits and gods. There were various reasons for this. Natural phenomena, such as storms, earthquakes and eclipses, happening in the world around him, filled him with fear and awe. There were also the hardships and disasters of daily life. All these seemed very mysterious, as he could neither understand nor find a cause for them. He realised that they could not be due to human agency, and the only explanation he could think of, was that they were brought about by invisible or supernatural beings. He naturally concluded that these beings had to be treated with great respect and even placated in various ways to avert the evil for which they could be responsible.

PSYCHIC EXPERIENCES

His belief in spirits was also fostered by certain individuals having psychic powers, and so being able to "see" or "hear" spirits. They would recognise some of these as spirits of dead relatives or friends, and would therefore realise that there was survival after death.

There are accounts of psychic dreams, spirit communications and appearances in the mythology and folk-lore of practically all nations, the psychic faculty being common to all races of mankind. This was recognised by Herodotus, who said that all ancient nations had similar psychic experiences. Such accounts are found in many ancient records—the inscribed tablets of Babylon, the Egyptian "Book of the Dead," the Hindu sacred books, and the writings of Homer, Sophocles, Herodotus and Cicero in Greece and Rome; as well as the Hebrew Scriptures.

ANCESTOR WORSHIP

In these early times man lived closer to nature and was less sophisticated in every way than in modern times. The belief that his ancestors survived death was very real to him, and he had also no doubt that they took an active interest in all his affairs and could affect them for good or ill. It was therefore essential to please them at all times and win their goodwill and help. To neglect them would cause their displeasure and might result in disaster to himself, his family and perhaps the community in which he lived. Thus *ancestor-worship* was one of the earliest forms of religion in all parts of the world.

Moreover, if any person was known to have clairvoyant powers, *i.e.*, "the open vision" of the Old Testament or "the second sight" of the Celts, he was consulted for spirit guidance and help on all matters of importance; it was essential to know whether the spirits approved, or disapproved, of one's manner of life or of any proposed course of action.

FOREKNOWLEDGE AND DIVINATION

Early man believed that the spirits and gods had also a knowledge of the future, which they could reveal to him, not only in psychic dreams, visions or other spirit manifestations, but also by external signs or omens, termed *auguries.* Cicero says, "As far as I know, there is no nation whatever, however polished and learned, or however barbarous and uncivilised, which does not believe that it is possible that future events may be indicated and understood and predicted by certain persons."

The recognition and interpretation of all such omens and psychic experiences was termed *divination.* This was practised from ancient times by many nations of the Near East and by the Greeks and Romans. It was regarded by these nations as of the greatest importance, and no matter of any consequence was undertaken unless all the omens and psychic manifestations were favourable.

The belief that supernatural beings could foresee and influence the future, and were willing to reveal their knowledge to mankind with their approval or disapproval of any course of action, led not only to the art of *augury* but also to an interest in *psychic practices.*

While augury was no doubt based largely on superstitious beliefs, it was nevertheless of spiritual significance to early races in that it was believed to show the will of the gods or spirits in relation to human affairs. Even the Ancient Hebrews and the Early Christians resorted to augury, as in the case of Gideon exposing a fleece to the dew (Judges 6. 37) and the apostles drawing lots in the appointment of a successor to Judas Iscariot (Acts 1. 26). Gideon and the apostles were fully convinced that God had influenced the results.

In this connection it must be borne in mind that with augury, the psychic element may have crept in occasionally to influence the results, especially if the augur himself had psychic powers. Dr. Rhine in recent years has demonstrated the power of the mind in influencing the results in the throwing of dice. Even in modern times, although the work of the witch-doctors and medicine-men of primitive tribes is based largely on superstition or magic, it may be in certain cases psychic in nature.

Augury played such an important part in the life of nations such as the Assyrians and Romans, that it must have had a profound effect on their religious outlook and acceptance of psychic phenomena. It might be said that in predicting the future the augur and the seer met on common ground. Hence it would appear to be desirable, before discussing ancient psychic practices, to mention briefly the various methods of augury.

DIVINATION BY AUGURY

METHODS OF AUGURY

The art of augury was organised by the Roman State. It was believed that Jupiter indicated by external signs his attitude to every proceeding, and that these could be interpreted by qualified persons, namely the *augurs*. There was a priestly college of augurs at Rome, founded according to tradition by Romulus, who himself was an augur. The members of this college were qualified in observing and interpreting the divine omens, and were consulted by the State when it was necessary to have the approval of the gods on matters of national importance. No action was taken until the auguries were favourable. Augurs were attached even to armies in the field, so that they could be consulted on the spot in the making of decisions.

By the time of the Christian Era, such practices were losing favour in Rome, being replaced by the consultation of oracles (see later) as in Greece, and by the Chaldean methods of astrology.

EXTERNAL OMENS FROM BIRDS: THE *AUSPICES*

The term auspices in its original sense applied only to bird signs, but the meaning was extended to include other omens.

From the earliest times birds were regarded as of special importance in augury. There were various reasons for this. Their speedy movements and general alertness gave rise to the belief that they were more spiritually developed than animals. In addition, their powers of flight, enabling them to travel far and wide, gave rise to the conviction that they had a knowledge of all things. ("A wee bird told me" used to be a common saying in Scotland.) Also, there was the fact that their movements gave sailors warning of oncoming storms, and the nearness of land.

The augur observed the kind of bird, the number, the flight and the cries. Certain birds were regarded as of special importance, *e.g.*, the eagle, hawk, heron, crow, owl and dove. Great significance was attached to the flight of birds of prey which fly high and alone, especially the eagle, regarded as the messenger of God. The cries of other birds, such as crows and ravens, were considered of good or evil omen depending on the direction from which they came. Even in Britain at the present day these beliefs still persist, *e.g.*, with regard to such birds as owls and magpies.

The auspices were favourable if the bird appeared in the east (the region of light), but unfavourable if in the west (the region of darkness). Homer tells how Calchas, the augur with the Greek army at the siege of Troy, foretold, by the number of sparrows he saw in flight, how many years would be required for the siege. Certain birds, as well as animals, were looked on as sacred to particular gods, and their mere appearance at the outset of an enterprise was regarded as favourable or otherwise. It was said that a certain general used to travel in a closed litter, so that it would not be possible for him to see any unfavourable signs.

The manner of feeding by birds was of special significance. This method of augury was used by armies in the field. Prior to any undertaking, the augur of the army fed the sacred fowls and if they ate so greedily that the food fell from their beaks, the omen was favourable. If they refused to eat, it was unfavourable.

It is related that Publius Claudius in the First Punic War was so annoyed when the fowls would not eat on being let out of their cage, that he sneered at the gods and ordered the fowls to be thrown into water, saying, "Let them drink, since they will not eat." He thereupon ordered the sailing of the fleet, only to suffer defeat. The Romans held his mocking of the gods to be responsible for this great calamity. In the same war, his colleague, Lucius Junius, also disregarded the auspices and lost his fleet in a storm.

In the Second Punic War, the horse of the Roman Consul, Flaminius, fell with him before a statue of Jupiter Stator, apparently without any cause. The augurs advised him not to engage in battle, but to wait and consult the consecrated fowls. He replied, "Fine auspices indeed, if we may only fight when the chickens are hungry, but must do nothing if they are full." Accordingly, he advanced to meet Hannibal, was slain and his army defeated. Caesar, however, disregarded the auspices in his successful invasion of Africa.

ANIMAL OMENS

In augury importance was also attached to the behaviour of animals. The howling of a dog was a bad omen. A dog, wolf or hare crossing one's path was also regarded as a portent to be interpreted by an augur. This type of superstition still persists, *e.g.*, with regard to black cats. Tacitus states that the races of Northern Europe regarded the neighing of horses as ominous, also the manner in which they walked over a set of rods. Homer tells how the divine horses of Achilles foretold their master's death. In this connection it must be remembered that certain birds and animals, especially the dog and the horse, appear to be psychic and may thus have forebodings of calamities, *e.g.*, their master's death.

Snakes in all countries were held in awe and reverence. This was no doubt largely due to their deadly bite and uncanny appearance. Also, as they lived in holes in the ground and were often found around graves, they were thought to be associated with the underworld and dead ancestors. It is on record that when Sylla was sacrificing in front of his tent, a snake suddenly glided out from beneath the altar. This was regarded as a good omen, so Sylla immediately advanced and defeated the Samnites before Nola. On the other hand, when a pet ape disturbed the written questions in the urn of the Oracle of Jupiter at Dodona, this was looked on as a bad sign.

Divination was also widely carried out by the inspection of the carcases of sacrificial victims, usually calves or oxen, lambs and goats. In important undertakings, *e.g.*, the founding of a city or going into battle, animals were sacrificed, and their viscera examined by augurs for any abnormality, especially of the liver (believed to be the seat of life). If there was injury or disease of an organ, the omens were considered to be unfavourable, and the enterprise was postponed or abandoned. It is said that when Julius Caesar went to preside at the Senate, there was a defective liver and no heart in the sacrificial ox. This was an exceedingly bad omen. (There was a belief that when an augur claimed that an organ was missing, it had been destroyed by the gods at the time of sacrifice.) This method of augury was common in Babylon, Chaldea, Greece and Egypt.

If an animal went willingly to be sacrificed, it was a good portent; also, if its carcase burned readily. The kind of flame and smoke was also observed.

SKY AND WEATHER OMENS

The sky and weather signs were thought to be of great importance. Thunder was regarded as a favourable omen only when it was heard on the left of the augur. Similarly, lightning flashing from left to right was a good sign. If a magistrate with the right of augury asserted that he had observed an unfavourable omen from a flash of lightning, no one could constitutionally contest this, and so any meeting for that day had to be postponed. A sudden storm was an unfavourable sign and would bring about the postponement of an enterprise or a meeting. Comets, meteors and eclipses were bad auguries, to be feared. A lunar eclipse just before dawn in the constellation of Leo was interpreted by the augurs to presage that the Persians would be defeated and King Darius overthrown by the Macedonians under Alexander the Great.

The Jews believed in such portents. For instance, the prophet Joel spoke of various sky and other omens, which would presage the "last day": "And I will give portents in the heavens and on the earth, blood and fire and columns of smoke. The sun shall be turned to darkness, and the moon to blood, before the great and terrible day of the Lord comes" (Joel 2. 30-31); "The sun and moon are darkened (eclipsed), and the stars withdraw their shining" (Joel 3. 15); and ". . . a day of darkness and gloom, a day of clouds and thick darkness" (Joel 2. 2).

Jesus, hundreds of years later, described somewhat similar portents of the "last day": "famines and earthquakes in various places, . . . the sun will be darkened, and the moon will not give its light, and the stars will fall from heaven" (*i.e.*, solar and lunar eclipses and shooting stars or meteors) (Matthew 24. 7, 29). "And there will be signs in sun and moon and stars, and upon the earth distress of nations in perplexity at the roaring of the sea and the waves, men fainting with fear and with foreboding of what is coming on the world; for the powers of the heavens will be shaken" (Luke 21. 25).

At the Crucifixion, it is said, "Now from the sixth hour there was darkness over all the land until the ninth hour" (Matthew 27. 45).

UNUSUAL OCCURRENCES

Any unusual occurrence, especially one likely to cause fear, was regarded as a warning from the gods, on no account to be ignored, *e.g.*, an earthquake, armour falling from the wall (like the modern superstition regarding the falling of a portrait). On the night that Alexander the Great was born, the Temple of Diana of the Ephesians was burned. The Magi claimed that this indicated a destroyer of Asia had been born that night. It is said that when Jesus died on the Cross, "And behold, the curtain of the Temple was torn in two, from top to bottom; and the earth shook and the rocks were split"—and spirits of the dead were seen by many (Matthew 27. 45, 52).

The sudden illness of a person at a meeting would lead to its abandonment. The spilling of salt, stumbling, and an eye-lid twitching were regarded as bad omens. A sneeze in some cases was a good omen, especially two sneezes. But sneezing in the morning before a person had put on his shoes was so bad a sign that the one concerned should go back to bed.

Abnormalities in offspring were also bad portents, *e.g.*, a neuter, a calf with two heads, or a mule with a foal.

THE DRAWING OF LOTS AND THROWING OF DICE

The drawing or casting of lots and the throwing of dice and knuckle-bones were widely employed in divination by ancient nations, including the Hebrews. The inquirer might cast coins into a bowl of water or a sacred pool. The water was believed to have a divine power (see later) which influenced the results, *i.e.*, which side of the coin fell uppermost, or the nature of the splash. For the same reason lots were sometimes drawn from a bowl of water. In the drawing of lots, oaken or bronze tablets might be used with a saying engraved on each. They were shuffled and drawn by a boy or a virgin.

The apostles cast lots to decide whom to appoint to replace Judas Iscariot. The teraphim were also probably used in this way for divination by the Hebrews, Egyptians and Carthaginians. Another method adopted by the Chaldeans and Hebrews was to shake some marked arrows in a quiver in front of an idol of their God, until one arrow fell out.

THE SIBYLLINE SCRIPTS

Instead of drawing lots, the Romans sometimes consulted the Sibylline scripts. These were in verse, believed to have been written under inspiration and to be prophetic in nature. Later, when books supplanted rolls, they were opened at random and the passage exposed was regarded as presaging the future. Christians have employed the Bible in this way.

OMENS FROM WORDS AND NAMES

Certain words or names were regarded as lucky, and care was taken to ensure that a person with such a name headed any list. The spoken word might also have an effect on the future, even although that was not intended by the speaker. The Romans believed that it was important to accept or reject such an omen. On the day Consul Lucius Paulus was given charge of the Roman army to fight against Perses, he went home at night and was met by his little daughter, Tertia. He noticed that she was very sad and asked her what was the matter. She replied, "Perses has perished." (Perses was the name of her dog.) The general at once accepted this as a good omen, and picking her up, said, "I embrace the omen, my daughter."

It could be said that Abraham's servant chose Rebekah to be the wife of Isaac by this method of augury, as the test he set was the wording of her reply to his opening question.

ASTROLOGY

Astrology was widely used for divination in ancient times, especially in Chaldea and Persia. The Chaldeans were famous for their predictions in this way. According to the Gospel of St. Matthew, the Magi who came to

Bethlehem at the birth of Jesus, obtained their information of the birth by astrology, but it is said that they were later "warned in a dream" not to return to Herod, so that they must have been psychic.

METHODS OF DIVINATION ADOPTED BY DIFFERENT NATIONS

Nations varied with regard to the particular kind of augury they preferred. The nature of the locality and the kind of life led, were to some extent responsible for this. In Egypt and Babylonia, there were wide stretches of plain and no hills, so that the people had extensive views of the sky. This favoured astrological practices. In Etruria they were more devoted to religious rites and animal sacrifices, so augury by the inspection of the viscera of sacrificial animals was widely used. There was also in that country great variation in the weather conditions, and this was considered to be of significance. In Arabia, Cilicia and Phrygia, the people went in for the rearing of cattle and sheep and were frequently moving about from place to place, and therefore the omens from birds were looked on as important.

It must again be emphasised that the various methods of augury were based not on genuine psychic practices, but as a rule on credulous ignorance, fostered in some cases by the augurs themselves. However, they have been dealt with in this work because of the impact they made on early religious beliefs.

The Romans, being highly superstitious, were entirely given to augury and the taking of auspices. On the other hand, the Ancient Greeks believed more in the prophetic utterances of their oracles and could therefore be regarded as a more spiritual people; the same may be said of the Ancient Hebrews, who were guided by a series of outstanding prophets.

Shakespeare in his plays not only describes visionary appearances, *e.g.*, the ghosts of Julius Caesar and Hamlet's father and Banquo, but also mentions a wide variety of auguries as presaging calamities: "The raven himself is hoarse that croaks the fatal entrance of Duncan under my battlements" (Macbeth); ". . . do ravens, crows and kites fly o'er our heads and downward look on us, as we were sickly prey; their shadows seem a canopy most fatal, under which our army lies, ready to give up the ghost" (Julius Caesar). He tells of many portents occurring just prior to Caesar's assassination: "And yesterday the bird of night did sit, even at noon-day, upon the market-place, hooting and shrieking." There was also during the night many other omens, *e.g.*, a violent thunder storm, a lioness whelping in the street, the neighing of horses, the ominous dreams of Calphurnia, Caesar's wife, and the failure of the augurs to find a heart in the sacrificial animal.

THE PSYCHIC PRACTICES OF ANCIENT NATIONS

SEERS OR PROPHETS

The psychic faculty would be developed at an early stage in the evolution of man. It is, as Homer says, "a gift from the gods," which is not dependent on the stage of civilisation or the degree of education. Thus certain individuals in early times would have clairvoyant and clairaudient experiences. As already mentioned, there are accounts of apparitions and other psychic phenomena in the folk-lore and literature of all ancient people.

Consequently, great importance was attached in early days, not only to the auguries, but also to the visions, psychic dreams and utterances of the seers or soothsayers. Cicero says, "There exists in the minds of men, a certain oracular and prophetic power of presentiment, whereby they anticipate future events, whether they are inspired by a divine ecstasy or as it were, disengaged from the body and act freely and easily during sleep." Seers, however, were consulted not only to divine the future, but also to find out the views of the gods on any course of action or mode of life.

MEDIUMSHIP

Individuals who were psychic would tell others of their psychic experiences, and some of these psychic sensitives would act as mediums for spirit communication on behalf of the rest of the community. They would be the seers, prophets, soothsayers, shamans or oracles of olden times. In some cases, as in Ancient Greece, these mediums were recognised by the State and consulted on all matters of importance. In other instances, as in Judaea, when in their utterances the actions of the Ruler or the State were condemned, or disaster to the nation prophesied, they were regarded as being guilty of treason and might have to flee, as in the case of Elijah, to avoid imprisonment or execution.

Seers and seeresses are frequently mentioned in the works of Homer and other ancient writers, as, for example, Cassandra, seeress of Troy, whose prophecies, even although true, were always disbelieved because of the curse laid upon her by Apollo; and Calchas, the seer of the Greek army at the siege of Troy. Certain seeresses, as a rule young maidens who lived in caves or at sacred springs, were known as Sibyls.

Even in those early days it was recognised that the psychic faculty tends to be inherited. For instance, the seer, Melampus, was the ancestor of a number of famous seers, including his great grandson, Amphiaraus of Argos and the latter's son, Amphilochus. The blind Theban seer, Teiresias, had a daughter, Manto, who was famous for her prophetic powers, and so also was her son, Mopsus.

According to the Hebrew Scriptures, those of the line of Ancient Patriarchs: Abraham, Isaac, Jacob and Joseph, were seers and so were their relatives, Lot and Laban.

Also, Philip the Evangelist "had four daughters which did prophesy" (Acts 29. 9).

THE PROMOTION OF CLAIRVOYANCE

Various practices were adopted in ancient times to induce clairvoyance or trance. For example, the seer might gaze into water, a crystal or a polished metal surface.

The Urim and Thummim and other semi-precious stones on the shoulders and breast-plate of the High Priest's garment appear to have been used for the purpose of divination. According to Josephus, the Jewish historian, these stones indicated by flashes the will of Jahveh. It is possible that this was a physical phenomenon somewhat similar to the production of psychic lights during modern séances, the conditions being favourable for this to occur if there was little or no light present when the stones were consulted. On the other hand, the stones may have been used to induce clairvoyance, as in crystal-gazing, the flashing being merely an associated phenomenon.

Joseph used a silver cup for divination. This was the cup which the steward put in Benjamin's sack of corn. "Is it not from this that my lord drinks, and by this that he divines?" To induce clairvoyance, Joseph may have simply gazed into the polished interior of the cup, or he may have filled it with water and looked into this. It has been suggested by some scholars that Joseph threw pieces of silver or gold into the water in the cup for purposes of divination, but why should he resort to this crude method, when he had such finely developed clairvoyant powers?

A more modern example is seen in the case of Jacob Boehme, who had a profound mystical experience, while gazing into a polished pewter dish, which reflected sunlight.

PREDICTION BY THE DYING

People in ancient times were aware that dying people frequently become clairvoyant and can foretell the future. Cicero says, "For it often happens that those who are attacked by a severe and mortal malady, foresee that their death is at hand. And in this state they often behold ghosts and phantoms of the dead." "And that the dying are often possessed by the gift of divination, Posidonius confirms by that notorious example of a certain Rhodian who, being on his death-bed, named six of his contemporaries, saying which of them would die first, which second, which next to him, and so on." Homer in the Iliad tells how the dying Hector foretold the early death of Achilles. Cicero also mentions how the Indian, Calanus, when led to execution, was asked by Alexander the Great if he had anything to say. "Yes," replied Calanus, "we shall soon meet again." This prophecy was fulfilled, for Alexander a few days later died in Babylon. (The Magi also foretold that Alexander would die shortly after reaching Babylon.)

The death-bed blessings of Isaac and Jacob were not mere pious benedictions, but prophetic clairvoyant utterances. This is shown by the fact that when Jacob was blessing Joseph's two children, he crossed his hands so that his right hand rested on the younger son's head, as he foresaw clairvoyantly that this son was to be the greater.

PSYCHIC DREAMS

PRECOGNITIVE DREAMS

From the earliest times visions during sleep have impressed mankind. Great importance has also been attached by all nations to dreams, as presaging future events. This is shown by the writings of Herodotus, Cicero and Iamblichus, and by the Hebrew and Christian Scriptures. Dreams were considered to be the way in which gods and the spirits of the dead communicated with man and warned him of the future. Homer tells us that Agamemnon believed that Zeus revealed his will through dreams. There was also a belief that Gaea, the Greek goddess of the Earth, was the sender of dreams at certain shrines. Cicero says, "Nor indeed have men of the greatest wisdom thought it beneath them to attend to the warnings of important dreams, if at any time any such appeared to have reference to the interests of the Republic."

INCUBATION OR TEMPLE SLEEP

The visions or dreams might occur naturally, or they might be sought for by "incubation or temple sleep." In the latter case the person seeking information would go to some holy place, *e.g.*, a temple, a sacred tree or spring. There he might undergo a ritual of purification and make a sacrifice to the associated god. Then he would spend the night in the temple or shrine, sleeping on the skin of the sacrificed animal, perhaps under a sacred tree beside a sacred stream. Dreams under such conditions were considered to be of special prophetic significance. Occasionally they were in symbolic form and had to be interpreted by the priest attached to the sanctuary.

Another method practised by certain races even in comparatively recent times to get into communication with the dead, was for the person to spend the night sleeping on the tomb of the departed, or on one of his relics, *e.g.*, his skull.

In the Celtic rite, known as Taghairm, practised formerly in the Highlands, a person was wrapped up in a bullock's hide, only his head being free, and was left overnight at some lonely spot beside a cataract or at the bottom of a precipice. It was believed that such conditions promoted spirit communications. An account is given in "The Lady of the Lake" by Sir Walter Scott, of how the seer, Brian, carried out this rite for Roderick Dhu.

PSYCHIC DREAMS IN THE OLD TESTAMENT

Like other Eastern people, the Hebrews recognised that dreams could be prophetic in nature, and instances of such dreams occur in their Scriptures. "For God speaks in one way, and in two, though man does not perceive it. In a dream, in a vision of the night, when deep sleep falls upon men, while they slumber on their beds, then he opens the ears of men, and terrifies them with warnings, that he may turn man aside from his deed, and cut off pride from man" (Job 33. 14-17).

In recording such dreams, it is generally said that God, or the Lord, or an angel, appeared and spoke to the person having the dream. Thus Abimelech, King of Gerar, had a dream in which God told him not to marry Sarah, as she was in reality Abraham's wife. Jacob had psychic dreams, one of which was symbolic, as he saw a ladder reaching up into heaven with angels ascending and descending, and the Lord spoke unto him in the dream. His son, Joseph, when a young lad, had two prophetic dreams both of which were symbolic in nature. In the first, his brothers' sheaves of corn bowed down to his sheaf, and in the second, the sun, moon and eleven stars, *i.e.*, his father, mother and brothers, did homage to him. Some biblical scholars have attributed his dreams to the wishful thinking of an egotistical and spoilt boy, but this does not take into account the facts that the dreams actually came to pass and that Joseph was clairvoyant and therefore likely to have psychic dreams.

Pharaoh's butler and baker had symbolic dreams which Joseph, owing to his psychic powers, was able to interpret. Pharaoh himself had two dreams. In the first he saw the fat and lean kine; in the second the full and the blasted ears of corn. Joseph interpreted the symbolism and Pharaoh, realising that Joseph was a man under divine guidance, appointed him to be Governor of Egypt, in spite of his youth and inexperience.

The Bible also tells how Solomon went to Gideon, a "high place," and offered burnt offerings, and the Lord appeared to him in a dream by night and spoke to him about his future. There is also the account of how Nebuchadnezzar had symbolic dreams, which the Hebrew seer, Daniel, was able to interpret.

PSYCHIC DREAMS IN THE NEW TESTAMENT

In the New Testament, it is said that the Magi from the East were warned by God in a dream that they should not return to Herod; also that an angel of the Lord (*i.e.* a spirit) appeared in a dream to Joseph, the husband of the Virgin Mary, and told him to flee with Mary and the child Jesus into Egypt. Later, an angel again appeared to him in a dream, telling him to return to the land of Israel, as Herod had died.

Some of the personages in the Bible, especially the Old Testament, may have been purely mythical, but the fact remains that the authors recognised that psychic dreams of a prophetic nature could occur.

PSYCHIC DREAMS OF OTHER NATIONS

Psychic dreams are also mentioned in the literature of other nations. Cicero gives many instances in his work "On Divination." He says, "Who, again, can despise those two dreams, which are so frequently dwelt upon by the Stoics?— one concerning Simonides, who, having found the dead body of a man who was a stranger to him lying in the road, buried it. Having performed this office, he was about to embark in a ship, when the man he had buried appeared to him in a dream at night, and warned him not to undertake the voyage, for that if he did he would perish by shipwreck.

Therefore, he returned home again, but all the other people who sailed in that vessel were lost."

Cicero goes on to say, "The other dream, which is a very celebrated one, is related in the following manner: Two Arcadians, who were intimate friends, were travelling together, and arriving at Megara, one of them took up his quarters at an inn, the other at a friend's house. After supper, when they had both gone to bed, the Arcadian who was staying at his friend's house, saw an apparition of his fellow-traveller at the inn, who prayed him to come to his assistance immediately, as the inn-keeper was going to murder him. Alarmed at this intimation, he started from his sleep; but thinking it nothing but an idle dream, he lay down again. Presently, the apparition appeared to him again in his sleep, and entreated him, though he would not come to his assistance while yet alive, at least not to leave his death unavenged. He told him further that the inn-keeper had first murdered him, and then cast him into a dung cart, where he lay covered with filth; and begged him to go early to the gate of the town, before any cart could leave the town. Much excited by this second vision, he went early next morning to the gate of the town, and met with the driver of the cart, and asked him what he had in his wagon. The driver, upon this question, ran away in a fright. The dead body was then discovered, and the inn-keeper, the evidence being clear against him, was brought to punishment."

FEES FOR MEDIUMSHIP

That the interpreters of dreams made charges for their services is shown by the writings of Chrysippus on dreams. He tells how "someone dreamed in the night that he saw an egg hanging on his bed-post. He consulted an interpreter, who informed him that the dream signified that a sum of money was hidden under his bed. He dug, and found a little gold surrounded by a heap of silver. Upon this, he sent the interpreter as much of the silver as he thought a fair reward. Then said the interpreter, "What none of the yolk?" For that part of the egg appeared to have intimated gold, while the rest meant silver. In connection with fees for mediumship, it may be noted here that the greatest charge that has ever been recorded was in the case of the classic seer, Melampus. He charged as his fee for healing the daughter of Proitus, King of Argos, marriage with the latter's daughter, the Princess Iphianassa, and one-third of his kingdom.

In 1 Samuel 9. 7-8, Saul discusses with his servant what fee should be payed to the seer or prophet, Samuel, for his services in finding the lost asses.

PSYCHIC DREAMS OF FAMOUS PEOPLE

Hannibal, the renowned Carthaginian general, had psychic dreams. In one of these, he was warned not to remove a golden column from a certain temple; in another he was advised to carry the war into Italy. Another Carthaginian general, Hamilcar, when besieging Syracuse, dreamt he heard a voice telling him that he would sup next day in Syracuse. In the morning, sedition arose in his camp, and the Syracusans, observing this, attacked and captured Hamilcar, so that his dream came true, but not in the way he had hoped.

Xerxes (519-465 B.C.), King of Persia, had visions in his sleep on two successive nights urging him, in spite of all advice to the contrary, to send a Persian army across the Hellespont to invade Greece.

Croesus (died 546 B.C.), King of Lydia, dreamt that his son, Atys, would be killed by a blow from an iron weapon. In spite of all precautions, the dream came true, the son being killed in this way in a boar hunt.

The great Greek poet and dramatist, Sophocles (495-406 B.C.), was clairvoyant. When a heavy golden goblet was stolen from the Temple of Herakles, the god appeared to him in a dream and revealed the identity of the thief. Sophocles paid no attention to the dream, but after it was repeated for several nights, he laid the matter before the Court of the Areopagus. The person named in the dreams was arrested, and under torture confessed his guilt and restored the goblet.

Xenophon (born about 431 B.C.) was a historian and essayist, and disciple of Socrates. He attached himself without any definite military rank to the army of the Younger Cyrus, and when the latter had been slain in battle and the Greek generals soon afterwards treacherously killed by the Persians, he was inspired by psychic dreams to take over the Greek Army of "The Ten Thousand" and direct their famous retreat from Mesopotamia through Armenia to the Black Sea and Byzantium.

When the great philosopher Socrates (469-399 B.C.) was in prison at Athens, he told his friend Crito that he would die in three days, because he had seen in a dream a woman of extreme beauty who called him by his name, and quoted in his presence this verse of Homer—"On the third day you'll reach the fruitful Phthia." The prophecy proved to be true.

Aristotle, the renowned philosopher, tells of the prophetic dream of his friend Eudemus. The latter was seriously ill and not expected to recover. He had a dream in which he saw a beautiful youth who told him that he would soon recover; also that Alexander, the Tyrant, would die shortly afterwards. In addition, he dreamt that he would return home after five years' absence. The first part of the dream was fulfilled, but Eudemus died at the end of five years, instead of returning to his home. Perhaps this was the true significance of the dream.

THE ORACLES

The oracles were gifted seers or mediums attached as a rule to a shrine or temple of some god, such as Apollo or Zeus. They gave clairvoyant messages or trance utterances to inquirers, and as the information might be in symbolic or cryptic form, a priest was usually present for its interpretation.

RITUAL AT THE ORACULAR SHRINES

The temples were frequently associated with a sacred spring or stream. In ancient days, many of these natural waters were regarded as sacred owing to the belief that there was present in the water a divine power or *mana*, later held to be a god or spirit. This could be harmful to an evil-doer bathing in the water, but could cleanse from all sin and bless the penitent and good. Moreover, if a good man drank the water he became united with the mana or the god, and thus became inspired. Hence it was a common practice at such oracular shrines for the oracle, after a preliminary purification process, to drink some of the sacred water prior to giving clairvoyance.

Before consulting the oracle, the inquirer might have to make special preparation by fasting and by drinking and washing in the sacred water. In addition, he might have to offer up a sacrifice, *e.g.*, a black lamb, to the god, and sleep on the skin overnight in the temple. This was known as temple or incubation sleep. The oracle was consulted the following morning. During the night the individual might have a psychic dream or a vision, and if this was symbolic or obscure, the oracle or the priest gave an interpretation.

The seeress or oracle at the shrine also carried out beforehand a definite ritual. For instance, in the Temple at Delphi she prepared herself by washing and purification; then in suitable attire she entered the sanctuary, drank water from the sacred fountain of Cassotis, ate some of the fruit of a bay tree which grew there, and finally sat on a seat mounted on a high gilded wooden tripod. The tripod was set over a cleft in the ground through which rose cold vapours, believed to induce an ecstatic state in the Oracle. A priest was present to note and interpret her message.

FAMOUS ORACLES

The most famous oracles were in Greece, *e.g.*, those at Delphi, Argos and Dodona, although others existed in great numbers throughout the Near East—Babylonia, Asia Minor, Libya, Egypt and later in Italy. Even in the West the Druids had oracular centres.

The leading Greek oracle was that in the Temple of Apollo at Delphi. It was in existence about 800 B.C., being mentioned in Homer's poems. The Delphic seeress was a maiden of noble birth. She was referred to as the Pythia or Pythoness, the Temple according to mythology being guarded at first by the serpent, Pytho, until slain by Apollo, who then became god of the shrine.

These oracles, especially the one at Delphi, were consulted by emperors, kings, statesmen, generals and others, on all matters of importance, such as war, law, religion and the founding of colonies. Pythagoras, Socrates, Plato and Herodotus held the Delphic Oracle in high esteem. Socrates advised Xenophon to consult the Pythia as to whether he should join the Persians under Cyrus.

THE TESTING OF THE DELPHIC ORACLE

Herodotus tells how Croesus, King of Lydia, wished to know whether he should go to war against the Persians led by Cyrus. He therefore tested a number of the oracles in Greece and one in Libya. He sent agents to each oracle, instructing them to ask on a certain day what he, Croesus, was doing that day. The Delphic Oracle gave the correct answer, "The smell has come to my sense of a hard-shelled tortoise boiling and bubbling with lamb's flesh in a bronze pot; the cauldron underneath is of bronze, and of bronze the lid." Croesus on that day had cut up a tortoise and a lamb and boiled them together in a bronze cauldron with a bronze lid.

Then he asked the Delphic and another oracle, whether he should fight the Persians or seek an alliance with them. The reply of both oracles was that if he attacked the Persians, he would destroy a great empire. He asked the Delphic Oracle a third question whether his reign would be a long one. The reply was that "when it comes to pass that a mule shall sit on the Median throne, he had to run and abide not." Croesus believed that it was unlikely that a mule would ever become King of the Medes, so he made war on Cyrus and was defeated. Cyrus was so impressed with his outstanding personality that he spared his life and made him his friend. Croesus later asked the Delphic Oracle why she had misled him, but she pointed out that he had misinterpreted the replies. Firstly, he did not ask whether the great empire was his own or that of Persia, and secondly, Cyrus was a mule metaphorically speaking. His parents were of different races, his mother being a princess of the Medes and his father a Persian of less noble birth.

To test the Delphic Oracle, the Roman Emperor Trajan on one occasion handed her a sealed packet, and requested an answer. The Pythia asked for paper, and much to the priest's astonishment, put a blank sheet in an envelope and sealed it. It was then found that the Emperor had given to the Oracle a blank sheet of paper instead of a written question.

THE TESTING OF OTHER ORACLES

In the days of Plutarch, there was a Governor of Sicily, a religious sceptic, who wished to test the renowned oracle,

Mopsus. He therefore sent a message in a sealed envelope to the seer, giving his messenger full instructions to guard against fraud or trickery. The messenger spent the night in the shrine of Mopsus, and in his sleep had a vision of a beautiful young man, who merely uttered the word, "Black," and vanished. The Governor was so overcome with emotion on hearing this message that he fell on his knees. In his note to the seer, he had asked the question, "Shall I sacrifice a white bull or a black?"

Herodotus tells how a person, called Mardonius, sent a man to consult various oracles on his behalf. Arriving at the Oracle of Apollo in Thebes, he chose three of the citizens to note down the message of the Oracle. They were unable to do so, as the message was not given in the Hellenic tongue, but in the Carian—a language known only to the messenger himself.

Herodotus also tells how the Roman Emperor Vespasian was visiting the Oracle at the Temple of Serapis in Egypt. Wishing to be alone in the temple, he ordered the doors to be shut to prevent other people entering. Much to his surprise he saw a well-known Egyptian who, he thought, was lying ill at his home eighty miles away. On making full inquiries he found that the Egyptian had never left his home.

PSYCHIC OR SPIRIT HEALING

Psychic healing was practised by all ancient nations. In some countries, *e.g.*, Greece, there were doctors, some with sound ideas on the promotion, of good health, *e.g.*, Hippocrates and Galen, but when their work did not meet with success, recourse was made to psychic healing carried out by seers, prophets or oracles. At certain healing shrines, doctors worked in association with psychic healers.

ILLNESS OF THE MIND AND BODY

In early times, no clear distinction was made between illness of the physical body and of the mind or "soul." Disease was believed to be due to the person having sinned or to his being possessed by a demon, and therefore it naturally followed that to effect a cure the sufferer had to be freed from sin or from the possessing demon. For this reason in many nations there was a close connection between religion and healing (medical or psychic), and the priest rather than the medical man was frequently summoned to deal with disease. The adepts of the Taoistic religion in China not only held that disease was evidence of sin, but that the sick should be imprisoned so that they could reflect on their sins.

In primitive races, even in modern times there is a close link between magic and medicine. It is held by some that no one dies a natural death but that all disease is due to magic; in other words, some evilly-disposed individual has projected his evil power over the sick person.

THE USE OF SUGGESTION

In psychic healing in ancient times, there is no doubt that suggestion played a part in the successful treatment of certain diseases. This is shown by the accounts of the healing "miracles" of Jesus in the New Testament. He would tell certain patients that their sins were forgiven or would assure them that the demons had been driven out. This set their minds at rest. He would then implant helpful ideas in their minds. He would also remove doubters and scorners from the room, as these would render conditions less favourable for healing; or he would take the sufferer away from the noise and clamour of the village to a quiet spot before healing him. An unstable patient would be advised to tell no man, lest as a result of scornful or critical remarks, doubts would arise in his mind, which might cause a relapse.

BELIEF IN THE DIVINE POWER OF SACRED STREAMS

The power of suggestion was also resorted to in the use of the water of sacred streams or wells at many healing temples. It was claimed that the divine power or god of such water gave it healing properties because a sick person who bathed in it was cleansed from all sin, believed to be the cause of disease. It was also held that if a sick person drank the water or threw one of his possessions into it, this united him with the healing power, and would bring about his recovery. The water in itself was not considered to be responsible for the healing. It was merely the means of uniting the sufferer with the divine power or god, who at the same time had to be invoked.

There were many sacred waters in ancient days. Some were noted for their success in the treatment of particular diseases, *e.g.*, leprosy, rabies, gout, complaints of children or of animals. Elisha told Naaman to bathe in the River Jordan seven times, so that he would be cured of leprosy. Of course, some of the healing springs had definite medicinal properties owing to the presence of various mineral salts, as is recognised in modern times.

Until comparatively recently, there was still a belief, even in Western Europe, regarding the divine power of water. For instance, there was the practice in Scotland of throwing a sixpence into a well or spring to determine whether a sick person would recover or not. The particular side of the coin which fell uppermost indicated the state of health or the likelihood of recovery—"gif the cross of the sixpence be up, then they are weill, gif not, they are not weill." There was a similar practice in England to find out whether a disease was due to witchcraft.

THE WATER TEST FOR WITCHES

The common practice of ducking persons suspected of witchcraft was based on the belief that the divine force in the water would reject a witch, so that she would float and could not be drowned, but it would accept an innocent person so that she would sink in the water and be drowned. King James the Sixth of Scotland and First of England says in his work on "Daemonologie," "It appears that God hath appointed (for a supernatural) signe of the monstrous impietie of witches) that the water shall refuse to receive them into her bosome that have shaken off the sacred waters of Baptisme and wilfully refused the benefite thereof." The utter ignorance shown by this statement was wide-spread and led to the wholesale torturing and burning of men and women during the Christian Era on the charge of witchcraft. At the instigation of King James himself and his Calvinistic advisers, there was in Scotland, in 1591, a mass trial followed by fiendish torturing and burning of two hundred male and female witches for "eine hellish conspiracie to bewitch and Browne his Majestic corning from Denmarke"—and all because his ship was held up by contrary winds for some weeks.

SACRED TREES AND SPRINGS

Certain trees, particularly the oak, were regarded as sacred, especially if growing beside a sacred well or stream, and they were believed to contribute to the healing forces of such places. At the healing shrine of the Oracle of Zeus and Dione at Dodona, the patient slept overnight underneath an oak tree beside the stream. Under such conditions he might have psychic dreams.

Psychic dreams and visions were always regarded as of importance in healing. There is the story of how Ptolemy, the friend of Alexander the Great, was cured of a poisoned wound. He was with Alexander on a campaign, when he was wounded by a poisoned arrow. He was lying in bed in great agony, apparently dying. Alexander was watching by his bedside, and falling asleep, dreamt he saw the pet serpent of his mother with a plant root in its mouth. He was told in the dream that the plant grew in the neighbourhood, and if its root were applied to Ptolemy's wound, it would cure him. Alexander told others of his dream. Some of the plant roots were obtained and when applied to the wound, Ptolemy was cured. In the same way others with similar wounds were successfully treated.

CELTIC PRACTICES

In Northern European countries, *e.g.*, among Celtic races, the belief in sacred trees and springs was also prevalent, but in this case the healing power or god of the spring might be invoked by hanging a rag or a piece of the clothing of the sick person on the tree. It was held that the cloth was the means by which the disease was passed from the patient to the tree, and at the same time the healing power was transmitted from the spring or tree to the patient. The Druids were not only seers, but were also skilled in medical lore, especially in the use of plants for the treatment of disease. Thus they used mistletoe to counteract poison and to promote animal fertility, and the plant Samolus to cure cattle diseases.

PSYCHIC HEALING BY THE ANCIENT GREEKS

Psychic healing was carried out in Ancient Greece and neighbouring countries hundreds of years before the Christian Era. Most of the healing centres were dedicated to the god Asklepios, and were therefore termed asklepeions. They were frequently associated with sacred springs or streams.

While the Early Christian leaders, *e.g.*, Origen and Celsus, admitted that such healing occurred outside the

Christian Church, they attributed its success to the work of demons or the devil, just as the Jewish leaders said the healing works of Jesus were due to Beelzebub. Some of the Early Christians claimed that God inflicted mankind with disease and pestilence to punish the enemies of Christianity and all other unbelievers.

THE CULT OF ASKLEPIOS

Asklepios (Latin Aesculapius) was, according to Homer and Pindar, a highly capable doctor of the Greek heroic age. It was believed that he travelled from place to place healing the sick. After his death, it was held that he continued his work through various healing mediums or oracles. He ultimately came to be regarded as a Saviour-God, and was worshipped throughout Greece and its colonies.

It was said that he revealed himself to mankind in the form of a snake, the symbol of prophecy and rejuvenescence. But snakes were also considered to be his valuable servants because of their knowledge of healing herbs. For these reasons tame and harmless snakes were kept at his healing shrines, and if they came in contact with the patients, the latter believed that it was the touch of the god, healing them. In ancient statues, the god is shown holding a staff with a serpent coiled round it, a symbol still used as an emblem by the medical profession. The belief in the power of snakes to cure disease was evidently held also by the Israelites, for it is said in the Book of Numbers (21. 9) of the Old Testament that Moses was commanded by the "Lord" to make "a bronze serpent, and set it on a pole" to cure the Israelites of snake bite.

There were about two hundred temples dedicated to Asklepios in Greece and neighbouring countries. The most celebrated one was at Epidaurus, a great festival being held there in the god's honour every five years. Other asklepeions were at Pergamos, Cos, Ephesus, Corinth, Athens and Rome.

His cult was introduced to the Romans in 293 B.C. There was a great plague at the time, and when the Sibylline books were consulted, the rulers were advised to appeal to the god Asklepios for help. Messengers were therefore sent in a ship to Epidaurus, and it was claimed that the god in the form of a serpent was brought from the temple there to Rome. Such a reptile was said to have left the Temple at Epidaurus and crept on board the ship. On the return to Rome it sprang from the boat on to an island in the River Tiber, where later a healing centre was established.

The Temple at Pergamos was devoted to healing, just as that at Delphi to other forms of mediumship. No medicine was given at this asklepeion, but simply psychic treatment. The patients were also encouraged to carry out physical exercises and to study music and drama.

THE PRACTICE AT HEALING CENTRES

In some of these healing centres, oracles, priests and doctors, all worked together. There were also sleep houses for the patients, providing for incubation or temple sleep. Thus the god might reveal in a dream to the sick person the nature of the disease and the remedy; or he might appear in a vision and give treatment, in one recorded case, restoring in this way sight to a blind man. In the morning the seer would be consulted and the priest would be in attendance to interpret, if necessary, the patient's dream and the trance utterance of the oracle. In this way diagnosis of the disease might be made and the best method of treatment revealed. In addition, the oracle might give psychic healing, transmitting the healing forces to the patient by the "laying on of hands" or other methods. In fact, if the oracle was a genuine healer, this would be by far the most important part of the treatment.

The power of suggestion at these healing centres would no doubt be marked. It would supplement the spirit healing forces and create the right conditions for these to act. It cannot, however, be claimed that psychic healing is due purely to the power of suggestion, as modern experience shows that it may be effective with unconscious patients and even with babies.

The cures were recorded on tablets, and if the remedies recommended by the god or oracle proved effective, they were used in later medical practice. It is on record that the Sophist, Polemon, who was suffering from arthritis, was told in a dream by the spirit of Asklepios that the cure for his complaint was to drink plenty of hot water. Inscriptions on tablets at Epidaurus told how forty-eight people were cured of a wide variety of diseases, including blindness. The walls of a passage-way were covered with such tablets erected by those who had been cured. Records at Rome tell also of cures at the asklepeion there of blindness, pleurisy, spitting blood and other conditions.

THE INFLUENCE OF ASKLEPIOS

Asklepios and the workers at his shrines were responsible for sound ideas of healthy living, the influence of which was felt for many centuries. He was held in such high esteem that in the end he came to be regarded as a Saviour-God, helpful and gracious in his healing work to mankind. In fact, he was revered as highly by the non-Christian nations, as Jesus was by the Christian, being referred to in "salvationist terminology" as "Lord Healer, Gentle One" and "Saviour of the World." He was amongst the last of the Pagan deities to go down in the advance of Christianity; his healing shrines were swept away, and their oracles or mediums persecuted. The Christian philosopher Justin said that "evil demons, in foreknowledge of Jesus, raised up Asklepios to detract from the Christian claims" of healing. This statement is so bigoted that it needs no comment.

EMPEDOCLES, HIPPOCRATES AND GALEN

Empedocles (490-430 B.C.) was a physician, and a great philosopher and social reformer. He was also a seer and a powerful psychic healer, and was said to have acquired information regarding the use of drugs by "unique" means. He realised the value of suggestion and music in the treatment of disease, the latter helping the patient to relax. It was claimed that he had cured a woman who had been in a deep coma (and therefore presumed to be dead) for 30 days. His healing work was cited by the Early Christian Fathers, Clement and Origen, in support of the Christian healing miracles.

Hippocrates, born at Cos about 460 B.C., was a celebrated Greek doctor, who, like Asklepios, had a considerable influence on medical practice for many centuries, and has been referred to as the father of medicine. He was a descendant of a priestly family, the Asklepiadae, who were followers of Asklepios, and who collected and preserved medical traditions and knowledge, and passed them in secret from father to son. He was responsible for the oath taken by the medical practitioner in olden times, the Hippocratic Jusjurandum, to lead a life of purity, to practise the art of medicine in an honourable and humane fashion, and not to divulge the secrets of the profession. He based his treatment on the belief that there is an essence in man, which in itself has a curative effect. He maintained that disease of the physical body can be detected by the eye of the "soul."

Galen, another celebrated doctor, was born at Pergamos in 130 A.D. In his writings, he tells how the patients at the healing sanctuaries were faithful in obeying the instructions of the oracle or priest.

PSYCHIC HEALING IN OTHER NATIONS

It must be remembered that, in addition to the Ancient Greeks, psychic healing was carried out in most nations by psychic individuals—seers, prophets (Elijah and Elisha), and shamans; and by Jesus and his apostles, and St. Paul. It was recognised as a spiritual gift in certain rulers, *e.g.*, Pyrrhus, King of Epirus, and the Roman Emperors Vespasian and Hadrian. Pliny tells of certain men being able to cure snakebite by touch. St. Paul was also able to do so. And Cicero records how the curative value of the herb, Aristolochia, for snake-bite, was revealed in a dream to the person after whom it was later named.

ABSENT HEALING

"Absent" healing or healing "in the silence" was also practised in ancient times, *e.g.*, by Elisha in the case of Naaman, the leper; and Jesus in his healing of the servant of the Centurion, and of the daughter of the Syrophenician woman. For such healing, articles "psychically charged" by the seer or medium might be used, as in the case of Elisha's staff in the treatment of the son of the Shunammite woman (2 Kings 4. 29); and St. Paul's handkerchiefs or aprons (Acts 19. 12).

HEALING IN LATER TIMES

Throughout the succeeding ages, psychic healing has been practised in almost all parts of the world, whether by kings, like Edward the Confessor of England, or Philip the First of France, or by saints or mystics, such as St. Bernard, and St. Patrick, or by the countless unrecorded seers or shamans of all nations, civilised or primitive. In all instances the methods have been essentially the same, being based on the application of psychic healing forces, supplemented frequently by the effect of suggestion on the mental outlook of the sick person. However, the manner in which the healing has been carried out, the exact procedure adopted, and the ritual, if any, observed have varied according to the religious beliefs of the healer and patient, the stage of civilisation, and the age in which they lived.

Healing takes place, no matter how divergent may be the ideas as to its source and its mode of action. No doubt there has been considerable embellishment in recording the cures in the past. In many cases the so-called cure has been merely temporary or purely fictitious. Nevertheless, to-day there are recorded in many healing sanctuaries in this and other countries countless lasting cures, and there can be no question of the fact that there is a psychic healing power in certain individuals, whether inherent in them or transmitted by them mediumistically from the spirit world. This power has been exercised throughout the ages, irrespective of colour, nation or creed.

MYSTICISM AND RELIGION

In all ages seers have claimed that they have had transcendent experiences in which they were in direct contact with the Divine Mind. This form of mediumship is known as *mysticism*, or in Central and Northern Asia, as *Shamanism*, the seers being also termed *mystics* or *shamans*. It is not confined to the higher forms of religion, being found in primitive races and in ancient times.

THE OCCURRENCE OF MYSTICAL EXPERIENCES

The deepest mystical experiences are beyond the powers of the ordinary psychic. Even with the true mystic, they cannot be made to occur merely by exertion of will-power. In a sense, they may be regarded as' given' by forces outwith the mystic's control. But experience has shown that they take place more readily under certain conditions. Thus various practices have been used in the past to promote their occurrence. The seers in many cases had to undergo a long course of training under an experienced leader. Then they might fast for a prolonged period in solitude and contemplation, until they made contact with higher spirit forces. At this stage they were frequently in a state of trance, the ordinary conscious mind being in complete abeyance, with no sense of time and surroundings. To induce trance, a practice adopted by certain mystics was to focus the attention on a single point or object by the constant repetition of a certain phrase or short prayer, or as in yoga, by rhythmical breathing. This procedure was continued until even the focal point faded away and the mind, now free from all conscious thoughts, became open to mystical impressions.

In the Quietist movement of mysticism, it was recognised that perfect communion with God could be attained only in a state of complete quietude, 'the stillness of the soul in the presence of God,' which St. Theresa termed, 'the prayer of quiet.' This passive, receptive attitude, free from any kind of active thought, was described by the Protestant mystic, Jacob Boehme (a Silesian cobbler), as to 'stand still from the thinking of self and the willing of self and become 'quiet and passive to the impressions of the eternal Word and Spirit.' (See *Mysticism and World Religion*.)

THE NATURE OF MYSTICAL EXPERIENCES

Such experiences are vivid and overwhelming, but quite indescribable. There is a profound sense of the life which permeates the Universe and of the basic unity of all things and creatures in it. This unity or oneness is not affected by space or time, but belongs to the Eternal Now and signifies union with God.

The mystics at such times have a feeling of the Supreme Good at the heart of the universe, of ineffable peace ("the peace of God which passeth all understanding") and of great exaltation or ecstasy.

While all such experiences are essentially the same in nature, there may be differences in their interpretation depending on the religious beliefs of the mystic. They create such a love of God in his heart that he is forced to express it in a life of love and service to his fellowmen. The realisation that there is a basic unity throughout the universe, gets rid of all sense of separateness, even between living creatures, including man, and this carries with it the conviction that man belongs to a vast Brotherhood of beings, in which there is no room for conceit or selfishness.

The most outstanding features of mystical experiences are the state of trance, the overwhelming sense of spiritual enlightenment or illumination, the awareness of the unity of all things, and the feeling of utter bliss and ecstasy.

Mysticism is essentially a psychic phenomenon, and the seers concerned may also be, clairvoyant, clairaudient, or may give trance utterances of prophetic nature. They may also have the power of healing.

In the past they were not merely individuals who spent their lives in contemplation. In many instances they were energetic, forceful characters whose mystical experiences appeared to spur them on to great activities, as in the case of Gautama the Buddha, Lao-Tsze, St. Paul, St. Augustine, Joan of Arc, St. Francis, St. Theresa of Avila, and Fox. Their mystical experiences were not due to some abnormal condition of the mind, such as hysteria, as has been suggested, but to the exercise of psychic power. Raynor C. Johnson points out in his work 'The Imprisoned Splendour,' that "If such men, whose personalities so profoundly impressed their contemporaries, and who contributed so enormously to the world's treasury, were self-deluded or psychopaths, we suggest that the world could do with many more of them! Their "delusion" is preferable to our sanity."

MYSTICISM IN INDIA-HINDUISM

Mysticism since ancient times has held a central place in the Hindu religions. The Hindu sacred books, the Upanishads, dating back to about 800 B.C. are based on the esoteric or secret teachings of ancient mystics. These books show a combination of mystical philosophy and deep intuitive insight, which has rendered them for almost 3000 years a source of great spiritual inspiration to millions of people. The seers claimed that as a result of self-discipline, fasting and meditation, they had had mystical experiences in which they had contacted the Divine Mind. They withdrew as a rule to the quiet of forest or mountain where each spent his life in contemplation and in the teaching of a group of followers or disciples.

Their work was continued throughout the ages by a long series of religious reformers, many of whom were mystics, including Gautama, the Buddha, founder of the Buddhist religion; Mahavira, the founder of the Jain religion; Nanak, the first Guru and founder of the Sikh religion; and Ramakrishna.

BUDDHISM—GAUTAMA

Prince Siddhartha Gautama (about 560-480 B.C.) was heir to the throne of the Sakya tribe of Hindus. He was so disturbed in mind by the occurrence of poverty, illness and the weaknesses of old age in the world, that he left his wife and child and wandered about without money as a monk in search of knowledge. After some years, while sitting in meditation under a wild fig tree, illumination came to him. He learned that the Key to Wisdom lay in the principle of the Law of the Deed or Karma, which states that "from good must come good and from evil must come evil." After this mystical experience he was known as "The Buddha, The Enlightened One," and the fig tree under which he sat was called "The Bo Tree" or "Tree of Wisdom."

In his mildness of manner, his simple way of living, his zeal, chastity and humility, he has been likened to St. Francis of Assisi. In his "boundless compassion" for his fellowmen, he has been likened to Jesus.

Gautama taught that pain and suffering are always associated with life on earth, and therefore the only way to get rid of these conditions is to free oneself from earthly existence by reaching the state of Nirvana, an ideal state of complete attunement to the Divine Existence. This can be done only by suppressing all desires and passions, and even by losing the sense of individual personality. To accomplish this, an ascending sequence of virtuous earth lives or incarnations is necessary, an individual being chained to "The Wheel of Life" until the state of Nirvana is reached.

Gautama set a high moral code and taught that the six fundamental virtues are charity, purity, patience, courage, contemplation and knowledge. An important difference between his religion and Brahminism, the original Hindu religion, was that while the latter upheld the caste system, which is based on class distinction according to birth, Gautama recognised that virtue, and not birth, is the true test of spirituality.

He founded the Buddhist religion, which spread from India, throughout Tibet, China, Burma, Siam and Japan, and is one of the great religions of the world.

Jainism differs from Buddhism in that its founder, Prince Mahavira, favoured ascetism in his followers, whereas Gautama, like Socrates, Lao-Tsze and Confucius, advocated moderation—"The Middle Path."

MYSTICISM IN CHINA—TAOISM

Mysticism was of importance in China, not only owing to the spread of Buddhism, but also because it entered largely into Taoism. This religion is based on the teaching of the mystic Lao-Tsze, who was born about 604 B.C. His teaching was readily accepted because the practice of contemplation was an essential element in the religious traditions of Ancient China. Certain individuals would retire from the ordinary affairs of the world and would exist as hermits, leading lives of simplicity and contemplation. These men were responsible in the early stages for the growth and development of Taoism.

A basic feature of religion in Ancient China was the offering of sacrifices through mediums or "shihs" to the spirits of ancestors. It was believed that in this way these spirits might be induced to enter or possess the mediums for the time being, and communicate with those still in earth-life. Information might thus be obtained as to whether the spirits were happy in the afterlife, and whether anything could be done to help them.

Later it was held that if a medium could cleanse the mind from all worldly thoughts, and could also still all physical and mental activities by certain practices, such as breath-control as in Indian yoga, it was possible to have intimate contact with higher spirit forces. Under such conditions the medium, like other mystics, might have ecstatic and transcendent experiences, and acquire power over his physical body, rendering it immune to injury and disease. In later Taoism, the "adepts" claimed that by leading an "inner life of vision and meditation," they could not only acquire immunity from all harm to their physical body, but could so "etherealise" that body as to render it immortal. It was believed that at death this "etherealised" body entered directly the Sacred Island of Paradise; what was left still on earth, the visible body, was merely an illusory form. As previously mentioned, it was held that physical weakness and disease were signs of sin.

In Taoism spontaneity and simplicity of life were regarded as of importance. It was said that "the sage loves kindness, sincerity and peace, and requites injuries with good deeds." The good Taoist avoids excess, extravagance and indulgence. He has "three treasures love, moderation and not venturing to go ahead of the world."

CONFUCIANISM

Mysticism also entered into the other Chinese religion, Confucianism. While Confucius (551-478 B.C.) does not appear to have had mystical experiences, he believed that he had been given a mission from "heaven" to teach and reform mankind, and this inspired him in his work. He devoted his attention to living and working in harmony with the Will of God, *i.e.*, to a way of life, whereas the Taoist sought for mystical contact with, and apprehension of, the Divine Mind, the "Supreme Reality." The way of life, according to Confucius, was to "fix your mind on the right way, hold fast to it in your moral character and follow it up in kindness to others." He advocated the avoidance of extreme, in all things; "Perfect is the virtue which is according to the Mean," *i.e.*, "The Path of the Mean" or "The Middle Path" of Gautama. He also enunciated The Golden rule "What you do not want done to yourself, do not do to others."

Religious leaders in China, who followed Confucius, continued and developed his teaching. Some of these were mystics, *e.g.*, Mencius. As a result of their teaching and also Taoistic and Buddhist influences, mystical elements were introduced into Confucianism resulting many centuries later (800 or 900 A.D.) in the school of thought known as Neo-Confucianism, a religion specially suited for scholars who were concerned with the deeper issues of life. These men with their fresh outlook on life introduced a new element into Confucianism and as a result the old religion gained fresh life and authority.

MYSTICISM IN ANCIENT GREECE

The religion of Ancient Greece was polytheistic. There was a large number of personal gods, who had to be worshipped and propitiated by prayer and sacrifice in order to obtain their goodwill and help. Mysticism does not appear to have entered to any great extent into the religious life. However, there were certain great philosophers whose teaching was somewhat mystical in nature. Belonging to this category were seers, such as Pythagoras, Empedocles (see earlier) and Socrates. These men were not true mystics in that they did not direct their whole lives to seeking direct contact or union with the Divine Mind, but they had great psychic gifts and devoted their lives to teaching and healing.

PYTHAGORAS

Pythagoras (born about 582 B.C.) was a seer with the gift of clairvoyance and prophecy, and, it was claimed, knowledge of the language of birds, and animals. He is said to have had mystical experience or illumination, whilst gazing at the stars. He recognised the superior psychic powers of women, and taught them so that they could take part in the church services. (In this respect his attitude is in marked contrast to that of St. Paul.) His disciples were required to lead lives of strict purity and simplicity. He was a great teacher and his philosophy influenced that of Socrates, Plato, Aristotle and others, including the Early Christian Fathers.

SOCRATES

Socrates (469-399 B.C.) was one of the greatest teachers and moral philosophers the world has ever known. He had powerful psychic gifts, including trance mediumship, clairvoyance and clairaudience. Thus he tells how he was guided throughout his life by a spirit voice in which he had implicit trust. There is the story of how after the Athenians lost the battle of Delium, he had to flee along with the defeated general, Laches. At length they reached a place where three roads met. Socrates refused to go by the same road as the others, and when asked the reason, said that he was restrained by a god. He managed to escape, but the others were overtaken by the enemy's cavalry. On another occasion, Socrates warned a friend, Crito, not to go by a certain path. The latter refused to take his advice, and as a result suffered an eye injury through contact with the branch of a tree.

Cicero says of him, "I cannot, however, avoid mentioning one fact in the history of this philosopher, which strikes me as magnificent, and almost divine; namely, that when he had been condemned by the sentence of impious men, he said he was prepared to die with the most perfect equanimity, because the god within him had not suffered him to be afflicted with any idea of impending evil, either when he left his home, or when he appeared before the court."

As already stated, he had a psychic dream foretelling his death in three days.

The teaching of Socrates, like that of Pythagoras, had a profound influence on the religious outlook of the people and also on the philosophy of Plato, Aristotle and Plotinus, and thus on the doctrine of Early Christian leaders, such as St. Augustine.

THE ELEUSINIAN AND DIONYSIAN MYSTERIES

There were also certain religious cults in Ancient Greece, most notably the Eleusinian and Dionysian Mysteries, where the followers carried out ceremonies in secret, and in which they seem to have had experiences of a mystical nature.

The Eleusinian Mysteries were based on the story of the earth goddess, Demeter, and her daughter, Persephone, and probably originated in a festival concerned with the growth of crops or fertility of the soil. The devotees after a preliminary purification and a prolonged fast, took part in a ceremony at the shrine of Eleusis. It was claimed that this evoked a sense of spiritual upliftment and aspiration, and of contact with spirit forces.

In the Dionysian Mysteries, the devotees took part in rites which were believed to cause them to become united with or possessed by the god, Dionysus or Bacchus, the god of vegetation. It was claimed that as a result of this union with their god, they could acquire the power of clairvoyance, prophecy, healing, and the controlling of natural forces.

The Orphic Movement

In the sixth century B.C., the worship of Dionysus was reformed to give rise to the Orphic movement. The members of this cult had mystical experiences of an ecstatic nature in which they believed they were in direct contact or in union with their god, Dionysus. They preached tidings of salvation, which were acceptable to all men, and so had a considerable influence on the religious views of the Ancient Greeks, including Pythagoras, Socrates, Plato and Aristotle. The philosophy of these men had a pronounced mystical aspect. This may also be said of that of Philo, several centuries later (25 B.C. to 40 or 50 A.D.), who although an orthodox Jew was influenced by Hellenistic as well as Jewish mysticism.

THE HERMETIC WRITINGS

Another development of Greek or Hellenistic mysticism was the Hermetic writings. These have been ascribed to Hermes Trismegistus, a prophet of Ancient Egypt, who was after his death believed to be the god Thoth or the Greek god Hermes, but they were probably the work of Greek settlers in Egypt in the first three centuries A.D. They were written primarily to teach men how to have personal or mystical experience of God. While the writers had no definite system of philosophy, their ideas were largely similar to those of Plato, Aristotle and Philo. They appear to have belonged to a small Brotherhood, having seers or mystics as their leaders and teachers.

GNOSTICISM AND NEO-PLATONISM

Hellenistic mysticism also entered to some extent into the teachings of the Gnostics, who stressed the mystical aspects of Christianity. It also affected the beliefs of Plotinus and the Neo-Platonists, who taught that it was possible to have mystical union with the Divine Mind. Their writings had a profound influence on the thought of the Christian mystics, including St. Augustine.

ISLAM

Mysticism spread from Hellenism or Neo-Platonism and Christianity to the Sufi movement of Islam. Mohammed does not appear to have stressed the importance of mystical experiences. In his teaching, God was so transcendent that there was too great a gulf between Him and man for the latter to seek union with Him. It was, however, man's duty to surrender himself entirely to God and to obey and pray to Him at all times. Thus mysticism entered to some extent into his teaching. In fact, the Sufis claim that he was a mystic. Sufism is based on mysticism, some of the Sufis being amongst the greatest of mystics. Their religion centres round entire trust in and surrender to God, the whole life being devoted to breaking down the barriers between the seeking spirit and God, so that in the end they are in at-one-ment.

THE HEBREW RELIGION

Mysticism was not a central feature of the Ancient Hebrew religion. This may have been due partly to the belief developed by the prophets that God was so transcendent that there was no possibility of man having close or immediate contact or union with Him. However, it can be seen from the Hebrew Scriptures (In the present work the Revised Standard Version of the Bible is used) that spirit communications and prophetic utterances, through a series of gifted seers, played an essential part in the development of the Jewish religion. In fact, the Old Testament is centred round the lives and utterances of these seers: the Ancient Patriarchs—Abraham, Isaac, Jacob and Joseph; the great leader, Moses; and the prophets— Samuel, Elijah, Elisha, Isaiah, Ezekiel, Jeremiah and others.

It must be borne in mind that there is little or no historical evidence to support the accounts of the Patriarchs and other early leaders of Israel, and scholars are now of the opinion that they are largely based on folk-lore. But it is recognised that folk-lore frequently centres round the lives of real personalities, though many of the details may be purely imaginative. And the supernatural happenings recorded in these stories are not inconsistent with modern psychic phenomena. In other words, they could have happened provided the persons concerned had the necessary spiritual gifts.

In the psychic manifestations recorded in the Bible, the spirit concerned is referred to as God, Lord, Jahveh, angel (or messenger) of the Lord, ghost or Holy Spirit. The term used would depend largely on the beliefs, not only of the person originally concerned with the psychic experience, but also of those handing it down by oral or written communication.

In ancient times spirits were frequently termed 'gods,' as when 'the woman of En-dor' spoke of the spirit of Samuel—"I see a god coming up out of the earth" (1 Samuel 28. 13). It is therefore a mistake to assume that when the term God or Lord is used in recording a spirit manifestation in the Old Testament, it means God Almighty, as in the case of the spirit who walked in the Garden of Eden in the cool of the evening, who ate a meal with Abraham, was laughed at by Sarah, Abraham's wife, or who wrestled with Jacob. (See "The Bible as Psychic History.")

THE PATRIARCHS

The Patriarchs were clairvoyant and clairaudient; they could "see" and "hear" spirits and had psychic dreams. For instance, in Genesis 46. 2, it is said "And God spoke to Israel (Jacob) in visions of the night, and said . . ." On one occasion Abraham entered the trance state; "As the sun was going down, a deep sleep fell on Abram; and lo, a dread and great darkness fell upon him. Then the Lord (or spirit) said to Abram . . ." (Genesis 15. 12-13). When these Patriarchs were in difficulty, they built altars, offered up sacrifices and held sittings "to call upon the name of the Lord." These sittings for spirit consultation took place as a rule in sacred places, frequently in the shade of large trees, particularly the oak, *e.g.*, in the case of Abraham the oaks of Mamre and Moreh, and with Jacob, the oak of Shecham. The deep shade of these trees would favour spirit manifestations.

Joseph had remarkable clairvoyant powers, and had prophetic dreams of a symbolic nature. He was able to interpret the dreams of others, *e.g.*, those of Pharaoh. He attributed this power to the spirit, "It is not in me; God (or the spirit) will give Pharaoh a favourable answer" (Genesis 41. 16). And Pharaoh recognised Joseph's great psychic gifts, and said unto his servants, "Can we find such a man as this, in whom is the Spirit of God (*i.e.*, who is a seer or medium)?" (Genesis 41. 38). And he made Joseph the Governor of Egypt.

Abraham and Jacob appear to have been physical or materialising mediums, for it is said that three spirits materialised and ate food which Abraham set before them; and Jacob on one occasion wrestled at night with a materialised spirit. Esau, the brother of Jacob, appears to have been a much finer character than the latter, but plays a minor part in the narrative as he had not his brother's psychic powers.

A number of other individuals appearing in the biblical records at the time of these Patriarchs were psychic, *e.g.*, Lot, Laban, Hagar, Pharaoh and Abimelech. They had psychic dreams or visions, or heard spirit voices.

MOSES

Moses was a great seer and leader. He was brought up as an adopted son by Pharaoh's daughter and would therefore receive the best education at court, and probably would have experience of the psychic practices of the priests. He was not only clairvoyant and clairaudient, but also a powerful physical medium, for according to the biblical narrative, "the Lord" materialised and spoke to him "face to face," *i.e.*, by direct voice. The "burning bush" may have been a clairvoyant experience, or it may have been due to the production of psychic lights by his own mediumship. That it was not merely a natural phenomenon is shown by the fact that Moses at the time heard (clairaudiently) a voice.

The inner room of the tabernacle in the wilderness was so screened off by a veil that it would be in darkness, and thus provide ideal conditions for the seer to "sit to the Lord" and receive His message, either by clairaudience or by direct voice. "There I will meet with you, and . . . I will speak with you" (Exodus 25. 22). The fact that it was known in these days that darkness or dim-light provides the best conditions for materialisation and direct-voice phenomena, is shown by various passages in the Bible. "Moses drew near to the thick darkness where God was. And the Lord said to Moses . . ." (Exodus 20. 21.) "These words the Lord spoke to all your assembly out of . . . the thick darkness with a loud voice (Deuteronomy 5. 22). And Solomon on the completion of the Temple at Jerusalem said, "The Lord . . . has said that he would dwell in thick darkness" (I Kings 8. 12). In Exodus 19. 9, the Lord said, "Lo, I am coming to you in a thick cloud that the people may hear when I speak with you."

It is stated that the face of Moses shone after some of his meetings with Jahveh; in other words, he had undergone transfiguration during these séances, as in the case of Jesus on the Mount. Mention is also made of the use of a trumpet at the direct voice manifestations. In Exodus 19. 19, it says "And as the sound of the trumpet grew louder and louder, Moses spoke, and God answered him in thunder." It is probable from this account that the trumpet was used to amplify the direct voice, as in modern séances. In this connection, it is worthy of note that in the Authorised and the English Revised Versions of the Bible, the expression "the voice of the trumpet" is used instead of "the sound of the trumpet."

THE SPIRIT CONTROL OF MOSES

The spirit, called Lord or Jahveh, who was the guide or control of Moses, has been commonly regarded as the Supreme or Almighty God of all the Universe, but there appears to be no justification for this assumption. God

Almighty is utterly beyond our powers of comprehension, and being transcendent in nature to man, we can never have any definite conception of His Being, nor meet Him face to face nor hold converse with Him. This is borne out by the words of Jesus, "No one has ever seen God" (John 1. 18); and in referring to the Father, "His voice you have never heard, his form you have never seen" (John 5. 37). It may be claimed that Jesus also said, "He who has seen me has seen the Father" (John 14. 9), but that does not mean that the apostles were face to face with God Almighty in person, when they were looking at the material body of Jesus. They were seeing the Spirit of the Father in him. This is shown by the context where he is explaining his condition of being at one with the Father; "Do you not believe that I am in the Father and the Father in me" (John 14. 10).

Hence it could not have been God Almighty that was referred to when it is said, "Thus the Lord used to speak to Moses face to face, as a man speaks to his friend" (Exodus 33. 11), or "There I will meet with you (Moses) and . . . I will speak with you . . ." (Exodus 25. 22). Nor could it have been God, who appeared in materialised form on Mount Sinai before seventy-four people, including Moses and the elders of Israel (Exodus 24. 9). This is also shown by the fact that on occasion Moses had to remonstrate with and even rebuke 'the Lord' and advise him not to vent his wrath on the Israelites; "And the Lord repented of the evil which he thought to do to his people" (Exodus 32. 14). Certainly, it was no Almighty Father, but a tribal deity or spirit, who commanded the Israelites to be merciless in their treatment of their enemies. It is commonly believed that the Commandments were given by God to Moses, but it is said in Acts 7. 53, "You who received the Law as delivered by angels . . ." (See also Galatians 3. 19, and Hebrews 2. 2.)

THE MOSAIC LAW

The Mosaic Law is frequently quoted at the present time against the consultation of mediums in general, but in this connection it must be remembered that Moses himself was a medium. What was condemned was the seeking to have spirit communications through individuals not officially recognised as seers or prophets, as some might not be genuine mediums, whilst others might not be properly developed or might be in touch with lower spirits and give false or harmful advice. In this connection, it is said in the New Testament, "Beloved, do not believe every spirit, but test the spirits, to see whether they are of God" (1 John 4. 1).

At the time of Moses there were many gods, and idolatry was rife. The people were also steeped in superstitious beliefs regarding augury and other methods of divining the future and of determining the Will of God. It was the desire of Moses and the other leaders of Israel that the people worship only their own particular or national God, Jahveh, and to this end they insisted that the only way to approach their God was through their own priests or officially recognised seers or prophets.

THE WOMAN OF EN-DOR

It is worthy of note that the "woman of En-dor" in the Authorised and English Revised Versions of the Bible is referred to as "a woman that hath a familiar spirit," whereas in the Revised Standard Version she is more correctly termed "a medium."

Sometimes mention is made at the present day of this woman (commonly misnamed "witch") to show the dangers of consulting mediums. In this connection it is pointed out that in 1 Chronicles 10. 13, Saul is said to have "consulted a medium, seeking guidance, and did not seek guidance from the Lord. Therefore the Lord slew him." But in 1 Samuel

28. 6, it is stated that he did inquire of the Lord, and "the Lord did not answer him, either by dreams, or by Urim (see earlier), or by prophets." Also, he was not slain in battle, but committed suicide after being defeated in battle.

According to the biblical narrative, the woman of En-dor, although not an officially recognised medium or prophet, was a genuine sensitive, because the prophetic message, which it was claimed came from the spirit Samuel, was subsequently fulfilled. Moreover, if she had been a fraud, she would have been afraid to have made up and delivered such a message of doom to King Saul, as it could have been regarded as treason and therefore punishable by death. A fraudulent medium would undoubtedly have given him a favourable and reassuring message. She was also kind-hearted and a woman of means, for when she noted Saul's distress on receiving the message, she killed a fatted calf and insisted that he should take a meal before setting out on his way.

Certain modern authorities on ancient religions, knowing little or nothing of psychic practices, have described the work of such seers as based on superstition, magic or witchcraft. For instance, Sir James G. Frazer in his work, "Folk-lore in the Old Testament," calls the "woman of En-dor" a witch, and says that by an act of ventriloquism, she faked the voice of the dead Samuel. This is an absurd suggestion in view of the facts already given. Also, in ventriloquism the deception depends on what is seen by the eyes, yet the séance at En-dor was probably held in dim light or darkness, for Saul "came to the woman by night."

BALAAM

Balaam was another psychic and, though not an Israelite, was renowned for his gift of prophecy. He apparently went into trance for in Numbers 24. 16, it is said "who (Balaam) sees the vision of the Almighty, falling down (*i.e.,* in trance), but having his eyes uncovered." However, he misused his psychic gifts in his greed for power and possessions and was in the end slain by the Israelites.

JOSHUA

Moses was succeeded by Joshua as leader of the Israelites. The latter was a powerful psychic, being clairvoyant and clairaudient. It is repeatedly said in The Book of Joshua that "the Lord spake unto Joshua." He was also a materialising or physical medium. This is shown by the fact that a spirit, "the Lord," materialised before him, after the crossing by the Israelites of the Jordan, and advised him how to proceed in order to capture Jericho. This spirit appears to have been a "national god," and certainly not the All-loving Father referred to by Jesus, otherwise he would never have told Joshua to carry out the bloody massacre of the men, women and children of Jericho, sparing only the household of the treacherous harlot who had harboured the Israelite spies.

Archaeological investigations have shown that Jericho was a peaceful city, without arms, on an important trade route.

DEBORAH

After the days of Joshua, there was a prophetess, Deborah, who "in her time judged Israel." Under spirit guidance she showed Barak how to defeat the army of Sisera, and so free the Israelites from Jabin, King of Canaan. Joan of Arc played a similar role hundreds of years later, and was condemned and burned by the Christian Church.

GIDEON

Gideon was another powerful psychic, who became leader of the Israelites. He was beating out wheat by the oak tree at Ophrah, when "the angel of the Lord" appeared under the tree and spoke to him, instructing him how he could defeat the Midianites. He sought assurance from the spirit by exposing a fleece of wool at night to the dew, a method used at that time in augury.

SAUL AND DAVID

Saul and David were made kings of Israel by the prophet, Samuel (see later), under spirit guidance. They appear to have been chosen because of their psychic powers, but Saul was said to have disobeyed his guiding spirit, and as a result his mediumship deteriorated, and being defeated in battle, he committed suicide.

David was a powerful medium—"And the Spirit of the Lord came mightily upon David" (1 Samuel 16. 13). He was said to have received the details for the building of the Temple at Jerusalem, and for its furnishings, in "writing from the hand of the Lord" (1 Chronicles 28. 19). This would appear to indicate that he obtained the information by automatic writing, a common method of spirit communication at the present day. It can hardly be said that he was of high moral integrity, but he "inquired of the Lord" or "went in and sat before the Lord," whenever he was in difficulty and so was "favoured by the Lord."

SOLOMON

King Solomon was clairvoyant and clairaudient and had psychic dreams. When asked by his guiding spirit, "the Lord," what gift he would like, he replied wisdom and understanding. He apparently received these in abundance from spirit sources, *i.e.*, under spirit inspiration or control, for we are told, "God (*i.e.*, the spirit) gave Solomon wisdom and understanding beyond measure, and largeness of mind like the sand on the sea shore" (1 Kings 4. 29). It is also said, "They (all Israel) stood in awe of the king, because they perceived that the wisdom of God was in him, to render justice" (1 Kings 3. 28).

THE PROPHETS IN ISRAEL

Apart from these rulers and leaders, there was a series of great prophets or seers in Israel. Unlike the priests, who were all Levites, these prophets belonged to no particular tribe or class. They were as a rule solitary individuals, holding no official position in the Church or State. They "stood apart" from the guilds of prophets or from the official body of prophets at the Court. In fact, they claimed that they received their messages from God and so were above all earthly authority. Their task, however, was not always an easy one. Their messages might not be accepted, and, if condemning the Church or State, might be regarded as sacrilege or treason. As a result they might be imprisoned or put to death, and often they had to flee from the land. But no matter the risks involved, they had to give forth their messages. "The lion has roared; who will not fear? The Lord God has spoken, who can but prophesy?" (Amos 3. 8).

Unlike the true mystics, the prophets seem to have been chosen for their psychic gifts, and not simply for high degree of spirituality. (The true mystics "by their inner life found their way to God"). Moreover, the prophets had specific work, which they felt that they were compelled to carry out—to proclaim a message from God to the people, whereas the sole aim of the mystics was union with God. The prophets, however, believed that at the time that they received the message from God, they were in some form of contact or even union with Him, which gave them, like the mystics, a feeling of ecstasy. Thus no hard and fast line can be drawn between the Hebrew prophets and the mystics of other nations. The former apparently had on certain occasions some form of mystical consciousness of the

Divine Mind; they were in the ecstatic state when, as stated in Ezekiel 1. 3, "the word of the Lord came to Ezekiel, the priest . . . and the hand of the Lord was there upon him." Isaiah and Ezekiel both claimed that they had such ecstatic experiences (Isaiah 6; Ezekiel 1). At the same time they had a sense of revelation or illumination, and a deep conviction of the truth of the message they had to proclaim. This in itself was a great source of strength to them.

SAMUEL

Samuel was the first of the great prophets. It is said in the Bible that when he was a child, "the word of the Lord was rare in those days; there was no frequent (or as the Authorised Version puts it "open") vision" (*i.e.*, clairvoyance) (1 Samuel 3. 1). He was clairaudient as shown by the incident when, as a boy serving in the Temple, he heard a spirit voice at night telling him of the oncoming fate of Eli, the High Priest, and his sons. He was clairvoyant and was thus able to tell Saul the whereabouts of his father's asses, and predict Saul's own future. It is worthy of note that in the account of the discussion between Saul and his servant as to whether they should seek help from a seer regarding the lost asses, it is said "Formerly in Israel, when a man went to inquire of God, he said, 'Come, let us go to the seer,' for he who is now called a prophet was formerly called a seer" (1 Samuel 9. 9). The question of giving the seer a present or payment for his services also arose.

ELIJAH AND ELISHA

The prophets, Elijah and Elisha, were clairvoyant and clairaudient; they "saw" and "heard" spirits. The "still small voice" which Elijah heard or the "voice which came to him" on Horeb, the Mount of God (1 Kings 19. 12) was not the voice of his conscience, but a spirit voice, which Elijah recognised as that of "the Lord," In 2 Chronicles 21. 12, it is said "And a letter came to him (King Jehoram) from Elijah the prophet." But Elijah had been dead for some time before Jehoram became king, so it would appear that this was a written spirit communication. Its contents, dealing with Jehoram's rule, show that it could not have been written whilst Elijah was still alive.

Elijah and Elisha were psychic or spirit healers. In each case an account is given of the curing of a young boy. Elisha was also able to carry out absent healing, as in the case of Naaman, who was suffering from leprosy. Part of the treatment was to bathe seven times in the Jordan. As already shown, bathing in water was frequently used in psychic healing in ancient days.

Elisha recognised the value of music in promoting clairaudience. He said, "But now bring me a minstrel," "And when the minstrel played, the power of the Lord came upon him. And he said, 'Thus says the Lord . . .'" (2 Kings 3. 15). The value of music for this purpose was evidently well known in these days, as indicated by the fact that the band of prophets whom Saul met, had musical instruments "before them" whilst prophesying (1 Samuel 10. 5).

Elisha's remarkable powers of clairvoyance is shown by his accurate prediction to the Kings of Israel, Judah and Edom, that their enemies, the Moabites, would be defeated; also by the account of how during the war between the King of Syria and the King of Israel, he was able to forewarn the latter about all the moves of the enemy forces. The King of Syria, realising that the King of Israel must be having this advance information, suggested to his men that there must be a traitor amongst them. "And one of his servants said, 'None, my lord, O King: but Elisha, the prophet, who is in Israel, tells the King of Israel the words that you speak in your bedchamber'" (2 Kings 6. 12).

THE LATER PROPHETS

After Elijah and Elisha, there was a long line of seers, noted for their psychic powers: Amos, Hosea, Isaiah, Micah, Jeremiah, Daniel, Ezekiel, Malachi, and others. It has been claimed by certain scholars, that these men were merely exceptionally capable and far-seeing national and religious leaders. However, this ignores entirely the fact that in practically all cases they were clairvoyant and clairaudient; they had visions, or saw and heard the spirit, angel or Lord, and passed his message to the rulers or the people. In the accounts of their lives, it is stated again and again, "thus saith the Lord," "the Lord said unto me," "the word of the Lord came to me saying," "And the Lord of hosts revealed himself in mine ears"—these statements clearly indicate a condition of clairaudience. And this is also shown by the fact that, as in the case of Jeremiah and Ezekiel, the date on which the communication was received is sometimes given.

ISAIAH

Isaiah was clairaudient; "Then the Lord said to me," and "The Lord spoke to me again" (Isaiah 8. 1, 5). He had also visions (Isaiah 6. 1), and made some remarkable prophecies regarding the Hebrew nation; and the destruction of the Assyrian Army of Sennacherib before Jerusalem (Isaiah 37. 36), and Sennacherib's death "by the sword in his own land" (Isaiah 37. 7).

JEREMIAH

Jeremiah, it has been said, was the greatest of all the prophets. He was clairaudient as shown by the oft-recurring statements, "The Lord said to me"; "The word of the Lord came to me saying"; "The word that came to Jeremiah from the Lord." He had symbolic visions, the meaning of which he received clairaudiently from the spirit. He appears to have been at times in trance. He made some remarkable prophecies, including the precise duration of the captivity of the Hebrews in Babylon; their return to Judaea; the fate of King Zedekiah, and the fall of Babylon.

DANIEL

The Book of Daniel is regarded by scholars as fictional in nature, but it is of interest as the chief character, Daniel, is depicted as having the gifts of a true sensitive, showing that the Jews at that time, about 165 B.C., must have been familiar with psychic phenomena.

Daniel was remarkable for his prophetic dreams, which, being symbolic, had to be interpreted by the spirit. He was able to reveal and interpret the symbolic dream of King Nebuchadnezzar, and to explain the meaning of that king's later dreams. He also interpreted the writing by the materialised spirit hand on the wall at Belshazzar's feast. He appears to have had visions during daytime under trance conditions, for it is said, "As he (the spirit) was speaking to me (Daniel), I fell into a deep sleep with my face to the ground; but he touched me and set me on my feet. He said . . ." (Daniel 8. 18-19). Also, in chapter 10, it says that he had a vision, while he was by the side of a river, but those with him did not see it. Then the spirit of the vision spoke to him. "Then I (Daniel) heard the sound of his words; and when I heard the sound of his words, I fell on my face in a deep sleep (*i.e.*, in trance) with my face to the ground" (Daniel 10. 9).

EZEKIEL

Ezekiel was a powerful psychic as is indicated by the remarkable events of his life. His clairaudient powers are repeatedly shown by the statements; "He (the spirit) said to me"; "And the hand of the Lord was there upon me; and he said to me . . ." (Ezekiel 3. 1, 4, 22). He had also symbolic visions.

At times he was apparently in trance under spirit control. For instance, it is stated, "Such was the appearance of the likeness of the glory of the Lord. And when I saw it, I fell upon my face, and I heard the voice of one speaking. And he said to me, 'Son of man, stand upon your feet, and I will speak with you.' And when he spoke to me, the Spirit entered into me and set me upon my feet; and I heard him speaking to me. And he said to me . . ." (Ezekiel 1. 28; 2. 1-3). This is an excellent account of the experience of a sensitive in trance under spirit control.

Ezekiel foretold the fall of Jerusalem and the future restoration of the Jews. He also appears to have been in the habit of giving sittings for spirit communication to the elders of Judah, the precise dates of these meetings being noted. "In the sixth year, in the sixth month, on the fifth day of the month, as I sat in my house with the elders of Judah sitting before me, the hand of the Lord God fell there upon me" (Ezekiel 8. 1). "In the seventh year, in the fifth month, on the tenth day of the month, certain of the elders of Israel came to inquire of the Lord, and sat before me. And the word of the Lord came to me" (Ezekiel 20. 1-2).

It is also said, "The hand of the Lord was upon me, and he brought me out by the Spirit of the Lord, and set me down in the midst of the valley; it was full of bones" (Ezekiel 37. 1). This appears to have been a purely clairvoyant experience or symbolic vision, and not actual transportation of his body. On the other hand, in chapter 3, verses 12 to 15, it is stated, "Then the Spirit lifted me up, and as the glory of the Lord arose from its place . . . The Spirit lifted me up and took me away, and I went in bitterness in the heat of my spirit, the hand of the Lord being strong upon me; and I came to the exiles at Telabib, who dwelt by the river Chebar. And I sat there overwhelmed (stupefied) among them seven days. And at the end of seven days, the word of the Lord came to me." It would appear from this account that his body was actually transported through space.

There is some evidence that the seemingly incredible phenomenon of transportation can occur at the present day. A number of authenticated cases are given in the Encyclopaedia of Psychic Science by Nandor Fodor, for instance, the transportation of the Marquis Centurione Scotto at Millesimo Castle in 1928, recorded by Ernesto Bozzano; and that of the two Pansini boys, reported in 1906 by Dr. Joseph Lapponi, medical officer to two recent popes. Sir Ernest Wallis Budge, for many years chief authority on Egyptology at the British Museum, reported its occurrence in the case of an African and an Indian. (See "The Bible as Psychic History," by the Rev. G. Maurice Elliott.)

It is also claimed that it has happened in the past with certain Eastern mystics and Christian saints, *e.g.*, St. Dunstan, St. Francis, St. Thomas Aquinas and St. Theresa.

According to the Old Testament, the prophet Elijah had a habit of disappearing to reappear elsewhere. Obadiah, the chief minister to Ahab, King of Israel, regarded this as being due to the prophet's power of transportation, as on being asked by Elijah to reveal the latter's whereabouts to King Ahab, he protested, saying, "And as soon as I have gone from you, the Spirit of the Lord will carry you whither I know not" (1 Kings 18. 12).

The occurrence of transportation is indicated in the New Testament in the case of Jesus, when he escaped from a mob; "but passing through the midst of them he went away" (Luke 4. 30); and in the case of St. Philip, "And when they came up out of the water, the Spirit of the Lord caught up Philip; and the eunuch saw him no more, and went on his way rejoicing. But Philip was found at Azotus" (Acts 8. 39-40).

THE TEACHING OF THE PROPHETS

There were many other prophets in Israel. They came from various walks of life and differed widely in their personalities, yet they had all more or less similar psychic gifts. They all felt that it was their bounden duty to proclaim the Will of God to the nation, and some were outstanding for their prophecies. From the early polytheistic beliefs of the Israelites, they developed a high monotheistic conception of an Almighty and Transcendent God.

THE CHRISTIAN SCRIPTURES—JESUS

THE GOSPELS

The Christian Gospels are centred round the last three years of the life of Jesus. His teaching and works have had such a profound influence on religious thought in the world, that it is desirable to consider in some detail the psychic aspects of his life and death. However, it must be remembered that the Gospels were written many years after his death (thirty or forty years in the case of those of St. Matthew, Mark and Luke, and seventy to one hundred years in that of St. John), and therefore the accounts of his life in these books cannot be regarded as infallible. It is possible that many of the details have not been accurately recorded. Except for some tiny fragments, none of the earliest New Testament manuscripts (*i.e.*, those written prior to 200 A.D.), is now in existence, and it is known that in the first few centuries the various scripts in use were altered and revised repeatedly in the determination to reconcile their statements on the doings and sayings of Jesus with the Church doctrines and practices prevailing in these later times. But the question as to the reliability of these New Testament books need not arise. It is sufficient for us to show that the happenings recorded therein are for the most part consistent with psychic facts.

Thus a Spiritualist in reading the New Testament, can see in it many manifestations of psychic phenomena, and accounts of people who were truly and wonderfully gifted sensitives. Others may not accept this interpretation, but it is the one we propose to bring as we are convinced it is the true one.

THE EARLY YEARS

Mary and Joseph, the parents of Jesus, were psychic, as also were their kinsfolk, Elizabeth and Zechariah, the parents of John the Baptist. According to the Bible, all these individuals saw or heard spirits (*i.e.*, were clairvoyant or clairaudient), or had psychic dreams in which a spirit, angel of the Lord, or Gabriel, gave them messages or advice. Zechariah and Elizabeth were also at times over-shadowed or controlled by the spirit or, as the Bible puts it, "filled with the Holy Spirit," and gave inspired or trance utterances of a prophetic nature (Luke 1. 41-42; 1. 67).

When Jesus was a baby, he was taken to the Temple at Jerusalem, and there he was seen by Simeon and Anna, both of whom were psychic. Anna is referred to as a prophetess. It is said of Simeon, "And it had been revealed to him by the Holy Spirit . . . And inspired by the Spirit he came into the temple" (Luke 2. 25-27). There, he received Jesus into his arms and blessed God, and said, "Lord, now lettest Thou thy servant depart in peace, according to thy word . . .," a prophetic utterance given probably under spirit inspiration or control.

HIS PSYCHIC POWERS

It is evident from the Gospels that Jesus had psychic experiences similar in nature to those of the great prophets of Israel. In fact, it may be said that he carried on the traditions of these prophets, and like them, was soon "in conflict with the legalism" of the rabbis, scribes and Pharisees. He was an extremely powerful psychic sensitive, being clairvoyant, clairaudient, a healer and a physical medium capable of such phenomena as levitation (walking on water) and materialisation. He developed his psychic faculties like the true mystics by prayer, meditation and fasting in solitude. In the account of his Temptation, it is stated that he fasted for forty days in the wilderness (Matthew 4. 2). He would also at times spend the whole night alone in prayer on the mountain-side.

He undoubtedly had mystical experiences. When he said, "I and the Father are one" (John 10. 30), and "I am in the Father and the Father in me" (John 14. 10), he would not be meaning that he was identical with the Father or merely that he was of like mind with Him, but that he was in at-one-ment or in direct contact or union in a mystical sense with the Father, the exalted Spirit who was his guide or spirit control (see later). These remarks are quite definitely mystical in significance. It is possible that he was initiated into mystical practices by the Essenes, a Jewish sect, the members of which lived a simple life and carried out ascetic practices. John the Baptist apparently belonged to this sect, and Jesus in his ministry showed their influence. He may have been initiated into their practices, especially spirit healing, during the early years of his life before he started his ministry.

THE BAPTISM

In the Gospel according to St. Mark, details are given of his baptism by John the Baptist It is said that "he (Jesus) saw the heavens opened and the Spirit descending upon him like a dove; and a voice came from heaven, 'Thou art my beloved son, with thee I am well pleased'" (Mark 1. 10-

11). This remarkable spirit manifestation was no doubt evoked, not only by his own psychic power, but also by that of John the Baptist. It was a symbolic representation of the fact that Jesus had now come to be under the direct inspiration or control of an extremely exalted spirit, to whom he referred as "the Father," and had thus become the "Son of God" a belief widely held by the Early Church. In this connection, Prof. Schmidt (Encyclopaedia Biblica) states, "It is possible that one of the earliest manuscripts and a large number of patristic quotations have preserved a more original reading of Luke 3. 22, namely, 'Thou art my beloved son, to-day I have begotten thee.'"

This spirit experience was his call to the service of God, resembling similar experiences in the life of Isaiah and Ezekiel. It must have made a profound impression on him, giving him a sense of the presence and power of the spirit, and of direct contact or union with the Divine. Throughout the rest of his life, he appears to have been at all times consciously aware of this exalted Spirit Presence, the Father, and devoted his whole life to His service. The Rev. Sidney Spencer in "Mysticism in World Religion," states, "A Christian Mystic, Gerlac Petersen, has said of the soul which is made one with God: 'It worketh all its works in God, or rather God doth work His own works in it.' No words can more aptly convey the essential secret of Jesus." This was the key note of all his ministry, and it rendered him, like the prophets of old, independent, self-reliant and fearless in the face of opposition from the Church and State.

THE TEACHING

He was a great teacher, his teaching being based upon the information and guidance which he obtained by inspiration or revelation from the Father. This is clearly shown by his sayings: "The words that I say to you I do not speak on my own authority; but the Father who dwells in me does his works" (John 14. 10); "the Son can do nothing of his own accord, but only what he sees the Father doing" (John 5. 19); "I can do nothing on my own authority" (John 5. 30).

That Jesus was directly inspired or controlled by this spirit is indicated by what happened after his baptism: "The Spirit immediately drove him out into the wilderness" (Mark 1. 12), to be tested. St. Matthew says he "was led up by the Spirit into the wilderness." And this may be the explanation of his last words on the Cross asking why the Spirit (or God) had forsaken him (Matthew 27. 46).

The fact that Jesus was undoubtedly an extremely powerful instrument for Spirit would be due to this close union with his Spirit Control and to his high psychic capacity to be "filled with the Spirit." It was this direct spirit inspiration which enabled him to teach "as one who had authority, and not as their scribes" (Matthew 7. 29). The teaching of the priests, rabbis and scribes, was concerned chiefly with ancient traditions and doctrines, and consisted largely of quotations from various authorities, and so, unlike that of Jesus, was of a second-hand character, and circumscribed with dogmas, petty rules and legal niceties.

The teaching of Jesus was essentially of a practical nature. He utterly condemned pride, selfishness and hypocrisy, but having a deep compassion for mankind, taught that love was everything—love not only of God but of one's fellow creatures. By this love only, can man become perfect and reach a state of at-one-ment with the Father and thus become a Son of God.

The Rev. Sidney Spencer says "Although there is little in the teaching of Jesus in the Synoptic Gospels which bears a specifically mystical character, yet the total impression which the gospel story leaves upon us is of one who lived in the constant awareness of the Divine Presence. It is significant that Arthur Drews, the author of "The Christ Myth," who regarded the gospel story as purely mythical, recognised its value as a symbol of the union of man with God. Union with God is in one aspect an entire self-giving to the divine; and it is that entire self-giving which we see in Jesus, and which is reflected in his ethical demands. The supreme law for him is the love which makes us one with God—by which we may share the divine perfection (Matthew 5. 43-48). The great sin is the self-seeking and self-exaltation which above all things stand in the way of that attainment. Jesus, like the Buddha, was moved by a boundless compassion. He identified himself with his fellows in their sufferings. The words of the Son of Man in the parable of Judgment are, clearly, an expression of his own attitude: "Truly, I say to you, as you did it to one of the least of these my brethren, you did it to me" (Matthew 25. 40).

In a special way Jesus identifies himself with his followers. They are to rise with him into the universal love which makes men sons of God. As his followers, they are an extension of his own personality, as he himself being the messenger of God, is an extension of the divine Personality: "He who receives you receives me, and he who receives me receives him who sent me" (Matthew to. 40).

THE CHOOSING OF THE APOSTLES

Jesus appears to have chosen his apostles because of their psychic powers, for it is said, all went under spirit control at Pentecost. Modern experience shows that a psychic can frequently tell if another individual is similarly gifted, and Jesus appears to have had this power. Samuel was able to do so in the case of Saul (1 Samuel 10. 6).

It can hardly be said that Jesus chose his apostles for their outstanding ability or intellectual powers, because he had on several occasions to upbraid them for their lack of understanding of his teaching and mission on earth. They were slow to learn even from the experiences they had in living with him. But there were great advantages to be gained in having psychic apostles. (1) They would be able to carry out spirit healing. (2) Although not highly educated, they would be able to spread his teaching under spirit inspiration or control. He could say from his own experience, "For it is not you who speak, but the Spirit of your Father speaking through you" (Matthew 10. 20). (3) He would be able to manifest to them in visionary or materialised form after his death, and thus prove his survival after death. (4) He would be enabled after his death to continue his teaching through them by inspiration or trance control. The address which St. Stephen gave prior to being stoned to death shows evidence of this (Acts 7. 2-53).

HIS CLAIRVOYANT POWERS

The clairvoyant powers of Jesus are shown by the following incidents:

"Jesus said to her (the Samaritan woman at the well), . . . 'You are right in saying, "I have no husband"; for you have had five husbands, and he whom you now have is not your husband.' The woman said to him, "Sir, I perceive that you are a prophet" (John 4. 17-19).

"And he sent two of his disciples, and said to them, "Go into the city, and a man carrying a jar of water will meet you; follow him, and wherever he enters, say to the householder, "The Teacher says, where is my guest-room, where I am to eat the passover with my disciples?" And he will show you a large upper room furnished and ready; there prepare for us.' And the disciples set out, and went to the city, and found it as he had told them." (Mark 14. 13-16).

"And when they drew near to Jerusalem, to Bethphage and Bethany, at the Mount of Olives, he sent two of his disciples, and said to them, 'Go into the village opposite you, and immediately as you enter it, you will find a colt tied, on which no one has ever sat; untie it and bring it. And if any one says to you, "Why are you doing this?" say, "The Lord has need of it and will send it back here immediately."' And they went away, and found a colt tied at the door in the open street; and they untied it. And those who stood there said to them, 'What are you doing, untying the colt?' And they told them what Jesus had said; and they let them go" (Mark 11. 1-6).

It is also possible that in the following instance, Jesus obtained the information clairvoyantly:

"And when he (Jesus) had ceased speaking, he said to Simon, 'Put out into the deep and let down your nets for a catch.' And Simon answered, Master, we toiled all night and took nothing! But at your word I will let down the nets.' And when they had done this, they enclosed a great shoal of fish; and as their nets were breaking . . ." (Luke 5. 4-6).

The following may have been cases of clairvoyance or merely instances of intuitive insight:

Andrew brought his brother to Jesus, "Jesus looked at him, and said, 'So you are Simon, the son of John? You shall he called Cephas'" (John 1. 42).

"But he (Jesus) knew their thoughts." (scribes and Pharisees) (Luke 6. 8).

"Jesus saw Nathanael coming to him, and said of him, 'Behold, an Israelite indeed, in whom is no guile'" (John, 1. 47).

There is also the story in the earlier versions of the Bible, now regarded by scholars as an interpolation, about the woman taken in adultery (John 8. 3). It is said that Jesus before passing judgment "wrote with his finger on the ground." He may have done this to give the guilt-stricken persons time to withdraw, but it may have been a case of obtaining spirit advice by automatic writing,

PROPHECY

The prophetic powers of Jesus are shown by the following instances:

"Jesus said to her, 'Woman, believe me, the hour is coming when neither on this mountain nor in Jerusalem will you worship the Father'" (John 4. 21).

"O Jerusalem, Jerusalem, . . . Behold, your house is forsaken and desolate" (Matthew 23. 37-38, and Luke 13. 34-35).

"But when you see Jerusalem surrounded by armies, then know that its desolation has come near . . . And Jerusalem will be trodden down by the Gentiles, until the times of the Gentiles are fulfilled" (Luke 21. 20-24).

SPIRIT HEALING

Jesus was a powerful psychic healer; "And the power of the Lord was with him to heal" (Luke 5. 17). He also helped his disciples to develop the gift of healing, otherwise they could not have obeyed his injunctions to "heal the sick, raise the dead, cleanse lepers, cast out demons" (Matthew 10. 8; Luke 10. 9).

Jesus, however, was not omnipotent and recognised that to ensure success even in his own healing certain conditions had to be observed:

(1) Trust of the patient or his kindred in his healing powers. This would render the sufferer more open to the curative action of psychic forces. It is said, "And he did not do many mighty works there (at Nazareth), because of their unbelief" (Matthew 13. 58). At Nazareth, the people would not only be doubting his powers to heal, but they would actually be scoffing at him.

Owing to the wide-spread belief that disease was caused by sin or demon possession, Jesus would assure the person that his sins were forgiven or that the demon was removed, thus easing the mental and emotional strain, and at the same time making use of the curative power of suggestion.

(2) Absence of antagonistic mental influences. To ensure this, Jesus turned doubters or scorners out of the room, as in the healing of Jairus's daughter; or he took the sick person outside the village before healing him; or he carried out the healing in the evening when quieter conditions would prevail. He would also advise certain patients after treatment "to tell no man," or "he sent him away to his home, saying, 'Do not even enter into the village'" (Mark 8. 26). He probably did this in case other people would suggest to the patients that the treatment had not really been effective or permanent, and thus would undermine their confidence in him. With certain diseases this might have caused a relapse. We are not told whether relapses ever occurred after his cures, but the possibility must have been in his mind.

(3) To supplement his own healing powers, and perhaps to overcome hostile mental influences, *e.g.*, those of scoffers and unbelievers, he would make use of his three apostles, Peter, James and John, who themselves appear to have been gifted healers (see Acts 3). Jesus in difficult cases, *e.g.*, the healing of Jairus's daughter, would be able to draw on them for more psychic power.

(4) After much healing work, Jesus would relax or rest by leaving the gatherings of people and retiring to a quiet and lonely place, *e.g.*, a mountain side or "wilderness," and might remain there in prayer all night. At such times he would be in mystical union with the Divine Mind and become recharged with psychic power (Luke 5. 16; 6. 12).

THE SPIRIT POWER TO HEAL

It has been claimed that all his healing "miracles" were carried out by suggestion, and there was no active or direct spirit power to heal. There is no doubt that the influence of suggestion would play a part in the cure of some types of illness, but it would not have enabled him to heal young children, including babies, or people who were unconscious or were in such a deep coma as to be thought to be dead, *e.g.*, Lazarus, Jairus's daughter and the widow's son. While there is no mention in the Gospels of his curing the very young, it does say that "he healed them all" (Matthew 12. 15). This must have included young children, as disease has always been rife in children of Eastern countries, and there would undoubtedly be mothers thronging around him pleading with him to heal their offspring. It is recorded that "Jesus said, 'Let the children come to me, and do not hinder them; for to such belongs the kingdom of heaven.' And he laid his hands on them and went away (Matthew 19. 14-15). It is also said, "Now they were bringing even infants to him (Jesus) that he might touch them" (Luke 18. 15). He would lay his hands on them, not simply to caress them, but to heal their complaints.

It is also possible that he treated sick animals, as he had compassion for all creatures. Further, he went about "healing every disease and every infirmity among the people" (Matthew 4, 23; 9. 35), and this must have included infectious diseases, such as leprosy. These are due to pathogenic organisms and are not curable by methods of suggestion.

The Gospels clearly indicate that Jesus was able to make use of psychic forces as our healers do at the present day. He was all the more able to do so, because he was in complete attunement with higher spirit powers. That he made use of such forces is shown by the incident, where the woman with the issue of blood touched his robe and was healed, "and Jesus, perceiving in himself that power had gone forth from him, immediately turned about in the crowd and said, 'Who touched my garments?'" (Mark 5, 30). (This incident reminds one of the statue of Asklepios with the sick woman touching his robe.) It is also stated, "And all the crowd sought to touch him, for *power* came forth from him and healed them all" (Luke 6. 19); and "the power of the Lord (spirit) was with him to heal" (Luke 5, 17). Jesus himself acknowledged that he made use of this spirit healing power, when he said, "But if it is by the Spirit of God that I cast out demons . . ." (Matthew 12. 28). At the present day, spirit healers claim that they feel the psychic force passing through them to the patient.

There is a Christian belief that spirit healing can occur only by the power of the "Holy Spirit" acting in the name of Jesus. But healing was carried out in Ancient Greece long before the Christian Era, and it is still practised by healers of non-Christian religions, such as Hinduism, Buddhism and Islam. The healing power has been the same in all ages and in all faiths, no matter what name is used for its source.

ABSENT HEALING

Jesus, like Elisha, was able to carry out absent healing, as shown by the curing of the servant of the Centurion (Matthew 8. 5), and the daughter of the Syrophenician woman (Matthew 15. 22). St. Paul also seems to have had this power (Acts 19. 12), using articles of his clothing as Elisha used his staff. It may be claimed that suggestion could play an important part in absent treatment, when the sufferer knows that he is being treated, but this would not apply to absent treatment being carried out unknown to the patient—here the healing must be due entirely to spirit or psychic forces. The same applies to prayer for the sick. It is useless to pray for the sick, as is commonly done in church, unless there is a definite power of the spirit to heal.

THE "DOUBLE WITNESS"

Healing works formed an important part of the ministry of Jesus; they constituted to a large extent the "signs and wonders" associated with his life and work. He carried out healing primarily to relieve suffering and cure the sick, but at the same time it demonstrated to the people the power of the spirit in him, and as it was associated with his preaching, it could be taken as evidence that his teaching was also divinely inspired. Thus it is stated, "And they went forth and preached everywhere, while the Lord worked with them and confirmed the message by the signs that attended it" (see Bible footnote, Mark 16. 20); "while God also bore witness by signs and wonders and various miracles . . ." (Hebrews 2. 4); ". . . speaking boldly for the Lord, who bore witness to the word of his grace, granting signs and wonders to be done by their (Paul and Barnabas') hands" (Acts 14. 3). As the Rev. G. Maurice Elliott puts it, "Note that there is always the 'double witness.' The preaching followed by a demonstration of 'signs and wonders' confirming the truth preached." (The Bible as Psychic History.)

It may be said, however, that if the healing as it has been claimed by certain scholars, was purely due to suggestion, the idea of the "double witness" is based on a fallacy as the healing "miracles" in that case are no more evidence of divine power than is the work of modern psychotherapists.

THE TRANSFIGURATION

Jesus was a powerful physical medium, as is indicated by his walking on the water (levitation), also by his transfiguration and at the same time the materialisation of Moses and Elijah on the Mount (Matthew 17. 1; Mark 9. 2; Luke 9. 28). In preparation for this transfiguration, he went to a solitary place on a mountain to pray. It was probably the evening and the climatic conditions would be very suitable in Palestine at that time for psychic phenomena to occur. He took with him Peter, John and James, three apostles who had strong psychic powers. "And as he was praying, the appearance of his countenance was altered ('his face did shine as the sun'), and his raiment became dazzling white (a typical case of transfiguration). And behold, two men talked with him, Moses and Elijah, who appeared in glory and spake of his departure, which he was to accomplish at Jerusalem." (Moses and Elijah would be in materialised form, their bodies being built up of ectoplasm drawn from Jesus and the three apostles.) "Now Peter and those who were with him were heavy with sleep but kept awake, and they saw his glory and the two men who stood with him" (Luke 9. 28-36). According to "The New English Bible," the apostles "meanwhile" had actually been in a deep sleep, but awoke in time to see Jesus still transfigured and the two spirits materialised beside him.

It has been commonly thought that the sleepy condition of the apostles was due to physical tiredness as a result of the activities of the preceding day, but the facts as given in the Gospels indicate clearly that the apostles were in trance, a common condition in the case of a medium when ectoplasm is being withdrawn from the body for a materialisation. This is also borne out by the fact that Peter was a physical medium (as shown by his walking on the water, and his escape from prison), and would be liable to go into trance during materialisations. Peter evidently recognised that the materialisation of Moses and Elijah had actually occurred as he suggested the making of three "booths" or cabinets, useful on these occasions to conserve the psychic power and build up the materialised forms.

Ectoplasmic materialisation is also indicated by the cloud which came and surrounded them. This was not an ordinary cloud or mist of the mountain side, otherwise why were they afraid? It would be an ectoplasmic mist which may occur during such manifestations due to the dispersal of ectoplasm. This is further shown by the fact that "a voice came out of the cloud"—in other words, the direct voice of a materialised vocal organ.

One can appreciate the difficulties of the translators of the Bible, knowing nothing about such psychic manifestations, trying to account for the state of trance in terms of ordinary fatigue or sleep. At the same time with such an explanation, they are faced with the further difficulty that the only three persons present during the occurrence of this stupendous phenomenon were half-asleep (or according to earlier versions, actually asleep for part of the time) and therefore could hardly be regarded as reliable witnesses.

(Transfiguration is a psychic phenomenon which occurs if there is much psychic power or high spiritual forces available, as in this case and in that of Moses on Mount Sinai. The body of Gautama, the Buddha, was said to shine in this way just prior to his death, and according to Bonaventura the whole body of St. Francis of Assisi on one occasion appeared to be wrapped in dazzling light. The face of St. Theresa of Avila also shone with light, when she was writing her mystical works).

After the Transfiguration, "as they were coming down the mountain, he (Jesus) charged them to tell no one what they had seen, until the Son of man should have risen from the dead" (Mark 9. 9). It is evident from this, that they had then to remember the experience, as it would help them to understand his own appearances after the Crucifixion—a lesson they apparently forgot, as they were slow to believe the testimony of the women who said that they had seen "the risen Lord."

Jesus seems to have held this séance, so that he could discuss with Moses and Elijah his coming death at Jerusalem. This should be borne in mind by those who claim that it is wrong to get into communication with the "dead" by such methods.

AFTER-DEATH APPEARANCES OF JESUS

The appearances of Jesus after his death may in some cases have been subjective or visionary in nature, the person concerned being clairvoyant. In other instances they were objective due to materialisations, his form consisting of the psychic substance, ectoplasm. He was able to appear in these ways, because his apostles and possibly some of his other followers, especially the women, were psychic.

The disappearance of his body from the tomb may have been due to its having undergone dematerialisation by psychic forces. The power would be available, as some of the individuals preparing the body for entombment were probably psychic sensitives, as in the case of the apostles and some of the women.

His first appearance was to Mary. That she did not see him clairvoyantly, *i.e.*, as a vision, is indicated by his words, "Do not hold me" (John 20. 17). It would seem to have been a materialisation, but the process being incomplete, perhaps owing to insufficient psychic power, he advised her, as the older versions probably more correctly put it, not even "to touch" him. One explanation by scholars of this warning to Mary is that whereas before his death she had approached him as a physical being, she was now to think of him in a purely spiritual manner. But if this is so, why did he allow certain women later to take "hold of his feet" (Matthew 28. 9), and the apostles in the Upper Room to touch him? The true explanation appears to be that in these cases more psychic power would be available, and the materialisation would be complete, enabling them to touch him. When he appeared to the two apostles on the road to Emmaus, the materialisation was evidently not at first perfect, as he was not recognised until he made them aware of his identity by breaking and blessing the bread in the house in the village. The comparative dimness of the interior of the house would also be more favourable than broad daylight for a perfect materialisation.

CONDITIONS AFFECTING MATERIALISATIONS

Materialisations do not readily occur in bright daylight, and it is worthy of note that the appearances of Jesus were as a rule in the early morning, "while it was yet dark," or in the dusk of the evening, or in the comparative dim light of the Upper Room. Here, the conditions would be ideal: a group of men and women, most of them psychic, semi-darkness, locked doors and no possibility of disturbance. Jesus appeared in their midst; his body was visible and tangible and he spoke to them and ate some food. It was a perfect materialisation, as happened also when Thomas was present, Jesus's body bearing even the wound marks to prove his identity. Then he faded away or vanished from their midst.

It could not possibly have been his physical body. A physical body could not pass through walls or closed doors, and be visible and tangible one moment and then shortly afterwards vanish into space. Those who argue that it must have been his physical body, as he had the wound marks and could eat and drink, do not realise that this could apply to a materialised or ectoplasmic body. They would also have to explain where the clothes came from, as a physical body would require ordinary material (not ectoplasmic) for clothing. Further, if it had been a physical body, he could have appeared before the leaders of the Church and State, but he could not do so, as he could materialise only under certain conditions—the presence of his mediumistic apostles, dim light and absence of any disturbing factors.

SURVIVAL AND RELIGION

All religions are based on survival; "If the dead are not raised, let us eat and drink, for tomorrow we die" (1

Corinthians 15. 32). The Christian religion is based on the survival of Jesus. There is no doubt that he placed great importance in proving to his followers that he survived after death, and he was enabled to do so because he had chosen for his apostles men who were psychic. His survival was not unique as is commonly claimed; even St. Paul recognised this, as he said, "But if there is no resurrection of the dead, then Christ has not been raised; if Christ has not been raised, then our preaching is in vain; . . . your faith is futile, and you are still in your sins." To emphasise his belief, he made this statement twice (1 Corinthians 15. 13-17).

The remarkable feature of the "resurrection" of Jesus was that he was able to prove survival to his followers. He actually gave them objective proof. They knew that he had survived; with them it was not simply a belief in ancient records or creeds, such as the Church relies on at the present time.

It may be noted that Jesus provided evidence of survival by the same methods as are used at the present day. This was recognised in the Majority Report of Archbishop Lang's Committee on Spiritualism, as it states: "It is certainly true that there are quite clear parallels between the miraculous events recorded in the Gospels and modern phenomena attested by Spiritualists. And if we assert that the latter must be doubted because they have not yet proved capable of scientific statement and verification, we must add that the miracles, and the Resurrection itself, are not capable of such verification either . . . If Spiritualism contains a truth, it is important to see that truth . . . as filling up gaps in our knowledge, so that where we already walked by faith, we may now have some measure of sight as well." (Psychic News.)

THE ASCENSION

Jesus seems to have appeared either in subjective (visionary) or objective (materialised) form on many occasions in the forty days after the Crucifixion, yet apparently he was not always recognised; "but some doubted" (Matthew 28. 17). With the objective appearances, this would be due to an imperfect materialisation. Even when he appeared at break of day on the shore of the Sea of Tiberias, there appears to have been some uncertainty: "Now none of the disciples dared ask him, 'Who are you?' They knew it was the Lord" (John 21, 12). In his final appearance at the Ascension, his materialised body disappeared in an ectoplasmic mist. Incidentally, he is said to have *ascended* into heaven. This is based on the old belief that heaven is in all cases upwards, an argument used by flat-earthers, for how could heaven be upwards both here and at the opposite side or antipodes of a round earth? Jesus after the Ascension was seen clairvoyantly and heard clairaudiently on various occasions, *e.g.*, by St. Paul on the road to Damascus.

PENTECOST

At Pentecost the apostles were all together in one place. They had probably met to develop their psychic powers and provide conditions for psychic manifestations, as Jesus had instructed them to do. The conditions must have been satisfactory, for they heard a sound "like the rush of a mighty wind" and saw "tongues of fire." A cold breeze and psychic lights are well-known phenomena in séances with physical mediums. "And they were all filled with the Holy Spirit (so all were mediumistic) and began to speak in other tongues, as the Spirit gave them utterance" (Acts 2. 2-4).

There were men of all nations standing around "And they were amazed and wondered, saying, 'Are not all these who are speaking Galileans? And how is it that we hear, each of us in his own native language?'" (Acts 2. 7-11). A long list of countries is then given of each of which the "tongue" was spoken. From this it would appear that all the apostles were controlled by different spirits, each speaking the particular language or dialect known to him in earth-life.

SPEAKING IN FOREIGN TONGUES

Some scholars hold that the apostles were merely muttering inarticulate sounds, giving rise to the belief that they were actually speaking in foreign tongues. Against this, it could be said that it is difficult to understand how such a purposeless phenomenon could be ascribed to inspiration by the Holy Spirit. But the Bible states quite definitely that they spoke under spirit inspiration in certain tongues (this could include dialects) and that what they said was understood by the people with a knowledge of these tongues. It must also be borne in mind that speech in a foreign tongue or even dialect might appear to be "muttering" to one ignorant of the language.

It is known from present day experience that muttering may occur with mediums, who are not being fully controlled by their spirit guides—in fact, it is an indication that their mediumship is not yet sufficiently developed to enable the spirit guides to act freely through them. This would probably be a common experience with the Early Christian Church owing to its lack of experience of mediumship or spirit control and the frequent occurrence of undeveloped mediums. Moreover, many of the church leaders would not appreciate fully the difference between an undeveloped and a fully developed medium. This is evident with St. Paul in his admonitions to the Corinthians (see later under St. Paul).

There is plenty of evidence at the present day that an experienced sensitive under certain circumstances may speak in a tongue unknown to her, but the earth-life tongue of the spirit control. An outstanding example of this was where messages from an Ancient Egyptian spirit were obtained through an English medium. These were in the Ancient Egyptian tongue and gave the hitherto unknown vowel sounds, thus enabling a vocabulary of the language to be built up. (See "Ancient Egypt Speaks" by Hulme and Wood.)

There is also the case of Dr. Whymant, a well-known authority on oriental languages. He was on a visit to New York, when he was invited to attend séances at which the spirit control of the medium was speaking in an unknown tongue. Whymant found that the control spoke in Ancient Chinese, and also explained the meaning of some ancient Chinese verse, which up to that time had not been understood.

ST. PETER

Peter was probably the most psychically gifted of all the apostles. His speech after Pentecost was evidently given under spirit inspiration or control. This was probably his first public speech, yet he was so eloquent that it is said that he converted three thousand people to the new faith.

He had the gift of healing, and an account is given of how he and John healed a lame man at the door of the Temple. It is further told that when Peter and John were afterwards brought before the rulers and elders, Peter, "filled with the Holy Spirit" (Acts 4. 8), stood up boldly and addressed them. "Now when they (the rulers) saw the boldness of Peter and John, and perceived that they were uneducated, common men, they wondered" (Acts 4. 13). From this it is evident that Peter was speaking under spirit inspiration or control. Jesus had warned them that they need not be concerned with what they should say when they were taken before the authorities, for the spirit of the Lord would tell them what to say, in other words, they would speak under spirit control or inspiration; "For it is not you who speak, but the Spirit of your Father speaking through you" (Matthew 10. 20).

St. Peter was a physical medium, as shown by his walking on the water, and by his escape from prison as a result of a materialised spirit unlocking the prison doors. Later, on the roof top of the house of Simon, the tanner, at Joppa, he was at prayer and went into trance, in which condition he had a symbolic vision and heard a voice.

St. Stephen

St. Stephen was psychic. The address which he gave prior to being stoned was apparently a trance speech, perhaps given under the control of Jesus himself. It was a brilliant exposition of how the Jewish Church in the past had persecuted the seers or prophets. At the end of his speech he became clairvoyant and had a vision.

St. Paul

St. Paul, when on the road to Damascus, had a vision of Jesus and heard him speak. At the same time he lost his power of sight, but had it restored to him by psychic treatment given to him by a Christian disciple, Ananias, who had been told by "the Lord" in a vision to do so. Zechariah had a somewhat similar experience, being struck dumb when he had a vision and was told of the birth of a son to be called John.

St. Paul was a psychic healer and used his handkerchiefs and aprons for absent treatment of disease, just as Elisha used his staff. He appears to have had a mystical experience in which, he said, he was "caught up to the third heaven" and "heard things that cannot be told, which man may not utter" (2 Corinthians 12. 2-4).

His Epistles contain many psychic references: "Do not despise prophesying; but test everything; hold fast what is good" (1 Thessalonians 5. 20-21).

"So, my brethren, earnestly desire to prophesy, and do not forbid speaking in tongues" (1 Corinthians 14. 39).

"Now concerning spiritual gifts, brethren, I do not want you to be uninformed . . . Now there are varieties of gifts, but the same Spirit; . . . to each is given the manifestation of the Spirit for the common good. To one is given through the Spirit the utterance of wisdom, and to another the utterance of knowledge (inspiration) . . ., to another gifts of healing . . ., to another working of miracles (psychic phenomena), to another prophecy, to another the ability to distinguish between spirits (clairvoyance), to another various kinds of tongues (trance control), to another the interpretation of tongues" (1 Corinthians 12. 1-10).

"And God has appointed in the church first apostles, second prophets, third teachers, then workers of miracles, then healers, helpers, administrators, speakers in various kinds of tongues. Are all apostles? Are all prophets? Are all teachers? Do all work miracles? Do all possess gifts of healing? Do all speak with tongues? Do all interpret?" (1 Corinthians 12, 28-30.)

"Make love your aim, and earnestly desire the spiritual gifts, especially that you may prophesy" (1 Corinthians 14. 1).

MEDIUMSHIP AND THE CHRISTIAN CHURCH

THE USE OF MEDIUMS IN THE EARLY CHURCH

It is quite evident from St. Paul's Epistles that the various kinds of mediumship played an important part in the life of the Early Christian Churches. In fact, the services were definitely spiritualistic in nature, mediums being used in the church services for clairvoyance, clairaudience, inspired or trance utterances and healing. The trance messages were given under spirit control, or as the Early Church puts it, when the speakers were "full of the Holy Spirit." St. Paul gives a detailed list of their work (1. Corinthians 12. 28-30); and shows how church meetings have to be conducted in an orderly fashion (1 Corinthians 14. 26-33). There would be plenty of individuals in the Early Church aspiring to be under spirit control, and they all would be eager to speak in public. As a result, confusion might arise due to several trying to speak at the same time. Hence the need for St. Paul's admonition to regulate their work in church so that they speak "in a tongue" or "prophesy one by one." "For God is not a God of confusion but of peace." In this connection, he wisely points out that "the spirits of prophets are subject to prophets"—in other words, mediums have the power to control their psychic utterances.

It would seem, however, from his admonitions to the Corinthians (1 Corinthians, chapters 12 and 14), that he was not clear in his own mind as to the exact nature and significance of the different forms of mediumship—clairvoyance, "speaking in tongues," interpretation of tongues, prophecy, etc. He had his own visions and his gift of healing but could not apparently distinguish between the undeveloped and the fully developed medium. Further, he would be completely out of his depths in Corinth, where he had to face a type of civilisation quite foreign to him. He was a strict Pharisee, serious, austere and full of zeal for his mission, whereas the Corinthians were light-hearted and volatile and devoted to the arts—painting, statuary and bronze work.

THE CLASH BETWEEN MEDIUMS AND THE CHURCH

Ignatius about the beginning of the second century tells of mediumistic activities, "Some in the churches do most certainly have knowledge of things to come (prophecy).

Some have visions, some give clairaudient messages and heal the sick by the laying on of hands, and others speak in many tongues." Further references to their work in the services of the Church occur up to the fourth century in the writings of Tatian, Justin Martyr, Irenaeus (Bishop of Lyons), Tertullian, Origen and Eusebius. (See "The Psychic Stream," by Arthur Findlay.) However, their spirit communications were not always in agreement with the dogmas and doctrines of the official Church and its scriptures, and as a result they were gradually ousted from the services. This was admitted by St. Jerome; he said, "We tell them that we do not so much reject prophecy as refuse to receive prophets whose utterances fail to accord with the Scriptures Old and New." He, therefore, advised Pope Damasus not to allow them to take part in the work of the Church, and this has been the position ever since.

THE EXCLUSION OF MEDIUMS FROM THE CHURCH

In the fourth century, Christianity was adopted as the State religion by the Emperor Constantine, and the Church dogmas and doctrines were creedalised by the Council of Nicaea. Later in the same century, the Emperor Theodosius, under the advice of St. Ambrose, Bishop of Milan, issued an edict against churches employing persons with psychic gifts and this was followed by the persecution and the slaying of their members. The Montanists (followers of Montanus, who lived in the second century A.D.) belonged to this category. They believed that the necessity for the psychic element in the Church, particularly prophetic ecstasy, was greater than ever. They held that the only true Christians were those who had "the inward prophetic illumination of the Holy Spirit, and the more highly gifted in this way were to be regarded as the genuine successors of the apostles, in preference to the more outwardly consecrated bishops." This sect of Christians was completely wiped out in the persecution which followed the issue of the edict of Theodosius.

THE PERSECUTION OF MEDIUMS

Accordingly, in the fourth century A.D., prophets or mediums were finally driven from the Christian Church. In the centuries which followed, the priests claimed that the Church was the only medium between God and man, and any divine guidance and help must come, not through prophets or seers, but through the "divinely" inspired priests. Thus the priests usurped the place held by mediums in the Early Church, a place only secondary to the apostles (1 Corinthians 12. 28). Further, the Church claimed that whereas it received direct inspiration from the Holy Spirit, the prophets or mediums were servants of the devil, and were controlled by lower or evil spirits. In fact, they were to be regarded as witches and, like sorcerers and heretics, had to be rooted out wherever possible.

The persecution, which followed lasted until about the beginning of the nineteenth century, and was responsible for up to a million innocent people being slain, often by torturing and burning. It reached its height in the fifteenth century with the publication of a celebrated Papal Bull of 1484, which sanctioned the discovering and putting to death of all such persons." Shortly afterwards the "Malleus Maleficarum" or "Hammer for Witches" was published, which systematised all form of trial and examination, and marked the beginning of the "witch mania," in which thousands perished after merciless torture. Even small children were not spared.

In Germany alone about one hundred thousand people were tortured and burned for witchcraft; in Scotland up to four thousand; in England many more—three thousand during the time of the Long Parliament alone; and in Northern Italy, one thousand in a single year. The prime movers in this persecution were the clergy of the Christian Church, Protestant as well as Roman Catholic. Many of the victims may have been genuine mediums, as in the case of Bessie Dunlop of Ayrshire, who was burned as a witch in 1576, because in her presence voices were heard, which claimed to be those of dead people. There was a somewhat similar case in Dundee about 100 years later. The disastrous effect on "open vision in the land" of all this persecution and killing is apparent, when it is remembered that mediumship is frequently inherited.

It is said in Chambers's Encyclopaedia, that the feeling (against witchcraft) zealously fostered by the clergy of the period, rose to a frenzy that for four centuries filled Europe with the most shocking bloodshed and cruelty. "Persecution for witchcraft formed one of the most deplorable episodes in human history. They (the episodes) show more strikingly than anything else has ever done what relentless cruelty human nature is capable of, under the influence of a fanatical delusion."

In this persecution the Christian Church forgot the All-loving and Merciful Father of Jesus, and could think only of the merciless Jahveh of the Early Israelites. If Jesus had lived in this period he would have been subjected to even worse torture than he received under the Romans.

THE CHURCH SERVICES BECOME FORMALISED

The Church, having thoroughly eradicated the prophets, lost the direct forms of spirit inspiration or communication which Jesus himself and the apostles had used, and its services became formalised, the teaching being based largely on its early traditions and dogmas. It insisted on all its members accepting its creeds, obeying its commands, and observing its ceremonies and rites. Thus it fell back into the error of the Early Hebrew Church, which had condemned the direct spirit-inspired teaching of Jesus and had insisted instead on a belief in the Faith of the Fathers and a strict obedience to the "Law." Consequently, after the fourth century there is little or no reference in the Christian literature to the inspired works of great contemporary prophets; there is just priestly teaching and dogma.

THE BELIEF IN THE HOLY SPIRIT

With regard to the belief of the Church in the inspiration by the "Holy Spirit," it may be said here that in the New Testament, the spirit communications and healing works are frequently attributed to the "Holy Spirit," although it would appear that in many of these cases *various* higher spirits, including Gabriel or some other angel or Jesus himself, were responsible for the manifestations. In fact, in their healing and other psychic works, the apostles invoked the help of Jesus. For instance, when Peter cured the lame man at the door of the Temple, he said, "In the name of Jesus Christ of Nazareth, walk" (Acts 3. 6). Also, at a meeting of the apostles, they prayed "While thou stretchest out thy hand to heal, and signs and wonders are performed through the name of thy holy servant Jesus" (Acts 4. 30). It may be noted that the expression "thy holy servant Jesus" shows that the apostles did not look on Jesus as co-equal with God; nor did Jesus himself and St. Paul. (See "The Search for God.").

That various spirits might be responsible for the manifestations is also shown by the admonition, "Beloved, do not believe every spirit, but test the spirits to see whether they are of God" (1 John 4. 1). The term, Holy Spirit, has never been clearly defined by the Church, and no clear conception of it can be formed from what is said of its activities in the New Testament. In this connection, Dr. Matthews, the Dean of St. Paul's Cathedral, states, "The New Testament evidence for a personal conception of the Holy Spirit is mixed, and I cannot resist the conclusion that, in many cases, the Holy Spirit is thought of as a power, influence or presence of God in Christ."

It seems that the expression, Holy Spirit, was used in the New Testament to describe in a collective sense God's activities in relation to man, activities in which the services of various higher spirit messengers or agents were used. It was only after several hundred years, at the Council of Nicaea, that the Holy Spirit or Ghost was officially adopted as the Third Person of the Trinity.

"THE SIN AGAINST THE HOLY SPIRIT"

Much thought has been given to the words of Jesus, "But whoever speaks against the Holy Spirit, it will not be forgiven" (Matthew 12. 32). It was the complete failure of the Jews to recognise the presence and workings of the Divine Spirit, which Jesus condemned. In the past God had given the Jews guidance and help through his inspired agents, the prophets; "As he spoke by the mouth of his holy prophets from of old" (Luke 1. 70). But only too often the Jews had failed to recognise these messengers and had rejected their teaching and even persecuted them. Finally, in the case of Jesus, instead of recognising his godlike nature and his Divine inspiration, they could only see in him the "work of the devil," and even claimed that his teaching was evil being inspired by the devil, and his healing was carried out by the help of Beelzebub, the prince of devils. It was this attitude that Jesus condemned, one in which the mind had become so warped that it had lost the God-given faculty of recognising truth when confronted with it; and only seeing evil in what was good.

The Early, Christians apparently thought that those who derided the spirit manifestations and healing works of their prophets or sensitives fell into the same error. Thus it is stated in "The Teaching of the Twelve Apostles" or "The Didache," a manuscript written about 130 to 150 A.D., that "every prophet that speaketh in the spirit (*i.e.*, under spirit control) ye shall not try nor judge, for every sin shall be forgiven but this sin shall not be forgiven." Yet, since the fourth century, the orthodox Christian Church has persistently set its face against these prophets or mediums; it has failed to recognise the spiritual nature of their inspiration, has scorned their messages and frequently subjected them to the most merciless persecution. In its blindness to the workings of the spirit and in its zeal to uphold its creeds and dogmas, it has turned its back on the truth. Because mediums are seldom theologically trained, it has despised the channels through which the Divine inspiration has come. Sir Winston S. Churchill in his book, "My Early Life," wrote, "If you are the recipient of a message which cheers your heart and fortifies your soul, which promises you reunion with those you have loved in a world of larger opportunity, why should you worry about the shape or colour of the travel-stained envelope?"

THE NEED FOR CONTINUED REVELATION

It has been claimed that in Jesus the Church has had the complete revelation, and that therefore there is no need for the direct or inspired teaching, which prophets or seers can give. In this connection it may be noted that Archbishop Temple said, "We (the Church) have created the impression that God was singularly active in one part of the world, Palestine, until A.D. 66, but He did not do anything anywhere else, and has not done anything since."

It may be said that at no time can revelation be complete; it tends to be affected by the age, and the stage of civilisation and the religious beliefs of the person concerned. St. Paul appears to have recognised that revelation at best can only be partial, as he said, "In many and various ways (in earlier versions by divers portions and in divers manners) God spoke of old to our fathers by the prophets" (Hebrews 1. 1). No one can reasonably contend that the revelation received nearly 2,000 years ago through Jesus and the apostles, and suitable for the conditions at that time, renders further revelation from God unnecessary. History shows that this is not the case. The world is still in desperate and urgent need of God-inspired wisdom. Such wisdom has come in the past and can still come through inspired seers or prophets.

THE PSYCHIC INSPIRATION OF GREAT RELIGIOUS LEADERS

All the great religious leaders from the beginning of civilisation were spirit inspired, whether seers, prophets or mediums God always spoke by the prophets; "As he spoke by the mouth of his holy prophets from of old" (Luke 1. 70).

In this connection, Tyrrell in his work, "The Personality of Man," quotes from Prof. Wm. fames, "You will in point of fact hardly find a religious leader of any kind in whose life there is no record of automatism (psychic phenomena, such as clairvoyance and trance utterances). I speak not only of savage priests and prophets, whose followers regard automatic utterance and action as by itself tantamount to inspiration. I speak of leaders of thought and subjects of intellectualised experience. St. Paul had his visions, his ecstasies, his gift of tongues, small as was the importance he attached to the latter. The whole array of Christian saints and heresiarchs, including the greatest, the Bernards, the Loyolas, the Luthers, the Foxes, the Wesleys, had their visions, voices, rapt conditions, guiding impressions and "openings." They had these things because they had exalted sensibility and to such things persons of exalted sensibility are liable."

Nevertheless, in all ages these prophets or psychics have been up against the Church of the time. This fact was in the mind of Jesus, when he told his disciples, "Blessed are you when men hate you, and when they exclude you, and revile you, and cast out your name as evil, on account of the Son of man! . . for so their fathers did to the prophets" (Luke 6. 22-23). And St. Stephen in his speech before the High Priest and Council used much the same words: "You always resist the Holy Spirit. As your fathers did, so do you. Which of the prophets did not your fathers persecute?" (Acts 7. 51-52). St. Stephen's speech could be applied with equal force to the way the Christian Church in later times persecuted psychic sensitives or mediums.

THE CHURCH'S BELIEF REGARDING SPIRIT AGENTS

There is the Christian belief that the members of their Church have through Jesus "direct, unhindered and first hand access to God," and therefore there is no need for other intermediaries, such as spirit agents, guides or guardian angels, between God and man. But surely it is only a commonsense and realistic view to hold that God has spirit agents or angels everywhere on earth as in spirit-life. If we are in difficulties in earth-life, our friends on earth are willing to help us. In doing so they act as God's agents, just as "the Good Samaritan" did in the parable. This should apply also to those in spirit-life, for they are unchanged in mind and personality after death. Thus discarnate spirits will try to help each other and, if possible, mankind on earth. In doing so, they do not come between man and God; they simply act as God's agents or intermediaries.

There is no reason why a person in his prayers should not appeal to God direct or through the intermediary of Jesus, but the answer to the prayers may actually come through his own spirit guide or some other spirit friend, or a friend still on earth, who perhaps has been prompted from the spirit world. For all should be God's agents, and any help that anyone can give will be in accordance with God's Will, even although the inspiration and prompting may have come through a number of intermediaries.

THE NEED FOR EVIDENCE OF SURVIVAL

The wiping out of prophets or mediums from the Church had another serious effect on its work. It was now unable to provide its members with evidence of survival, apart from that of the ancient Gospel records concerning Jesus. Nor could it give any information with regard to what happens after death—in fact it had the most fantastic ideas of the nature of the after-life, derived from ancient beliefs and works, such as The Revelation. For instance, until recent times, there was the belief in a physical resurrection. (See "The After-Life.")

Survival is the basic feature of all religions. Christianity is centred round the survival of Jesus; but for his after-death appearances, there would have been no Christian religion. After the Crucifixion, the apostles were in a panic through fear of the rulers, and were utterly dispirited by the fact that their leader, on whom they had built such high hopes of establishing an earthly kingdom, had been put to death in what to them seemed to be a most ignominious manner. But Christ's after-death appearances, put new life and courage into them. They became changed men, and were only too eager to continue the mission he had given them, to teach the people and heal the sick.

Although at the present time some people have a profound inner conviction of the continuing presence of Jesus in their lives, others, many of whom are Christians, have not this conviction, nor will they accept the personal experience of others as evidence of survival. In fact, non-Christians, especially atheists, might claim that this inner personal feeling was merely self-delusion or imagination.

There is therefore a need at the present day for proof of survival.

In the past the Church has insisted on an implicit belief in its creeds and dogmas regarding the survival of Jesus and of mankind in general. It has claimed that the evidence which Jesus provided of his survival should be sufficient for true Christians for all time. In fact, faith in this evidence is regarded by the Church as in itself a Christian virtue, so that as Archbishop Temple stated in a Gifford lecture in Glasgow in 1934, "It is positively undesirable that there should be experimental proof of survival." "I am convinced that direct proof of survival is not only impossible, but undesirable." This was a strange statement for a leading churchman to make as Jesus himself considered it necessary to provide proof of survival to his apostles and other followers, and actually was able to do so. It also ignored the fact that similar proof can be had at the present day, and by the same methods.

The fact remains that as a result of the wave of materialism, which has swept over the Western World, many Christians have not this blind faith in the Church creeds and dogmas. They refuse to accept these ancient records of Christ's "resurrection," unless they can also have evidence of survival at the present time. And this the Church cannot provide, as it refuses to employ psychic individuals with the gifts of clairvoyance and materialisation. Such psychic evidence, being factual in nature, is more convincing than all the creeds and dogmas in existence. For as Burns said, "But Facts are chiels that winna ding, an' downa be disputed."

The physical and the spiritual worlds intermingle; there is no hard and fast line or impenetrable barrier between them. Heaven is not far away but in our midst.

"Earth's crammed with heaven
And every common bush afire with God;
But only he who sees, takes off his shoes."

Man in earth-life in virtue of his spirit nature is always in touch, though as a rule subconsciously, with other-world conditions; he may be said to walk "hand in hand with angels." Early man was keenly aware of the existence of these spirits; they were very real to him. He was of the opinion that they played an active part in his life, affecting for good or ill all that he did. It is only in modern times that as a result of the growth of materialism, a spirit of agnosticism and even atheism has arisen. Hence the existence of ministering spirits is apt to be overlooked or even denied entirely, and man chooses to think that he can walk alone. He fails to see the absurdity of the belief that he can do all things in his own strength and face up by himself to the vast universe in which he lives, ignoring completely the unseen world around and the Almighty Power which sustains all things. But in spite of all that he thinks, he is a member of a vast Brotherhood of Spirits, whether incarnate or discarnate. He is never alone—he is surrounded at all times by "a cloud of witnesses."

"The angels keep their ancient places;
Turn but a stone, and start a wing!
'Tis ye, 'tis your estranged faces,
That miss the many-splendoured thing."

THE
UNIVERSE AND MAN

THE UNIVERSE AND MAN

The Universe comprises everything in existence, whether physical or spiritual in nature. Man belongs to the *physical universe* because he has a physical body, but he is also of the *spirit universe* as he is a spirit and has a spirit body.

THE ORIGIN AND NATURE OF THE PHYSICAL UNIVERSE

"The heavens are telling the glory of God;
and the firmament proclaims his handiwork.
Day to day pours forth speech,
and night to night declares knowledge.
There is no speech, nor are there words;
their voice is not heard;
yet their voice goes out through all the earth,
and their words to the end of the world." Psalm 19.

THE STUDY OF THE STARS

It has been said, "If our earth had been so clouded that the stars were hidden from men's eyes, the whole history of our race would have been different. For it was through his leisure-time observations of the stars that early man discovered the regularity of the year and got his fundamental impressions of the order of Nature—on which all his science is founded" ("Outline of Science," Newnes).

The science of astronomy is concerned with the largest aspects of the physical universe. Alone of all living creatures on earth, man has ventured to search out into the vast depths of space and probe into the nature and origin, not only of our sun and its attendant planets, but of the countless star systems around.

On a clear cloudless night, millions of stars can be seen in the sky. These stars are actually distant suns.

They are arranged in huge clusters, termed galaxies. Our own sun, a star of moderate size, occurs in the galaxy known as the Milky Way. Round many of the stars rotate smaller bodies, like our earth, and these are termed planets. A sun with its associated planets is referred to as a solar system.

THE THEOLOGICAL IMPORTANCE OF ASTRONOMY

The study of astronomy is of great theological importance. In all the great religions of the world, it is claimed that there is a God behind the universe, a God who is its Creator and Sustainer. Man knows from his everyday experiences that there is a cause behind every effect in his earthly environment, and scientific investigations have confirmed the universal nature of this law of causation. Hence man argues that there must be a Cause behind the whole universe, a Power which was responsible for its creation and which can be referred to as God. Thus he regards the sun, moon and stars as evidence of God's handiwork, as expressions of the Divine Spirit in matter, and as giving him an insight into the ways and workings of the Divine Mind.

EARLY SPECULATIONS

From the dawn of civilisation, the sun, moon and stars have kindled feelings of awe and wonder in the human mind. It has been said that "the simple contemplation of the vault of the sky produces a religious experience in primitive consciousness." Early man spent most of his life in the open. He saw the sun by day and the moon and stars by night and must have given much thought to their nature and origin. These shining bodies, which seemed to move across the sky, were they gods or the homes of gods? Could they influence for good or ill his life on earth—his success in hunting, in tilling the soil and in defending himself from his enemies?

The chief or "high gods" of primitive people are in general "sky gods."

From such crude speculations and imaginings originated the science of astronomy, although until a few hundred years ago the chief interest in this subject lay in astrological issues—the supposed effects of the stars and planets on the ways and doings of man.

THE CREATION OF THE UNIVERSE

In the folk-lore and mythology of ancient nations there are many differing accounts of the creation of the earth and the stars. That of the Ancient Israelites, given in Genesis, is outstanding in its simplicity and grandeur. It appears to have been written by Jewish scribes (not by Moses, as was formerly believed) between 900 and 400 B.C., a period in which occurred the Babylonian Captivity. These scribes apparently made use, not only of ancient Jewish beliefs and traditions, but also of early Babylonian records of the Creation, the Deluge and the Tower of Babel, as the account in Genesis bears close resemblances to that of the Gilgamesh Epic tablets from the Royal Assyrian Library, which were inscribed prior to 2,000 B.C.

Most of the early astronomers and philosophers, including Aristotle and Ptolemy, believed like the writers of Genesis that the earth was the centre of the universe, with the sun, moon and stars revolving round it. This geocentric belief was not held by Aristarchus of Samos, an astronomer of the third century B.C., who claimed that the earth and other planets revolved round the sun. His views, however, received little consideration until restated by Copernicus about 1,800 years later. It can be readily understood why the claims of this early astronomer were not easily accepted. It was difficult to believe that this massive and apparently fixed and immovable earth on which they lived was actually in motion; this appeared to be contrary to all reason and to the seeming facts of everyday observation and experience. Moreover, theologians refused to accept any view which suggested that the earth was not fixed and at the centre of a universe of sun and stars. They also insisted that the universe had been created at a particular time in the past and was not only finite in time but also in space. Any ideas contrary to these beliefs were rigidly and even violently suppressed, as in the case of Bruno and Galileo. Even when it was at last accepted (in the seventeenth century) that the earth and other planets moved round the sun, it was still believed until comparatively recent times that our solar system was the centre of the universe of fixed stars.

It is now known that there are millions and millions of other solar systems in the universe and probably trillions and trillions of planets. These modern scientific findings require a conception of God and the Universe, which is grander and more vast by far than that of Genesis and the Christian theology.

THE NATURE OF THE UNIVERSE

The universe consists of a stupendous number of huge starry clusters or galaxies, which appear to exist in groups distributed in a highly uniform manner throughout space. Our galaxy, the Milky Way, occurs in a group of about twenty-five. This is a small group compared with that known as Virgo, which contains over a thousand galaxies.

In the vast area within the range of observation by our optical telescopes, *i.e.*, up to two thousand million light years distance, there are about one hundred million of these huge galaxies or groups of galaxies. (Light travels at a speed of 186,000 miles a second and therefore a light year is six million, million miles.) The light from the galaxies at the extreme limits of observation (two thousand million light years away) takes two thousand million years to reach the earth and therefore these galaxies appear to us as they actually were two thousand million years ago.

Each of these galaxies contains thousands of millions of stars. It is estimated that in our galaxy alone, *i.e.*, the Milky Way, there are a hundred thousand million stars. Thus there must be billions of stars, *i.e.*, suns, in the universe.

All the galaxies are apparently receding from each other at very high speeds. The speed of recession is proportional to the distance between them. The most distant galaxy observable by our optical telescopes is receding from our galaxy, the Milky Way, with a speed of about one-fifth of that of light. A galaxy at double the distance away will be moving at about the same speed as that of light. Beyond that point the light of a galaxy can never reach us, and it will be no longer visible by optical telescopes, no matter how great the magnification. However, there is evidence from radio telescopes that there are galaxies at far vaster distances in space. Hence it would appear that the universe is expanding at an inconceivable rate.

THE ORIGIN OF THE UNIVERSE

There are various theories with regard to the origin of the universe. These can be divided into the evolutionary, and the *continuous creation* theories.

According to the *evolutionary* theory, the universe originated at a definite time in the remote past (from twenty to sixty thousand million years ago) as a single mass of electrically charged particles, the so-called "primeval atom," which was only a few million miles in diameter. This mass was unstable and, owing to the disruptive action of radioactive forces, it disintegrated with explosive violence. As a result, the primeval matter was hurled outwards into space with such great force that it continued to disperse as a vast gaseous cloud for thousands of millions of years. At a certain stage in the process of dispersion, *i.e.*, about nine thousand million years ago, this cosmic cloud began to condense to form galaxies. According to this evolutionary theory, all the basic matter of the universe was present in the primeval atom and no more is being created. If this is the case, the average spatial density of the galaxies is gradually becoming less owing to their recession in space.

On the other hand, in the *continuous creation* or *"steady state"* theory, the primary matter of the universe is being created continuously throughout space. From this basic matter, hydrogen gas is formed which then condenses to form galaxies. In this theory, the expansion of the universe is attributed, not to the effects of an explosion of a primeval atom, but to the continuous creation of new material which subjects the entire universe to outward pressure, and thus causes it to expand in all directions and the galaxies present to move outwards or recede rapidly in space. However, in spite of this recession movement, the average density of the galaxies in space should remain fairly constant because new ones are being continuously created. Also, as there is no end to space, there must be an infinite number of galaxies.

It has been estimated that the spatial density of the galaxies in the observable universe could be maintained in this way by the creation of only a few atoms of hydrogen per cubic mile of space in the year. This may appear infinitesimal but the observable universe is so vast that it would amount to some hundred million, million, million, million, million tons per second.

In both these cosmological theories there is agreement that the universe is not static but in a dynamic state of expansion. The fundamental difference between them is that in the evolutionary theory *all* the basic matter and *all* the energy in the universe were present in the primeval atom, the creation of which took place once and for all at the first moment of finite time in the far distant past; and the universe will continue to exist until no more energy is available for the production of heat, light and chemical or nuclear change. When this stage is reached, there will be no radiant solar masses, no illuminated planets; only cold, dark bodies moving forever onwards in space. On the other hand, in the continuous creation theory, the creation of new matter is going on continuously throughout all time—past, present and future—and the new matter makes up for all that has condensed into galaxies. In this theory, there is no end to space, and finite time had no beginning and will have no end. The universe will remain, as it has always been, in a state of continuous creation. Differences may occur in the details of its structure, but it will always remain the same as a whole—hence the term "steady-state" universe.

With both theories, no attempt is made to suggest an origin for the primeval matter of the universe. Was it formed, or is it being formed, by some physical or chemical process which is capable of being investigated by scientific methods, or has it arisen out of nothing as a result of Divine creative action outwith the bounds of human understanding? Modern scientific methods are not yet, and may never be, capable of investigating the ultimate origin of the universe; there is always "a time and conditions beyond the utmost mental horizon."

FORMATION OF GALAXIES

The basic matter of the universe, no matter the manner of its origin, appears to consist almost entirely of hydrogen, although other elements may be present from the gases and dust of disrupting stars. The density of the hydrogen is extremely low, but as the universe is in a state of expansion, the gas is continually moving outwards in all directions. This movement causes the development of irregularities and, as a result of gravitational action, the gas in each of these gradually becomes denser and denser and begins to rotate in the form of a vast disc. Thus a galaxy is formed. At first no stars are present, but the rotating movement of the disc causes eddies to occur in its gaseous matter, especially near the rim, just as small eddies occur in a whirlpool of water. The gas in each eddy gradually becomes denser until first a separate cloud of matter and then a star or sun is formed. Millions of these stars may occur in the one galaxy; our galaxy, the Milky Way, is believed to contain one hundred thousand million. Many of these stars appear to have been formed about the same time, eight or nine thousand million years ago.

THE STARS OR SUNS

The temperature of the gas in the galaxy is at first low, but once each star is formed and begins to shrink (owing to further condensation), high pressures are created in its interior and as a result the temperature rises until it is sufficiently high for the hydrogen to be converted into helium. Then, as the temperature rises still further, the helium is changed into higher elements, *e.g.*, iron. These nuclear processes increase in intensity with the rise in temperature and result in the generation of much energy, which is radiated from the star's surface as light and heat. With stars, such as our sun, the rate of generation of energy in the interior is the same as the rate of radiation of energy from the surface, so that the size of the star remains constant. (It is believed that the temperature of the interior of our sun is about 15,000,000°C. and of the surface, 6,000°C.).

Certain large stars, in some cases ten times the size of our sun, are known as *supergiants*. They have a short existence as their hydrogen is rapidly converted into helium. There is excessive loss of energy by radiation from the surface of such stars, and as a result they gradually shrink and rotate more and more rapidly until they begin to break up, steadily throwing off matter into space. The star at this stage is termed an *ordinary nova*. In some cases, supergiants shrink very rapidly and owing to the extremely high internal pressure and temperature, nuclear processes may be set up which, instead of liberating energy, actually require it. As a result, the supergiants collapse and disintegrate with explosive violence, ejecting far into space a vast cloud of gaseous matter consisting not only of hydrogen and helium, but also of the higher elements, *e.g.*, the metals. These exploding stars are termed *supernovae*.

As the stars generally consist largely of hydrogen, it has been inferred that the galaxies observable in space by our optical telescopes are of relatively recent origin. Our galaxy may be about 9,000 million years old; it is still at an early stage in its life. It has been estimated that the hydrogen in our sun will last another 50,000 million years, so that our solar system may be said to be still in its childhood.

THE MILKY WAY

Our galaxy is a vast disc of stars, thicker in the centre than at the rim. It is up to 100,000 light years in diameter. The huge belt of stars, which is popularly referred to as the Milky Way, is made up of the countless stars of the galaxy we see when we look along or in the direction of the plane of the disc. These stars are mostly within 50,000 light years of the earth. Owing to the presence of interstellar clouds of gas and dust, only about ten percent of the light of the stars reaches us, and for the same reason the central region of our galactic disc is obscured.

The disc rotates like a vast wheel, a complete rotation taking about 200 million years. Thus the galaxy may have made only twenty to forty of such complete revolutions since its origin. Nevertheless, this rotation imparts to our solar system a speed of 500,000 miles an hour. (In addition, the earth rotates round the Polar axis at about 1,000 miles an hour at the equator, and it has also an orbital movement round the sun of 70,000 miles an hour).

THE FORMATION OF PLANETS

Most modern astronomers believe that the earth and other planets originated from a primeval cloud of diffuse gas and particles of dust, which rotated like a vast disc-shaped nebula round the sun. There is, however, great difference of opinion with regard to the origin of this solar cloud. Was it thrown off as a ring from a rapidly rotating sun, or was it acquired by the fully formed sun at a much later period owing to the latter having passed through a dense cloud of interstellar dust and gas?

As the matter in this solar cloud cooled to a low temperature, it began to condense into solid particles. Many of these particles came into contact with each other and by a process of accretion gradually formed larger and larger aggregates of matter. There was much disturbance, however, in the rotating gas cloud and as a result there were many collisions between the aggregates, causing them to be shattered into fragments again. A few which were not broken up in this way, gradually grew in size owing to the accretion of dust and fragments with which they came into contact, until they were large enough to sweep in by gravitational attraction the surrounding matter. Then they rapidly increased in size until they became planets. The formation of planets from the solar nebular matter must have taken from three to six thousand million years. All the planets must have added further to their size by gathering up the gas and dust which they encountered in their passage through space.

It is highly probable that planets are frequently formed in this way amongst the stars of the cosmos. Thus, many of the stars in our galactic system may have planets, and this may hold good for other galaxies, so that there may be millions and millions of planets in existence. They may be as countless as are the grains of sand in the Sahara Desert. Dr. R. C. Johnson mentions in his work, "Nurslings of Immortality," that an eminent astronomer has "suggested that if God sent forth an angel to find the Earth, his task would be like looking for a particular grain of sand on all the sea-shores of the world." The astronomer apparently did not realise that spirits are not under spatial limitations.

THE MOON

There are different theories about the origin of the moon. Some believe that shortly after the earth's formation, the moon was thrown off or torn from it as a result either of the rapid rotation of the earth or its close approach to the sun. Others are of the opinion that, like the planets, the moon was formed by an accretionary process from the solar nebula and being in the proximity of the earth, became attached to it, as a satellite, by gravitational forces.

THE EARTH

It is now commonly accepted that the age of the earth and other planets is three or four thousand million years, *i.e.*, five or six thousand million years younger than the sun. The age of the earth is shown by the rate and degree of disintegration of the radio-active ores present in its crust; also, by the rate of deposition and the thickness of sedimentary rocks, and by the occurrence of plant and animal fossils in these rocks. It is worthy of note that, according to the genealogical trees of the Old Testament, the earth is only from four to seven thousand years old. Archbishop Ussher, 1650, actually put the Creation precisely at 4,004 B.C. and this date was widely accepted by the Church until comparatively recent times, as shown by the fact that it was given in the marginal notes of many editions of the Authorised English Version of the Bible.

Until recently it was believed that the earth, like the other planets, was at first in the molten state owing to its material having been derived directly from the sun, and that its surface then gradually cooled until a crust was formed. However, it is now generally accepted that, if all the planets have been formed by the accretion of matter (probably at a low temperature) from space, the earth would have had at first a low temperature. As its matter condensed under the force of gravity, a great pressure would be set up in the interior of the mass and as a result of this and also perhaps of radio-active changes, the heat of the earth's core would rise to such an extent (according to Hoyle, 5,000 °C.) that the matter present would become liquid and undergo a "slow boiling process," the lighter substances tending to rise to the surface, and the heavier to sink to the depths. The outer crust of the earth, however, would remain cool throughout this period, except at weaker places where the molten rock or lava was forced up from the depths giving rise to volcanic eruptions. As the earth shrank owing to the condensation of the matter in its interior, the crust would become wrinkled into folds.

At first there would be no masses of water on the earth's surface, but ultimately water exuding from the crust or condensing from the atmosphere, would begin to gather on the surface and collect in the deeper hollows to form seas and lakes. The higher ridges would form the dry land.

As the outer crust of the earth would remain cool from the first, living organisms may have appeared on its surface at a very early stage in its existence, especially if water, oxygen, carbon dioxide and nitrogen were swept up and retained by it from the gaseous matter which it encountered in its orbit round the sun.

THE NATURE OF THE PHYSICAL MATTER OF THE UNIVERSE

All forms of physical matter in the universe have a common origin and are essentially the same in nature. They are made up of extremely small units, termed atoms, consisting of electrically charged particles. Each atom has a central particle, the nucleus, which has a positive charge of electricity. Around the nucleus rotate one or more other particles, the electrons. These have negative charges of electricity and may travel round the nucleus at great speeds, over 100,000 miles a second. The atom may be likened to an extremely small solar system in which the nucleus represents the sun, and the electrons, the planets. All the particles are infinitely small, and in relation to their size, the distances between the electrons and the nucleus are comparable to those between the planets and the sun. Thus the atom consists almost entirely of empty space, and this applies also to every substance in the universe as all are atomic in nature.

The nucleus, unlike the electron, is massive in character and gives almost all the weight to the atom. It may be simple in structure, having only a single particle with a positive charge of electricity (a proton), or it may be complex, consisting of several particles, perhaps of different types. With increase in the complexity of its structure, there is an increase in its mass or weight and in its positive electric charge. There is also a corresponding increase in the number of electrons which it can retain rotating around it, as there must be always sufficient electrons to neutralise its positive charge. Although all electrons are similar in nature, atoms differ in their chemical properties according to the number and arrangement of electrons present.

Atoms occur as a rule in combination with other atoms to form molecules. If all the atoms in the molecules are of the same type, the substance is termed an element.

There are about ninety-two different types of atoms and therefore elements in the world. These elements can in general be arranged in a regular series according to the weight of their atoms and the number of electrons present. The element hydrogen has the simplest and lightest atom. It has a simple nucleus and a single electron. The heavy metals, *e.g.*, gold, mercury, lead and uranium, are at the other end of the series. Their atoms have complicated nuclei and large numbers of electrons.

Different types of atoms (*i.e.*, atoms of different elements) may combine to form the molecules of a compound. In some cases they can combine in more than one proportion, giving rise to different compounds. There is a vast number, hundreds of thousands, of compounds in existence.

The carbon atom can link up with other carbon atoms and such linkages can combine readily with the atoms of other elements, especially hydrogen, oxygen and nitrogen. As a result there are countless carbon compounds or, as they are termed, organic compounds in existence. The living principle of animals and plants in earth-life has made use of this combining property of carbon for the development and maintenance of the tissues of the physical body. These tissues consist of organic compounds.

Accordingly, all the physical matter of the universe consists essentially of electrically charged particles. These particles make up the atoms and the latter under certain conditions unite in definite proportions to form all the vast range of substances in existence. Hence there is a fundamental unity running through all physical matter, and a system of law and order in the changes which it undergoes at any time.

The simplest element is hydrogen. It is not known how it originated in the universe, but it is possible that it is formed from some primary stuff present in space.

However, nothing is known as to whether such basic matter actually exists. At the high temperatures prevailing in certain stars, hydrogen becomes converted into helium and this, under certain conditions, undergoes further nuclear changes with formation of higher and higher elements until ultimately the heavy metals are produced. It has been claimed that there is nothing haphazard in this series of changes, but that it is the result of a definite evolutionary process showing evidence of Purpose and Design.

MODERN SCIENCE AND MAN'S CONCEPTION OF GOD

A study of the physical universe broadens man's conception of the Almightiness of God. In all ages, man's views of God have been based largely on his ideas of the universe. The spectacle of the skies by day and night—the rising and setting of the sun and moon, and the apparent movement of the stars—must have caused primitive man to speculate vaguely as to the nature and origin of these heavenly bodies. In his mind there would gradually develop the idea, perhaps dim at first but becoming more definite later, that there must be a Cause behind it all, some Almighty Force which had brought it into being and which continues to sustain it. And early man, from a knowledge of his own creative powers, conceived of this Almighty Creative Force as a Divine Person—a God in human form. But to him this God, although Almighty in that He had created the universe and still ruled over it, was only a little higher in His personal traits than man himself. He was swayed by the same emotions and passions as man. He could enjoy walking in a garden in the cool of the evening. He could be jealous and capricious in nature and become angry when man was disobedient. He could even be argued with and threatened on occasion.

Accordingly, the God of most theologies throughout the ages was a very human God, not far removed from ordinary man in character and temperament. This narrow conception of God was based largely on the supposition that the earth was the centre of the universe, and that the whole universe was created primarily for the life of human beings on earth—a belief held until the beginning of the present century.

In recent years man has had to revise his ideas about the size of the universe. He now knows that the earth is really one of the smaller planets of a relatively small solar system, which is part of a huge galaxy containing one hundred thousand million stars or suns. Our sun is situated far from the centre of the galaxy and ranks merely as a star of moderate size and of rather less than average brightness. It is probable that many, if not most, of these other stars have planets. Also, far out in the depths of space, there are millions of other enormous star clusters, like our galaxy, in course of evolution, each with its millions of solar systems and millions and millions of planets. This new knowledge is bound to make man alter his ideas of the Almighty Power, commonly referred to as God, behind the Universe. The old theologies—Hebrew, Christian and others—will have to be readjusted in the light of the new cosmology to admit of a far wider conception of God.

A systematic examination of the stars shows that they are distributed in no haphazard fashion. They occur in huge clusters or galaxies which are arranged in a highly uniform and orderly manner throughout space. There appears to be a design and purpose behind all this. Further, the countless stars and their attendant planets which make up these galaxies, are apparently governed by definite laws. As a result, their movements are regulated so that their positions at any time, past, present or future, can be more or less accurately determined. These facts indicate that the Almighty Power or Being, who was responsible for the creation of all these star systems, is a God of purpose, law and order.

This is also borne out by the essential unity in the constitution of all forms of matter in the physical universe. The countless physical and chemical changes which occur in such matter are all governed by definite and immutable laws so that these changes proceed in a precise and predictable manner. There is nothing haphazard in the response of electrical particles and atoms to the natural forces acting upon them at any time.

Thus a knowledge of the physical universe is of great importance in forming any conception of God. All forms of matter, whether electrical particles or huge star systems, are expressions of the Infinite. They tell of His ways and methods, and show that there is a purpose and design in all His activities. They reveal that there is a Divine Mind at the heart of all things.

What is now known about the stars shows that the popular conceptions of the Almightiness of God bear no relationship whatsoever to His Power as displayed in the utter vastness of the star systems in space; it is quite impossible for man to apprehend the Power responsible for the creation and sustenance of the seemingly boundless Universe.

THE ORIGIN AND EVOLUTION OF LIVING ORGANISMS ON THE EARTH

"Life sleeps in the mineral, stirs in the vegetable dreams in the animal and awakes in man."

THE ORIGIN OF LIFE

On the assumption that the crust of the earth was at first in a molten condition, it was commonly believed that the first forms of life appeared in the warm primeval seas about one thousand million years ago. However, if the crust was cool from the first, as is now widely accepted by astronomers, it is probable that the dawn of life in the world was at a much earlier period; in fact, carbonaceous residues, believed to be from primitive algae (seaweeds) and bacteria, have recently been found in ancient rocks, which indicate that the dawn of life on the earth may have been as far back as 3,000 million years ago, *i.e.*, at the time when water first began to collect on its surface.

No one knows how the first forms of life originated on the earth or what precisely was the nature of these primitive organisms. The most rudimentary and smallest forms of life known at the present time are the viruses. In certain cases they apparently consist of little more than a nucleo-protein molecule, and some are crystalline in nature. It is doubtful whether some are actually living organisms, being apparently on the border line between animate and inanimate matter. But, they can hardly be regarded as representatives of the most primitive forms of life as in all cases they are parasitic on plants and animals.

From early times, there was a general belief in many nations: Greek, Roman, Hebrew and Arab, that new generations of all kinds of plants and animals were continuously being created in rivers and the sea, and from the mud of swamps and from dust. The Creation described in Genesis was but the same process on a grand scale. This belief in *spontaneous generation* was widely held even in European countries, including Britain, until a few centuries ago, as shown by writings in the seventeenth century on the creation of mice from wheat stored in barns, of maggots from meat or of insects from manure heaps.

It was found in the seventeenth and eighteenth centuries that when foods and other organic substances were protected to prevent access of insects and animals, these organisms did not develop in the material. Hence it became generally accepted that spontaneous generation did not occur in the higher forms of life, although many biologists still believed that it might occur in lower organisms, such as bacteria, and these might later develop into higher organisms. About a hundred years ago, Louis Pasteur showed that under laboratory conditions spontaneous generation did not occur even in the case of bacteria. This left the question as to how life originated in the world still unanswered.

Lord Kelvin and others suggested that living organisms, perhaps in the form of spores, may have been carried to the earth in cosmic dust or in the fissures of meteorites. This theory only transferred the question of the origin of life from the earth to some other place in the universe. The spores of bacteria have great powers of resistance to adverse conditions and may live for years in a dormant condition in absence of water and at extremely low temperatures (conditions likely to be present in interstellar dust), but for the *active* existence of all known forms of life, water in the liquid state and temperatures above freezing point are essential.

Another theory of the origin of life on earth is based on the possibility that under certain natural conditions highly complex carbon compounds, *i.e.*, organic substances, may be formed by ultra-violet rays or catalytic or other agents, from carbon dioxide, water and ammonia. (Some of these organic substances have actually been synthesised in the laboratory by purely physical or chemical processes). The surface water of the primeval seas would be brightly illuminated and well aerated, and the shallow water near the shore would contain an abundance of mineral matter. Thus the conditions might be favourable for the formation of these organic substances, and in the absence of any form of life to use them as food, they might accumulate and become highly concentrated in the water. Such an environment might provide ideal conditions for the generation of living organisms. However, no one has succeeded as yet in causing such Complex carbon compounds to acquire the properties of living matter or protoplasm, but for all we know it may occur at the present time under natural conditions, *e.g.*, in the sea.

THE LIVING PRINCIPLE

No one knows what constitutes life. Is it a vital activating principle generated within certain forms of organic matter as a result of the action of various conditions, or is it a principle which is taken up by the organic matter from extraneous sources? Many scientists even refuse to accept that there is such a principle, but are faced with the difficulty that for some reason, which they cannot explain, animate or living organic matter has certain characters, *e.g.*, reproduction, nutrition and growth, which inanimate organic matter under no circumstances can be made to show.

It is a belief common to all the world's great religions that there is this vital principle or source of energy in all living organisms, plant and animal, and that it is inherent in the spirit of each; as God is Spirit, it is also a character of His Divine nature. Further, as God is the Creator and Sustainer of the universe, there must be throughout it an infinite and all-pervading supply of this Vital Principle. Under certain conditions this may cause various complex forms of inanimate organic matter, *e.g.*, nucleoproteins, to develop into extremely rudimentary living organisms. Whether these conditions may arise in the world to-day and thus enable spontaneous generation of life to occur has never been proved by experimental methods.

Quite apart from the question of whether spontaneous generation may occur or not, one can readily understand that all living organisms which are already in existence can renew their vitality throughout their lives by absorbing and

259

retaining the vital energy from this Universal and Infinite supply. Certain facts indicate that there is this source of power. For instance, the renewal of vitality during sleep is not due merely to the resting of the body and the brain. There is also the sustaining effect of prayer and meditation in which the mind is brought into attunement with higher spirit forces; and the curative effect of psychic treatment of disease.

THE EVOLUTION OF THE HIGHER ORGANISMS

The first forms of life would be very simple in nature, consisting of minute unicellular (single-celled) structures. From these earliest types all other living organisms were evolved. The theory of how this occurred, namely, the theory of Evolution, was developed largely as a result of the work of Lamarck, Charles Darwin and Alfred Russel Wallace. According to this theory, the descendants of the first group of primitive organisms have undergone in the course of some two or three thousand million years a progressive series of changes in form and structure to give rise to all the species of plants and animals, including man, now in existence.

The general truth of evolution is now accepted by practically all leading biologists and is shown by the following facts: (1) The simplest forms of life in the world at the present time, *i.e.*, unicellular organisms, are linked with the highest forms of plants and animals through a large gradation of types which in structure are definitely related to one another.

(2) The fossilised remains of various kinds of plants and animals found in the rock formations of the earth's surface, show a definite succession of evolving, yet related, types of living organisms in the past. Environmental conditions throughout the ages have had a definite influence on the development of the new types. This has to some extent

been responsible for the typical flora and fauna found in different parts of the world, *e.g.*, Australia, Central Africa, Brazil and the Polar regions.

Important confirmation of the theory is also shown by the fact that in man and the higher animals, the evolutionary history is recapitulated by the developing embryo of each individual. At first the embryo consists of a simple cell like that of the earliest unicellular organisms; then it develops tissues similar to the muscular structures of the earliest aquatic animals. At a later stage, the embryonic heart and system of blood vessels resemble the heart and circulation system of the gills of fishes; only to be modified later to the heart and lung circulation, typical of land animals and man. These embryonic structures are similar, not so much to the actual corresponding structures of the adult ancestors as to those of the embryos of these ancestors. For instance, the embryo mammal has gill pouches which resemble more closely the gill pouches of the embryo fish than the fully developed gill slits of the adult fish.

Evolution is a process which is going on continuously, with the development of new types of plants and animals. Many of these new types may be unable to persist under the conditions of their environment and in face of competition with other organisms, and as a result die out. Other types may be able to persist in the environment and then evolve further. Since the dawn of life there has been on the whole a gradual progress upwards; birds and mammals in the present age are more highly developed in body and in brain power than their far distant ancestors. As will be shown later, evolution tends to lift organisms upwards to a fuller sense of awareness and a greater freedom of expression and of will; also, a greater reasoning power and a greater sense of personal responsibility. The advance in itself shows a directive power behind the process.

THE EARLIEST FORMS OF LIFE

The earliest organisms would be very simple in their mode of life, feeding on the organic substances already elaborated in the sea by purely physical or chemical processes. At an early stage certain organisms might be evolved, which could utilise the carbon dioxide and perhaps the ammonia of the atmosphere, and the mineral salts in solution in the water, and build these up into the organic compounds of their cell substance. They would obtain the energy for this process from the oxidation of ammonium compounds, sulphides or other oxidisable substances present in their environment. Thus these organisms would be similar in their modes of nutrition to certain soil and water bacteria of the present time.

All these primitive organisms, being unicellular, would multiply by simple cell division or fission, the single cell of the organism dividing to form two independent daughter cells. This is a very rapid method of reproduction, so that there could be several new generations of organisms in the course of a few hours or even in an hour, and innumerable generations in a week. In the countless organisms, which would be produced in this way, variations would arise in form, structure and mode of life, and all these variations would be subject to the selective action of environmental conditions. A certain type or variety of organism would tend to persist or to die out according to whether a new variation in its cell structure or mode of life was beneficial or useless to it.

THE DIFFERENTIATION OF PLANTS AND ANIMALS

Modifications would also soon arise in the modes of nutrition, and this would ultimately lead to the great division of living organisms into plants and animals Thus certain organisms by producing the green colouring substance, chlorophyll, became adapted to use sunlight as a source of energy. This enabled them to utilise in their nutrition entirely inorganic substances, namely carbon dioxide, water and minerals. From these green unicellular forms of life all species of plants were evolved. Other organisms, never became adapted to feed in this manner, but used for their nutrition only preformed organic matter, *e.g.*, that of other organisms, dead or alive. Some of these organisms remained simple in their mode of life and developed into bacteria bringing about changes, such as putrefaction and fermentation, as at the present day, but others evolved further and developed into animals.

THE EARLIEST MULTICELLULAR ORGANISMS

Many of the early unicellular organisms would occur singly in the environment, but others would occur in chains or clusters owing to the cells after cell-division remaining in adherence. Each cell in these aggregates would as a rule retain its independent nature. In certain cases, the cells might become to some extent interdependent; there might even be a certain amount of division of labour in the aggregate, certain cells becoming specialised to carry out particular functions, *e.g.*, reproduction, feeding, growth, locomotion or fixing the organism to some surface. This would constitute an important step forward in the evolutionary scale; it would be the first step in the development of a multicellular body.

These earliest multicellular forms would be free-swimming in the water, or would become fixed to rocks. They might be somewhat similar to the present Higher Bacteria or certain Algae (seaweeds). At first their multicellular bodies would be very simple in nature, but with the passage of millions of years they would become more and more complex until finally the massive and highly complicated bodies of the higher plants and animals were evolved.

BACKBONED ANIMALS OR VERTEBRATES

At first all the animals were backboneless or invertebrate in type, like sponges, jelly-fish, molluscs and worms, but after some five hundred million years, vertebrates (backboned animals) in the form of true fishes, breathing by means of gills, appeared in the seas. The development of a backbone and other bony structures gave the organisms certain advantages, which were to be even more fully exploited at a much later period when their descendants left the seas and invaded the dry land. These skeletal structures provided support for the body cells and helped to retain the shape of the body. They protected the delicate internal organs, gave rigid attachment for the muscles and acted as levers for muscular action. Without the skeleton, the animal would not be capable of the rapid and precise movements it can carry out in the sea or on the land. Fishes are expert at moving freely through their watery environment. Their eyes are well developed, the vision being sharp, especially for moving objects, but they have no eyelids and cannot therefore close their eyes.

LAND PLANTS

About the same period as the true fishes were evolved (about five hundred million years ago), plants from the sea invaded the land surfaces. These terrestrial plants developed roots, stems and leaves, but were flowerless as they reproduced by spores and not by seeds. Before plants became established on the dry land, there would be few or no living organisms there, except perhaps for bacterial or seaweed types living in moist places near the shores of seas and lakes. The early land plants would require plenty of moisture and so would take longer to become established in very dry areas. Hence the main land surfaces would be at first bleak and desolate, completely bare of vegetation. Even after plants had become established on the land, there would be no flowering plants or grass until millions of years later.

LAND ANIMALS

The growth of terrestrial plants prepared the way for the invasion of the land at a much later period by animals from the sea. These animals had become adapted to use air for respiration, and included invertebrates, such as worms, centipedes, spiders, scorpions and insects; and vertebrates, such as lung-fishes or mud-fishes. These lung-fishes had lungs as well as gills, and so could live both on land and in water. This was a great advantage when they lived in pools which might become dried up—in fact, the lungs may have been developed in the first place to meet this contingency. The lung-fishes were an important stage in evolution as they were the ancestors of the amphibians, reptiles, birds and mammals.

Flowering plants would begin to appear about this time and as the vegetation would be swarming with insects, cross-fertilisation of plants by these organisms would be possible.

Aquatic creatures gained many advantages by invasion of the land. The new environment enabled them to carry out a higher mode of life with much greater prospects of further development. The move to invade the land may have been due to some extent to curiosity (a common trait in animals) or to the urge for adventure; it may have been necessary owing to the shallow pools, in which they were living, becoming dried up or overcrowded with creatures; or it may have been to escape from enemy or predatory types. The terrestrial mode of life would also enable the creatures to obtain more oxygen, but as oxygen could not be absorbed readily through a dry hard protective skin, lungs had to be developed so that the oxygen could be absorbed by the blood through a moist internal surface. Insects for the same purpose developed air tubes instead of lungs.

Life on land involved for most organisms the production of legs for locomotion and for raising the body from the ground; and to facilitate movement, the body became more compact. As a protection against injury and extremes of heat and cold, the organism acquired a hard, tough skin, covered in many cases with hair or fur. The eggs had to be deposited in a safe place (not so easy as in aquatic life), or carried in the body until the embryo had fully formed. Moreover, for safety and for the supply of food, the organisms might adopt an arboreal mode of life, or invade the air, burrow underground, or even return to the sea. But some of these changes in mode of life occurred only at a much later stage in evolutionary history.

As amphibians became adapted to life on land, they gradually lost their gills (gill pouches or rudimentary gills occur in the embryos of all reptiles, birds and mammals, including man), but evolved lungs and a more highly organised heart. The paired fins of the true fishes became replaced with limbs having fingers or toes for feeling, holding and grasping objects, including food. The tongue became movable; and eyelids, eardrums and vocal organs were developed. These air-breathing amphibia would be the first creatures of any kind to utter true vocal sounds. They would produce at first mainly mating, and then also maternal and infantile calls, and later perhaps sounds expressing pain, fear, rage or pleasure. The use of the fingers and toes for feeling and holding objects, and the employment of the vocal cords for the utterance of various sounds had an important influence in the development of the brain.

REPTILES AND BIRDS

From a relatively small and primitive group of these amphibians, reptiles were evolved. The latter were capable of living entirely on dry land and were an important advance in evolution as they could carry out a much wider range of activities than their amphibian ancestors and had a more highly developed brain. From them, tortoises, lizards and snakes were developed and, most important of all, birds.

In the evolution of birds, a group of small lizard-like reptiles, too weak to maintain themselves against their enemies on the ground, sought refuge in the trees. After ages of this arboreal life, they became adapted to glide from one tree to another or from the tree to the ground, and then gradually, and probably through many intermediate forms, they acquired the power of sustained flight. Mastery of the air gave birds great advantages. They could readily escape from their ground enemies; they could range much more widely for food and water; they could nest and rear their young in safe places, and they could migrate from one country to another at different seasons to avoid extremes of climate. The power of flight enabled birds to spread rapidly over the earth and become an important group of animals.

There have been in the past four successful invasions of the air by animals: insects, pterodactyls (now extinct), birds and bats. Each solved the problem of flight in a different way. In insects, the wings consist of light, hollow, flattened sacs, which grow out from the body and in flight are kept in rapid motion by powerful muscles. Pterodactyls and bats produced wings of specially developed folds of skin, which stretched between the limbs and the body. In the case of birds, the power of flight is based on feathers, which cover the fore-limbs to form two coherent vanes or fans for beating the air and thus propelling the creature forward. The feather is a unique feature of birds. It is not only required for flying, but it protects the body from injury and keeps it warm. The covering of feathers also encloses a layer of air over the body surface and so enables birds, such as gulls, ducks and geese, to float high in water and swim more readily. Birds show other characters associated with the power of flight, *e.g.*, lighter and more porous bones containing air cavities; a more compact and stream-lined body; specially formed fore-limbs with very powerful muscles to move the wings; large heart for rapid circulation of the blood to carry plenty of oxygen and food to the muscles. The breast bone has a deep keel for the adequate insertion of the heavy wing muscles; and the dorsal vertebrae have become fused to give a firm basis for the movement of the wings. The tail has become short and bears a fan of feathers.

Birds are bipeds using only their hind limbs for walking or hopping. The fore limbs are devoted almost entirely to flight, and cannot be used for feeding so this operation has to be done almost entirely by the mouth (sometimes assisted by the feet), using a hard beak and a long highly flexible neck. Associated with their mastery of the air, are keen senses of sight and hearing, and an alertness of mind and body, giving a life full of zest and spirit.

Mammals

Another group of reptiles after long ages evolved into mammals—animals with mammary glands, a coating of hair on their skin, a highly developed brain, and limbs which enabled them to carry out a wide variety of actions, some of which entailed the use of great skill, *e.g.*, grasping and holding. The mammals became specialised for different modes of life—on the ground, in the trees, below ground, in the rivers and lakes, and in the air (bats). Many developed highly specialised limbs, as in the case of the ox, the horse, the elephant and the whale. One group of small creatures, to enable them to survive, took to the trees and were able to persist without losing the five digits on each limb originally possessed by their ancestors, the fishes and amphibians. And it was these limb structures, which, once the brain had developed sufficiently, enabled them to carry out skilful and precise activities, and thus acquire valuable information and experience of their environment. The fact that this group had delayed specialising their limbs until a relatively late period, when the brain had become much more highly developed, was to give them a great advantage over other animals; in fact, it was from this group that apes and man were evolved.

ARBOREAL CREATURES AND MAN

Man is at the highest point in the scale of evolution. He is a recent comer to the world as he has been in existence only a mere fraction of the time since the first organisms appeared. His ancestors sixty million years ago were lemur-like animals which lived in trees. This arboreal mode of life was particularly suitable for man's ascent from the animal world. In the first place, life in the trees led to the eyes being shifted from the side of the head (where they looked sideways) to the front of the face, and becoming directed forward. Thus the animal could observe and appreciate depths, *i.e.*, it had stereoscopic or three-dimensional vision. It was therefore able to estimate distances and thus to judge the strength of the leaps it would require to make in jumping from branch to branch. Defective vision would be disastrous to an arboreal creature. The ears, unlike the eyes, did not move forward, but retained their lateral position on either side of the head. This was an advantage, as the head acted as a screen between the ears and so provided for binaural hearing.

Another feature, which was developed as a result of this tree-dwelling life, was the first digit of each fore-limb became a thumb, which could be worked independently of, or in opposition to the fingers. Thus the animal could grasp firmly objects, such as the branches of trees. At the same time, the hand acquired a more delicate sense of touch and so became more useful in its ability to appreciate the shape and nature of the object grasped. A keen sense of touch is essential in arboreal creatures for the skilful and delicately adjusted movements of their bodies. An erect posture was also acquired to relieve the hands from the work of moving the body from place to place. Man differs from animals in that he can stand bolt upright.

The possession of forwardly directed eyes led eventually to the reduction of the size of the nose or snout, so that an unobscured field of vision was obtained. The smaller nose was responsible naturally for a somewhat diminished sense of smell. To compensate for this, the sense of hearing became more acute, especially in the ability to discriminate between different sounds, a faculty which led eventually to the development of speech. The brain is the organ which distinguishes to the greatest extent man from animals; and the increased sense of vision and also to some extent that of hearing, were largely responsible for the enlargement and development of the brain and thus for the evolution of man. In this connection it must be remembered that the brain is the instrument through which the mind expresses itself, and the more highly developed the brain, the more efficient and sensitive an instrument it is. As the brain developed, so also did the ability to control and direct the actions of the body and at the same time there was a wider range of awareness of environmental conditions. Also, the power of speech was gradually acquired. At first, the speech would consist largely of sex, parental and infantile calls; or sounds expressing pain, pleasure, fear or anger; or recognition signals, especially at night or in a forest. Then man would develop sounds or words for food, home and so on. In this way a vocabulary would gradually be formed for use in conversation.

Thus the peculiar conditions of a group of animals, taking to life in the tree-tops, has led to the evolution of monkeys (including the manlike apes) and man. The two groups were evolved from a common stock of arboreal creatures, but on independent lines. The human body is very similar to that of the anthropoid ape, *e.g.*, the gorilla or chimpanzee, and the fact that man is akin to the anthropoid ape is shown by the close relationship in their blood reactions compared with those of other mammals.

The earliest human beings of which we have any knowledge lived about one and three quarter million years ago, so that it has taken about two or three thousand million years for man to be evolved from the first forms of life. In his physical characters: strength of body, fleetness of movement, senses of hearing and smell, he is markedly inferior to many animals, and, of course, he is incapable of flying and his swimming powers are limited; but his highly developed brain and his dexterity in the use of his limbs, especially his arms and hands, has enabled him to climb higher in the evolutionary scale than all the other animals.

THE DEVELOPMENT OF THE MIND

Animals in general have shown in the whole course of their evolution, not only a certain awareness of the conditions around them, but also an urge to adapt themselves to these conditions by learning to carry out efficiently useful or needful activities and to suppress those that are useless. The knowledge thus acquired has frequently become in the course of many generations an inborn or inherited trait, as in the case of birds knowing how to build their nests. These inherited traits may be responsible for the simple responses of the brain and nervous system to sensory impressions, or for the more complex types of behaviour which are said to be instinctive in nature. Speaking generally, such instinctive behaviour becomes of less importance in the life of the animal as it ascends the evolutionary scale.

THE MIND OF LOWER ANIMALS, FISHES AND BIRDS

The lower animals, *e.g.*, insects, such as bees and ants, are richly endowed with specialised instinctive powers, but they do not as a rule learn readily from experience and are therefore said to be of low intelligence. Thus they know instinctively how to conduct their lives under normal conditions, but if subjected to new or unusual circumstances, they have only low powers of adaptation.

Fish also are largely governed by their instincts and their responses to sensory impressions, but they may rapidly learn to make use of beneficial sensory associations and to discard useless ones. They are, however, of low mentality; in fact, a high degree of intelligence is not required for their mode of life, because as a rule they can readily procure their food and do not require to take any special steps for the care of their offspring, their prodigious powers of multiplication compensating for a high infantile mortality.

Reptiles have a more highly developed brain than their ancestors, the fish and amphibia. They are more sensitive and adaptive to external influences and show a higher mentality in their behaviour.

Birds are still more intelligent. In their activities they are not so dependent on their instincts and have an alert mind which in many cases can be educated. With their powers of flight they lead an active life. They are highly emotional, expressing their feelings in their songs.

THE MIND OF MAMMALS

Mammals, the highest order of animals, are less instinctive in their behaviour than lower animals and are much more intelligent. Thus they have a much higher capacity of learning how to do things or of acquiring knowledge from experience, *i.e.*, they are more educable and more adaptive in nature. They also take a greater interest in their surroundings and may readily make mental associations in response to sensory stimuli. They may be even experimental in their activities, especially in their play. The horse, dog, cat, elephant and monkey are amongst the most highly intelligent of these big-brain types, but even they show a lower mentality than one would expect from the size of their brains, as their minds are concerned largely with sensory impressions or perceptual influences (what they see, hear, smell, taste and feel), and with the thoughts associated therewith. They appear to have little or no power of reasoning. They seem to be well fitted for, and contented with the circumstances in which they live and have little urge to experiment or learn new ways of life. Although much less instinctive in their activities than are the lower animals, nevertheless, even with them, much of their behaviour is basically instinctive in nature, being determined by hunger, sex, maternal affection for the young, and fear of their hereditary enemies.

The dawn of mind is more evident in monkeys than in other mammals. The former are alert, quick in their powers of perception, are expert at manipulating their fingers and toes and co-ordinating these with their eyes. They are always active, curious and ready to explore and make experiments, but in spite of these indications of intelligence there is little evidence of reasoning power.

THE HUMAN MIND

On the other hand, not only can man make inferences from what he perceives of the world around him, *i.e.*, from his sensory impressions or perceptions (as can certain animals), but he has, in addition, reasoning powers. Thus he differs from animals in that he can draw conclusions from general ideas or concepts. He is also in every way more capable of solving problems, recalling readily for this purpose past knowledge and experience. Although the instincts, which he has inherited from his animal ancestors, still play an important part in his activities or behaviour, their effects may be modified considerably according to circumstances. An important factor in his advance of mentality has been his power of speech and later his ability to write. This has enabled him to discuss and compare his experiences and ideas with other men; also, to pass on to others what he has learned from his forebears, and any original knowledge of his own. Animals, owing to their lack of power of speech, have been unable to acquire or pass on knowledge in these ways.

Finally, it may be said that although with animals in general there has been a gradual advance in mental fitness since the dawn of life on earth, in man evolution has also brought about the power of reasoning, a fuller sense or range of awareness, a greater degree of self-control and a sense of personal responsibility. For these reasons, man is by far the highest expression of life on earth.

THE DIRECTIVE POWER BEHIND EVOLUTION

The facts of evolution are clear; the higher plants and animals have undoubtedly evolved from primitive unicellular forms of life. But it is not known what initiated the process of evolution, and what is responsible for the urge behind it and which sustains it. It has been claimed that the process can be accounted for by physical or chemical factors or by powers of adaptation alone. There is no doubt that variation in itself, disciplined by the current environment, would automatically have led to evolutionary advance throughout the vast ages at the disposal of the process. Nevertheless, it is difficult to conceive how such a process, with its tendencies for the development of higher forms of consciousness and greater states of awareness, can be entirely accounted for by the physical and chemical properties of substances, no matter how complex in chemical nature these substances may be. After all, the other phenomena of life can not readily be accounted for on a purely physical or chemical basis. In fact, no biologist knows what constitutes life, or in other words, what is responsible for an organism, whether plant or animal, being alive.

Against the purely materialistic conception of evolution it may be said that there are indications of a Directive Power in evolutionary advance. There is evidence of purposive and experimental features, which can be taken as an indication of a Master Mind or Planner Thus in the past ages, many types of plants and animals were evolved, which could not maintain themselves indefinitely in the changing environmental conditions of the earth and died out, as in the case of the giant reptiles of the Mesozoic Period, *e.g.*, the dinosaur. Such failure-lines were not repeated. On the other hand, the types which could persist, were frequently evolved further and new types formed from them. The dying out of the failure-lines was no doubt due to the elimination of unsatisfactory types by natural selection, but one has still to account for the origin of the property of living matter (mutation) to develop new types, and the urge behind it to develop further the successful types.

Further evidence of a Planner behind the process of evolution is shown by the development of highly specialised and complex structures, such as the eye and ear, in which difficult problems with regard to vision and hearing had to be solved. No doubt there were many transient intermediate forms in the long ages before the organs reached the final stage, but it is difficult to believe that such a complicated series of changes as was necessary in these cases could have occurred in a purely fortuitous manner. Further, at certain stages in evolution, when animals have made a complete change in mode of life, for example, when aquatic animals first invaded the land or when land creatures invaded the air, a complicated series of changes, some of a major nature, had to be made, as already described, to enable the animals to live in the new environment. All these evolutionary changes had to take place before the organism could deal adequately with the new form of environment. Although there must have been many transient intermediate forms, for example, lung-fishes bridging the aquatic-amphibian gap, yet there must have been some definite mental conception of the ultimate form necessary; there must have been a Planner behind it all.

The Master Mind behind evolution is also shown by the exquisite artistry and beauty of design, colouring and structure of many forms of life, for example, the brightly coloured flowers with their perfumes, the birds with beautiful plumage and remarkable powers of song, the insects, such as butterflies, with marvellous colouring. Mechanistic, purely chemical or physical factors or powers of adaptation alone, cannot account for such characters; there must have been a Directive Power behind all.

It may be claimed that it has never been proved that there is such a thing as Spirit, or that there is a Directive or Spirit Force responsible for the urge behind the process of evolution and for its direction and control, but even materialists must admit that in the "something" which is known as "life," there appears to be a tremendous force to survive, multiply, vary and in many cases advance to more highly developed forms; yet they have never been able to say what is responsible for this force.

THE RISE OF MAN

> "What is man, that thou dost make so much of him, and that thou dost set thy mind upon him." Job 7. 17.

PRIMITIVE MAN

The first human types appear to have evolved within the past two million years. At an early stage, primitive man left the forests and, like the horse, ox and deer, took up life in the more open country which by that time was becoming covered with grass. This change in mode of life may have been caused by the desire for more freedom of movement, or it may have been forced on him by the shrinkage of the forests, perhaps as a result of increased dryness of the climate or the destruction of young trees by animals. In the new life on the ground he retained his erect posture, and the hands, which were originally adapted to grasp branches, were now available for holding sticks, flints and stones, which he was gradually learning to use as weapons and tools. The manipulative skill thus acquired had an important educative effect on the developing mind.

At first man would lead a life very similar to that of wild animals. There would be a merciless struggle for existence in which as a rule only the fittest would survive. He would be weak compared with many animals and so would have to rely on his intelligence for his protection. Like animals, he would be controlled largely by the needs of his body, *e.g.*, hunger and thirst, and by his instincts, especially those of self-preservation, fear, sex and curiosity. He would spend most of his time in searching for food and in hunting. To protect himself from the weather and from his enemies, he would live in rock shelters or caves.

EARLY PROGRESS

He appears to have been gregarious in his habits, usually preferring to live in family groups or in small communities rather than to lead a solitary life. Living in such groups provided him with more protection from human enemies and wild beasts. At the same time, it brought about a certain amount of division of labour, the most able-bodied men taking on the duties of hunting and fishing, and the women and old men attending to the children and the homes. (Even the lower animals, *e.g.*, ants and bees, may live in colonies for mutual assistance and protection; and individuals in these communities may make sacrifices for the common welfare).

The communal life and the development of a common language enabled individuals to discuss and pass on any new information or experience and thus fostered the growth of knowledge. All this also promoted a feeling of kinship or fellowship among the members of the group and taught them to be less self-centred. The education and training of the children in the traditions and customs of the community would play an important part in raising the general standard of knowledge and behaviour.

At an early stage man discovered the use of fire and made use of undressed flints and stones for tools. Later he began to make tools by breaking off pieces from a flint or stone until it was of the required shape (core tools), or by chipping off flakes from it until a flake with a cutting edge was obtained (flake tools). These tools, although roughly dressed, were frequently skilfully made, even in the case of Neanderthal man who lived as long as two hundred and fifty thousand years ago. In addition, early man made spears of wood, bone or horn.

MODERN MAN

The early human types, including Neanderthal man, did not persist, and modern man has sprung from a later offshoot of the original humanoid stock, which seems to have appeared from thirty to fifty thousand years ago. At first, modern man's stone implements were roughly dressed (the Palaeolithic period), but later he learned to polish them (the Neolithic period). With further progress the stone tools were replaced by copper or bronze implements and then by iron. At an early stage he made boats and discovered the art of pottery. Later, he learned to spin and weave and made a great step forward by inventing the wheel.

Man at first acquired knowledge very slowly. He preferred to follow traditional practices rather than to experiment and initiate new ones. But each new discovery or invention increased his range of knowledge and frequently proved the basis for further advance. Moreover, with increase in knowledge of the use of tools he was able to improve the primitive conditions under which he lived. Instead of having to adapt himself, like animals, by evolutionary changes to his environment, he could now modify its conditions to suit himself.

At first he obtained his food by collecting fruit, shellfish and vegetation, and later by hunting and fishing. Less than ten thousand years ago to meet his requirements better, he domesticated certain animals, *e.g.*, the ox, sheep, goat, camel and horse, and started to grow grain crops and fruit trees. He then developed the practices of agriculture and the milling of grain for food.

As life became less arduous, man became more interested in personal comfort and appearance. He used skins and fibres for clothing and for furnishing his home. He made statuettes from wood; and necklaces and armlets from shells, horn, bone, wood or stone. His paintings and engravings of animals and other objects on the walls of caves show great artistic skill, even although they were made up to fifty thousand years ago.

THE DEVELOPING MIND

As the human mind developed, its powers of perception or range of awareness, and its memory would also increase. The ability to remember things would be of great importance in the development of intelligence in primitive man, as it would enable him to make use of past experiences and to acquire and store up knowledge obtained from others. Such knowledge cannot be inherited from the parents; it has to be acquired by learning during earth-life.

At the same time the power of forethought and planning for the future would be increasing. In this case the provision of food for a season of scarcity, *e.g.*, the winter, might be the main incentive; also, the provision of shelter for a cold or wet season. (Animals show forethought, as in the case of bees storing honey, squirrels storing nuts and dogs burying bones).

Thus man would gradually acquire the ability to plan for the future and to make up his mind or decide on certain courses of action—the first step towards the possession of the power of self-determination and of a sense of free will. Although his conduct would be determined largely by his instincts and the needs of his body, he would also have to think of what was best for the welfare of his family and the rest of the community in which he lived. He would be largely selfish in his actions, but would be swayed to some extent by affection for his family and by a feeling of kinship and even sympathy for the others of his group. He would gradually realise that in such communal life it was wiser to be less self-centred and to pay more heed to the feelings of others, as this made for harmony and happiness. Selfishness could lead only to strife and chaos, just as failure to respect the rights and property of others could only give rise to insecurity with regard to his own. He would also recognise the fact that in thinking of others, he was helping in reality to protect himself and his family, as there was a greater chance of a community surviving where all the individuals were prepared to make sacrifices for the common good.

Further, in the interests of the community certain practices or customs would have to be rigidly observed otherwise evil or hardship might befall its members. Each individual would have to learn that he alone was responsible for any of his transgressions against these customs, and that he might be punished by the community for such misdeeds. This would teach him that he could not now follow his natural impulses blindly but would have to exercise some self-control. In this way he would acquire a sense of personal responsibility. With the possession of more self-control, he would be able to choose the right course of action, *i.e.*, the one most beneficial to the group, and reject the wrong or harmful one. Hence he would come to realise that in deciding what was right and what was wrong, he had to think of others in addition to himself. In acquiring in this way a sense of right and wrong, or good and evil, man was developing a conscience. He had taken a definite step in the ascent from the animal creation and was now showing a faint gleam of Divinity.

THE BELIEF IN SPIRITS

Another factor which played an important part in the development of a conscience in man was a belief in spirits and gods. From the earliest times, primitive man in all parts of the world apparently believed that invisible beings or spirits were responsible for all the phenomena of nature: earthquakes, volcanic eruptions, thunderstorms, tornadoes, floods, droughts and forest fires. He also believed that there was a spirit in man and that at death this spirit left the body and existed in a spirit state. This belief in survival was held even by Neanderthal man as shown by the fact that he buried his dead with great reverence and furnished them as for a long journey; and modern man from the Early Stone age has had elaborate burial customs, indicating his belief in survival.

These beliefs about spirits and the life after death would arise to some extent from the fact that certain individuals with clairvoyant or clairaudient powers would be able to "see" or "hear" spirits. The psychic faculty was probably developed at an early stage in the evolution of man as there is evidence of extra-sensory perception even in animals, *e.g.*, the horse and dog. This faculty would be more likely to function freely in these early days as man lived a simpler and more natural life than in modern times. Accounts of psychic experiences occur in the folk-lore and mythology of most of the ancient nations: Hebrew, Greek, Persian, Indian and others.

Thus early man had no doubts about the existence of spirits. He also believed that the spirits of the dead could affect for good or ill those left behind on earth. These spirits had to be recognised still as members of the family or community. Naturally, they came to be regarded as gods, especially in the case of those of the chiefs of the community. These spirits or gods were interested in their surviving kinsmen and could be appealed to for advice and help. Man talked to them as if he were in their presence. He told them of his needs and desires, perhaps aloud, but later in thought as he believed that they could read his mind. At the same time they had to be respected and even propitiated in various ways to prevent them from haunting the locality and to avert ills which might befall the family or kinsmen through their displeasure. Tribal practices and customs were therefore drawn up with a view of placating them and of winning their favour and protection.

PRACTICES ARISING FROM BELIEFS IN SPIRITS

Arising also from these beliefs, certain races adopted practices to enable them to utilise the spirit powers of a dead person for special purposes. For instance, in building a fort, a human victim might be immured alive in the wall or crushed to death under the foundation stone. It was believed that the spirit of the dead body gave strength and durability to the building, or that the vindictive spirit haunted the place and protected it from enemies. In the same way, a human victim might be sacrificed at each corner of the wall of a city or fortress. (See "The Golden Bough," by Sir James Frazer.) Even in modern times certain Pacific islanders place the dead bodies of their kinsmen on high hills or rocks, so that the spirits of the latter can watch over and protect the villages and crops.

Sacrificial practices were also carried out in the growing of food crops. Early man would not realise at first the connection between the seed and the growing plant. It is possible that he acquired this knowledge to begin with as a result of leaving cereal grains at burial places as food offerings to the spirits of the dead. He would observe that cereal plants grew from the grains. These cereals would be more luxuriant than those growing in the wild state, owing to the soil at the burial place having been dug up and perhaps kept relatively free from other plants. He would, however, attribute the luxuriant growth to the animation or vitalisation of the seed by the spirit of the dead person. From this supposed action of the spirit would develop the idea of a corn-god.

To propitiate the corn-god and so ensure a good crop, it was necessary to offer a human (later an animal) sacrifice. The person thus slain was supposed to represent or to be the incarnation of the corn-god, and his spirit was believed to enter the seed and give life to the growing crop. The blood of the victim was sprinkled on the seed, or his dead body was buried in the field at the time the seed was sown. Thus the spirit was believed to come to life again in the growing crop. This resurrection was celebrated at harvesting by festivals at which the people partook of the first-fruits; later, bread and wine were substituted as symbolising the flesh and blood of the slain god.

These early gods were supposed to be very human in their traits and not greatly superior in their powers to man himself. When they appeared to be unwilling to carry out his wishes, he might bribe or threaten them in various ways to force them to do so. Even until recent times certain tribes during solar or lunar eclipses have beaten drums and shouted threats to scare away some malevolent spirit who was believed to be stealing or destroying the sun or moon.

At the same time, it has been a common belief in all ages that man himself can exercise powers over nature (supernatural powers) by carrying out practices, which may be described as magical in character. Such a belief forms to some extent the basis of the witchcraft found in savage tribes even at the present time. But witchcraft may also be based on practices whereby the spirits of nature or of dead ancestors are invoked to take action.

POLYTHEISM AND MONOTHEISM

In ancient times therefore there were gods of nature, and family and tribal gods, and man fully believed that they could affect for good or ill all that he did, whether in the home or in hunting, tilling the soil or building a house. Hence these gods had to be respected and even propitiated in various ways otherwise evil might befall the family or tribe. In fact, the only way to do certain things was that ordained by tribal custom to appease the gods, and so ensure the welfare of the man himself, his family and the community.

From these early crude beliefs in many gods and spirits (animism and polytheism) was to come at a much later stage in man's history, the conception of the One Almighty God who ruled over these minor gods and spirits. This monotheistic conception was vague at first and varied widely with different peoples, but in most cases the God was in human form (anthropomorphism), and was frequently symbolised by the sun, as in Mithraism. He was the Supreme God and was therefore ultimately responsible for all the alarming and mysterious forces of nature and any calamities befalling mankind. Hence if men did wrong, they had to propitiate their God by making sacrifices or by doing penance. On the other hand, God could protect them from all "ills" if they obeyed His commands and prayed to Him for help.

Early man may not only have speculated as to the nature of God, but also have wondered at the nature and purpose of his own life on earth. He may have yearned dimly for some higher state of existence in which all the hardships of earth-life would disappear. He may have had a hope or belief that at death (a most mysterious change to him) his life would continue in company with his dead ancestors and friends in some such blissful region, ruled by his Supreme God. In these ways would first come the dawn of religion.

FREE WILL AND DETERMINISM

In developing a conscience, early man with his sense of free will would become aware that he could obey or ignore its guidance. He would be still largely swayed in his actions by his instincts and the needs and desires of the body, and seldom would his will power be exercised to control these deterministic factors. Self-control through the action of free will is a character which is not readily acquired. Even at the present time there is considerable difference of opinion as to whether man can successfully resist and overcome deterministic factors by the exercise of his free will—in fact, the problem of free will and determinism has occupied the minds of philosophers and religious scholars since the days of Ancient Greece. This question has been discussed in "The Nature of Man" and so only a brief mention of it need be made here.

According to the free-will theory, man has complete freedom of choice in making decisions, so that he is responsible for his own actions. Thus he is a being with real moral freedom and a sense of duty and responsibility. On the other hand, the determinists believe that all man's decisions are determined by external or internal factors over which he has no control.

There is no doubt that such factors as environment, education, health, and the laws governing the society in which we live, are bound to influence our minds in making decisions, but the fact remains that we are all quite certain that no matter the circumstances, we have freedom of will, *i.e.*, the power to choose what we think to be the right course. We fully believe that the final decision always rests with ourselves and that we are morally responsible beings.

It is of vital importance to man that he should have free will to choose between right and wrong. If his behaviour was controlled entirely by deterministic factors, he would not be capable of making spiritual progress and could not rise above the animal creation. (It must not be assumed that animals are controlled entirely by deterministic factors. Many show an element of free will in the spontaneous nature of their play and in the care and defence of their young.)

The amount of free will, however, possessed by a human being depends upon his spiritual development. A really good man can resist or control deterministic factors. A man of low spirituality may be controlled almost entirely by them. The latter can widen the scope of his free will by being less self-centred and by striving for greater self-control. Otherwise he remains a mere slave to his own passions and selfish desires. God, being free from all inhibitions, is not influenced in any way by deterministic factors; in the Divine Mind free will reaches Completeness and Infallibility of expression.

The Divine plan of our lives appears to have been outlined for us beforehand but we are responsible for filling in the details or completing the pattern. Having free will, we can refuse to do so; we can insist on leading evil, self-centred lives. On the other hand, if we are willing to accept the Divine plan, help, should we desire it, will at all times be given to us from higher spirits.

THE OCCURRENCE OF EVIL AND SUFFERING IN THE WORLD

In all ages the problem of the occurrence of evil in the world has occupied the minds of philosophers, and the question has been asked, why should an Omnipotent and All-loving God permit evil to exist, especially as it is the cause of much pain and suffering to man and animals.

Theologians in the past have tried to answer this question by claiming that all evil is due to the activities of a malevolent spirit or god (the Devil of the mediaeval Christians, the god Ahriman of the Zoroastrians and the goddess Kali of the Hindus) who preys upon mankind, tempting them to do evil. But it is difficult to understand how an All-just and Loving Father, who has created mankind "in his own image," can also be responsible for creating and setting loose and uncontrolled in the world an arch-fiend with vast powers of causing pain and suffering. Such a doctrine carries little weight with the modern mind and does not promote the cause of any religion, based on a belief in a just God with particular interest in mankind.

There is no doubt that evils do befall mankind and animals, bringing about much suffering. Many of these evils arise from the fact that all living beings have physical bodies and are therefore liable to be affected by the natural forces around them, such as volcanic eruptions, earthquakes, tempests, lightning and fire. They are also liable to suffer if the needs of their physical bodies in regard to food, water and temperature, cannot be satisfied; or as a result of disease.

Suffering is also caused by animals preying on others for food; fighting for food, water or shelter; or attempting to advance their own species at the expense of others. Man himself, of course, has been responsible for much suffering, not only amongst his fellowmen but also in animals.

In many of these cases the factors responsible for the suffering are outwith a person's control. On the other hand, many evils are brought about by the fact that man has free will and is making wrong decisions owing to ignorance, greed, conceit or selfishness. Thus he causes suffering to others, including animals, and to himself.

If God is Omnipotent it was in his power to create a race of perfect beings with no free will, but such creatures would be mere robots, reacting in a perfectly correct and consistent manner to all factors whether inherent in their own nature or present in the world around them. Under such conditions, they could not develop a sense of responsibility and conscience. They would have no knowledge of good and evil, would be unable to appreciate the harmful effects of making wrong decisions and would be incapable of making spiritual progress.

"THE FALL OF MAN"

The doctrine of the Fall of Man from a state of primeval perfection was an attempt to explain the occurrence of evil and suffering in the world. It formed an important dogma in the teaching of the Jewish and Christian Churches. It had also an important bearing on the Christian dogma of the Vicarious Atonement of Christ. However, in the light of modern knowledge, the doctrine of the Fall is not now generally accepted.

In the first place, it is based on the account in Genesis of the Creation of the first human beings, Adam and Eve, from dust of the earth, and their subsequent fall from a state of innocence as a result of their eating the forbidden fruit of a tree in the Garden of Eden. But the facts of evolution have shown that man was not created directly or in a single step from dust. Instead, he was gradually evolved from the earliest forms of life over a period of some several thousand million years. In the course of this long period, the highly complex human body was developed, and although certain early types, *e.g.*, Neanderthal man, did not persist, there was no general fall or set-back in his physical evolution.

The vitalising principle in all forms of life (plant and animal) is spirit, but as nothing is known with regard to its nature, it is not possible to determine whether there has been any form of spiritual evolution corresponding to the physical. It would appear, however, that there are different grades or degrees of spirit development according to whether the spirit is manifesting itself in plant, animal (lower or higher) or man. It may be inferred therefore that the spirits of the early organisms would be, on the whole, of much lower development than those of later organisms of the same kind. This would apply also to the spirits of the earliest humanoid species as compared with those of Neanderthal and modern man. Thus there has been in all probability some form of spiritual development concomitant with physical evolution. In this connection it must be borne in mind that the more the physical body evolves into higher and higher types, the more suitable it becomes as an instrument for spirit.

According to the doctrine of the Fall, the first of mankind were in a condition of primitive innocence. Anthropologists claim that this was not so; early man was in a state of savagery, governed entirely by his bodily desires and his instincts, and thus little higher than the wild animal in his mode of life. In the course of the last twenty or thirty thousand years, he has gradually become more civilised and has advanced to higher ethical standards of living. During this period, set-backs have occurred with different races or nations, but there has been no general fall throughout the world. Instead, there has been on the whole a gradual spiritual advance.

THE DISCIPLINE OF EARTH-LIFE

The spirit on entering earth-life takes on a physical body, so that it can function and have experiences in a material environment along with other incarnate spirits, and thus develop its spiritual nature. At the same time the body restricts the activities of the spirit and isolates it to some extent from other spirits. This apparently enables it to become individualised and develop a distinct and fixed personality, capable of adapting itself to changes in conditions of environment.

The world may be likened to a school in which the human spirit is tested and disciplined to fit it for life in the spirit state. Life on earth is seldom without hardship, pain and suffering. But if these conditions can be met with fortitude, they strengthen the character and have a refining effect on the spiritual nature. In fact, they frequently act as stimuli for fresh efforts. An easy comfortable life without any hardships leads to self-complacency, indolence and spiritual and mental stagnation.

The difficulties of earth-life may at times appear to be overwhelming, but they will never seem so great if they can be looked at in proper perspective, *i.e.*, in the light of the spiritual purpose of man's evolution. This purpose appears to have been the production of a type of spiritual being with a knowledge of good and evil, a sense of conscience and the power of free will. Such beings could make mistakes and do evil, but they could also appreciate the harmful effects of wrong-doing and realise the merits of a moral and spiritual life, and could of their own free will try to follow that kind of life to the heights of spiritual greatness. Beings with these qualities could be evolved from the animal creation only after ages of pain and suffering, of sifting and sorting, but they would be closely akin to the Divine.

THE PRESSING NEED FOR SPIRITUAL PROGRESS IN THE WORLD

Man's spiritual progress throughout the ages has been slow. He is still content to lead a life of no high ethical and moral standard. His material achievements in science and industry have far outstripped his spiritual development and as a result there is a danger that new discoveries and inventions, for instance, in nuclear physics, may be used for wrong purposes—for warfare instead of for the welfare and advancement of the human race. Sir Winston S. Churchill, in referring to the new discoveries of atomic energy, said some years ago, "Under the impact of war, man became aware of the vast powers of atomic energy, a discovery for which he was not spiritually fitted. Man's inventiveness had outstripped his spiritual progress. We and all nations stand at this hour of human history before the portals of supreme catastrophe or of measureless reward. My faith is that in God's mercy we shall choose aright."

It would appear that with advance in knowledge, the need for spiritual progress becomes more pressing, to ensure that the knowledge will be put to the right use. Spiritual progress has undoubtedly been made. In the world to-day there is with many nations a higher ethical and moral standard, less cruelty, more respect for the rights, beliefs and welfare of others, and more charity. There is also a greater appreciation of the eternal values of life, namely Goodness, Truth, Justice and Beauty, and a more widespread sense of a Supreme Power or Intelligence behind the Universe. But in spite of this spiritual advance with its strengthening of the forces of good, there have been disastrous setbacks due to outbursts of evil, as shown by the extreme cruelty and ruthlessness only too often manifested in the modern world, *e.g.*, in the Great Wars. It would appear that with advance of civilisation, man not only becomes more sensitive to higher spirit forces, but also, if he ignores these forces, he renders himself more susceptible to lower or evil influences.

For real spiritual advancement to be made throughout the world, men must not only make progress themselves, but they must also help others to do so by promoting a universal spirit of Brotherhood, Justice, Peace and Goodwill, together with a reverence for all life. What with the ease and rapidity of modern travel and communication, nations at one time regarded as being far apart are now in close contact. The world has become like a single neighbourhood, and men of all nations must learn to live together as good neighbours, instead of yielding to the forces of evil and dissipating their energies and resources in unrest, slaughter and bloodshed.

By living in attunement with God and thus by co-operating in the Divine Scheme, man can move forward, although perhaps slowly, to heights of spiritual greatness. Already he can catch glimpses of these heights in moments of exalted inspiration. At these times he can dimly sense the Divine Presence in all its qualities of Timelessness, Goodness, Truth, Justice and Beauty. With further spiritual progress, the powers of apprehension of these Divine qualities will increase until the human spirit will be able to realise them in all their fullness. Then man will also be aware that he is in truth a Son of God.

THE NATURE OF GOD

The universe is of such utter vastness with its millions and millions of galaxies, suns and planets, that it is quite impossible for man to have even the slightest conception of the Infinite and Almighty Power responsible for its creation and sustenance. However, throughout all things, animate and inanimate, there is evidence of purpose, planning and guidance. It can therefore be postulated that there is a Universal Mind or Principle, which has not only infinite creative powers but is also All-loving, Omniscient and Omnipotent. This Mind has a vitalising and sustaining power on all forms of life, including mankind.

The Eastern mystics have regarded this Divine Mind as purely impersonal in nature, although having a benevolent influence on man. Aristotle also believed that this Universal Mind was impersonal in nature but he thought that It was transcendent and quite aloof from the world and not actively interested in mankind.

On the other hand, with many nations, the early anthropomorphic ideas of God have persisted throughout the ages; they still believe in the personal nature of the Divine Mind or God. He was the Zeus of the Ancient Greeks, the Mithra of the Persians and Romans, and is still the Jahveh of the Jews, the Heavenly Father of the Christians and the Allah of the Mohammedans. And this Divine Mind, no matter the name applied: God, Jahveh, Allah, Brahman or Heavenly Father, is accessible to all mankind, whatever their race, colour or religion. As the Hindu God, Krishna, in the Bhagavad-Gita says, "By whatsoever path you come to Me, I shall welcome you, for the paths men take from every side are Mine."

> "One Life through all the immense creation runs,
> One Spirit is the moon's, the sea's, the sun's;
> All forms in the air that fly, on the earth that creep,
> And the unknown nameless monsters of the deep—
> Each breathing thing obeys one Mind's control,
> And in all substance is a single Soul."
>
> Aeneid, VI. Virgil.
> (F. W. H. MYERS)

293

SDU PUBLICATIONS

SDU Publications' aim is to print books about mediumship.

During the period we call 'Modern Spiritualism', 1848 to the current day, there have been some outstanding mediums. By keeping these books in print we preserve for future generations a record of their achievements and thereby keep their names alive.

We currently have in stock books by or about the following mediums:

- J. J. Morse
- Helen Hughes
- Judith Seaman
- Estelle Roberts
- Emma Hardinge
- Margery Crandon
- Kathleen Goligher
- Daniel Dunglas Home
- Nettie Colburn Maynard

for our current catalogue contact:

Minister Steven Upton
Tel: +44 (0)1909 489828
Email: mail@s-upton.com
Website: www.sdu3.com